W9-BND-945

FEELING GLOBAL

CULTURAL FRONT

GENERAL EDITOR: MICHAEL BÉRUBÉ

MANIFESTO OF A TENURED RADICAL
BY CARY NELSON

**BAD SUBJECTS: POLITICAL EDUCATION
FOR EVERYDAY LIFE**
EDITED BY THE *BAD SUJBECTS* PRODUCTION TEAM

CLAIMING DISABILITY: KNOWLEDGE AND IDENTITY
BY SIMI LINTON

**THE EMPLOYMENT OF ENGLISH: THEORY, JOBS,
AND THE FUTURE OF LITERARY STUDIES**
BY MICHAEL BÉRUBÉ

FEELING GLOBAL: INTERNATIONALISM IN DISTRESS
BY BRUCE ROBBINS

FEELING GLOBAL
INTERNATIONALISM IN DISTRESS

BRUCE ROBBINS

NEW YORK UNIVERSITY PRESS
NEW YORK AND LONDON

NEW YORK UNIVERSITY PRESS
New York and London

Library of Congress Cataloging-in-Publication Data
Robbins, Bruce.
Feeling global : internationalism in distress / Bruce Robbins.
p.   cm.
ISBN 0-8147-7513-6
ISBN 0-8147-7514-4
1. Internationalism.   2. World politics—1989–   I. Title.
JC362.R553   1999
327.1'01—ddc21   98-58005
                                    CIP

New York University Press books are printed on acid-free paper
and their binding materials are chosen for strength and durability.

Manufactured in the United States of America
10 9 8 7 6 5 4 3 2 1

THIS BOOK IS DEDICATED TO MY MOTHER,
LYNNE PETERS ROBBINS.

CONTENTS

ACKNOWLEDGMENTS

A mong the many friends and colleagues who have generously taken the time to read, comment, and argue, I thank Amanda Anderson, Perry Anderson, Kwame Anthony Appiah, Lauren Berlant, Richard Bernstein, Jacqueline Bhabha, Carol Breckenridge, Pheng Cheah, James Clifford, Nicholas Dirks, Wimal Dissanayeke, Tom Dumm, Nancy Fraser, Dilip Gaonkar, Gerald Graff, Jean Gregorek, David Hollinger, Tom Keenan, Dominick LaCapra, Benjamin Lee, George Levine, Scott Malcomson, Franco Moretti, Benita Parry, Richard Rorty, Andrew Ross, Edward Said, Sohnya Sayres, Naomi Schor, Kalpana Seshadri-Crooks, Neil Smith, Gayatri Chakravorty Spivak, Michael Sprinker, Ann Stoler, Charles Taylor, Fengzhen Wang, Gauri Viswanathan, Jeff Williams, Rob Wilson, George Yúdice, Linda Zerilli, and Xudong Zhang. I have benefited enormously from those challenging and mercifully constructive students at Rutgers, New York University, and Cornell who were willing to take on the unlikely topic of cosmopolitanism, as well as from the never-ending surprises offered up by my fellow editors of *Social Text*. Michael Bérubé and Eric Zinner know how much this book owes to them. For emergency help at the last minute and long-term intellectual sustenance well beyond my deserts, I am especially grateful to Jonathan Arac, Ken Hirschkop, Bonnie Honig, Aamir Mufti, Peter Osborne, Louisa Schein, and Elsa Stamatopoulou. Friends and faux-French speakers Marjorie Howes, Jim Livingston, John McClure, Marc Manganaro, and Lisa Salem lent their skepticism and belief in just the right proportions.

Earlier versions of chapters 2 through 7 appeared in the following periodicals: "Some Versions of U.S. Internationalism," *Social Text*, 45 (Winter 1995), 97–123; "The Weird Heights: Cosmopolitanism, Feeling, and Power," *differences* 7, 1 (Spring 1995), 165–87; "Feeling Global: John Berger and Experience," *boundary 2* 11, 1–2 (Winter 1981–82), 291–308; "Upward Mobility in the Postcolonial Era: Kincaid, Mukherjee, and the Cosmopolitan Au Pair," *Modernism/Modernity* 1, 2 (1994), 133–51; "Secularism, Elitism, Progress, and Other Transgressions: On Edward Said's 'Voyage In,'" *Social Text*, 40 (1994), 25–37; "Sad Stories in the International Public Sphere: Richard Rorty on Culture and Human Rights," *Public Culture* 9, 2 (Winter 1997), 209–32 and *Tamkang Review* (Taipei) 26, 1–2 (Autumn/Winter 1995), 19–39. A portion of chapter 8 appeared as "Cosmopolitanism and Boredom" in *Theory and Event* 1, 2 (April 1997) and in *Radical Philosophy*, 85 (Sept./Oct. 1997), 28–32. I am grateful to the editors for permission to reprint.

The photographs on the cover and facing each chapter were taken by my father, Eugene Robbins, while serving as a pilot in the 305th Bomb Group, Army Air Corps.

INTRODUCTION

Bombs are falling. I watch them through the open bomb-bay doors of my father's B-17. Clusters of bombs drop off into space, wobbly but still symmetrical. I notice a different symmetry far below—dark smoke in overlapping circles that blot out the ground.

Later, when World War II is over, my father pilots the Flying Fortress on a mapping mission over southern Europe, while his navigator, relaxed now, takes more photographs. There is time for detours over Florence, Rome, Naples, Athens. It's a kind of government-issue Grand Tour, an aerial overview of some cultures and monuments my father might have studied in college, if he had gone to college.

As a child, I slip down to the basement and open the latch on his wooden ammunition box, mysteriously marked "Oben. Nicht Werfen!" I take out those large, square, black-and-white pictures from among the other souvenirs (two bayonets, one with a polished wooden handle and still very sharp, the other handleless and disappointingly dull). I look down—sometimes straight down, sometimes at a less dizzying angle—on the bombs falling and on the famous sites of Florence, Rome, Naples, Athens. Seen from directly overhead, the ruins of the Coliseum look like a bomb crater. I pore over these photos, letting the record of modern explosives merge in my mind with the record of ancient civilizations. Florence, Rome, Naples, Athens—these are places I will want to go.

Time would have to pass, but it feels like a short step from wanting to visit these fragile foreign monuments to becoming a student and then a teacher of culture. This thought is not very appealing. Yes, I expanded my horizons. It was an odd satisfaction to find out, among other things, that "Oben. Nicht Werfen!" means "This Side Up. Don't Throw!" Germans, it appears, were also worried about accidents. But the photographs from that ammunition box are a reminder that knowledge of cultural sameness and difference is explosive and needs to be handled with care.

It cannot be accidental that I associate worldliness with world war, the desire to know with the view through a bombsight, a wider horizon with the altitude of an aircraft. What does it mean to take your slant on things from a B-17? Much as I would like to, I cannot altogether resist the notion that to look at culture as I looked at those photographs is to relive the collecting of trophies after a battle. This was Walter Benjamin's idea, though Benjamin didn't spell out the degree of aggression, displaced from the battlefield onto the objects of culture, that his metaphor would ask critics to recognize in themselves. Readers of this book will undoubtedly recognize some of that aggression here—for example, when I argue that deference to culture has become a useful disguise for American nationalism.

Still, I would like to think that my identification with the aerial perspective was more complicated. It was, of course, an identification with the victors, and it was both filial and patriotic. The view from above seemed to promise power, superiority, mobility, security. (Not that there was actually anything secure about flying combat missions in World War II, I remind myself.) Once the war is over and the threat of death or injury is removed, the aerial viewpoint can seem to represent an unambiguous privilege. But ambiguities remain. The distance this perspective captures is also the social distance between those who do and do not have an education, those who can and cannot appreciate the finer things, those who are and are not members. The bombsight perspective that seems to threaten also provokes a longing to overcome these distances. Collecting also means protecting. There is a wish to possess, but also a wish to belong. Like the servant, the refugee, and the economic migrant, the soldier is an unwilling and ambivalent cosmopolitan. None of these figures is a simple duplicate of the leisured traveler, not even those who join the armed forces to see the world, and not even when they pause to take snapshots from a high vantage point.

The half century since the end of World War II has been a period of unprecedented American hegemony over the rest of the planet. The confident mobility and the implicit threat that go with an aerial perspective have helped give a face to that hegemony. In Vietnam and the Persian Gulf, images of projectiles plummeting from the sky became as ordinary as television, and it is not hard to see television itself as an extension of the same roving, all-penetrating viewpoint. Whether in its self-appointed cold war role of world policeman, propping up and pulling down regimes in Asia, Latin America, Africa, and the Middle East, or in its less-obtrusive support for the free flow of capital, the United States has demanded, as a sort of natural right, that its citizens and media be able to pass unhindered across the borders of nations and continents. For fifty years, the assumed mobility of the view from above has been a virtually unavoidable component in a sort of unconscious popular cosmopolitanism, a set of expectations about the openness and submissiveness of the world that are shared widely even among Americans who never leave their country.

It is no wonder, then, that critics of American power have been severe in their judgments both of cosmopolitanism and of the view from above. This is especially true of critics who are also students and teachers of culture; for custodianship of the monuments, whether these be Roman ruins or English literature, entails a commitment to preserving and transmitting meanings that are observed from up close. As indicated by its frequent references to panopticism and surveillance, today's critical standpoint tends to look at heights and distances with mistrust. With Timothy Brennan, it sees cosmopolitanism as "specious mastery of the whole."[1] With Mary Louise Pratt, it draws back from the "monarch-of-all-I-survey scene" in European travel writing (discussed in chapter 3) and from the "planetary consciousness" for which it stands. And at its best, it takes such political forms as Judith Butler's angry and eloquent response to the Persian Gulf War of 1991.

In that response, Butler points out the dangerous connections between the war and its "visual record," which is "not a *reflection* on the war, but the enactment of its phantasmatic structure, indeed, part of the very means by which it is socially constituted and maintained as a war. The so-called 'smart bomb' records its target as it moves in to destroy it—a bomb with a camera attached in front, a kind of optical phallus; it relays that film back to a command control and that film is refilmed on television, effectively constituting the television screen and its viewer as the extended apparatus of the bomb itself. In this sense, by viewing we are bombing, identified with both bomber and bomb, flying through space, transported from the North American continent to Iraq, and yet securely wedged in the couch in one's own living room" (11).[2] Thus the viewer, in safety and at a distance, reenacts "the allegory of military triumph" (11). Watching from "the aerial, global view" means becoming, at least in imagination, "the disembodied killer who can never be killed, the sniper as figure for imperialist military power" (11).

Writing at a moment (February 1998) when the United States has been gearing up for still another lunatic exercise in diplomacy by bombardment, it is impossible for me not to feel the force of Butler's case against the "aerial, global view." And yet, I try to balance it against another moment, not long after the end of the Gulf War, when many voices appealed for American air strikes against the Bosnian Serb forces that were shelling the inhabitants of Sarajevo. If ever a good reason existed for reconsidering one's extreme mistrust of any and all American intervention, it was so-called ethnic cleansing. Commentators recalled the air strikes that might have disrupted the train lines into Auschwitz — air strikes that never happened. I remembered the air strikes that my father had led as commander of his squadron. Much may be said about the inhuman consequences of such tactics, and even about their relative inefficacy. But they had come in a war that had to be fought — to the extent that war can ever be good, a good war. And to rule out even the theoretical possibility of a good war is to come very close to ruling out political action altogether.

This is a reason not to give up on the perspective from above — not as long as politics remains likely to present itself, as it did in World War II and in Bosnia, as a matter of unforeseeable but urgent collective action in an imperfect world (with allies and under circumstances that one might not have chosen for oneself), rather than as a radical refusal of all imperfection and, with it, of all action. The moral messiness of politics in this sense, a preference for the profane or this-worldly as opposed to versions of politics that assume the sacredness of their own side and the perfect coherence of their cause, is one thing I defend in this book when I adopt Edward Said's polemical usage of the word *worldly*.[3]

A worldly politics that takes for granted both the need for transnational mobility of viewpoint and action, on the one hand, and the inescapable reliance of such mobility on existing inequalities of power, on the other, will look to some people like a specifically *American* program — a program that could only be proposed by and for representatives of the most powerful nation in the world, however critical of that nation they may be. After all, the poorer citizens of the weaker nations have their hands full at home. They will not find it natural even to imagine intervening elsewhere in the world, let alone to carry out the intention. Like humanitarianism, this type of worldliness may seem available only to those who are free of the most dire necessity, who already have more than minimal access to resources, publicity, leverage. It may seem to display a culpable negligence of which side is up.

It is certainly not my intention to speak exclusively to the powerful. I imagine readers of this book largely will be people who have a personal, and perhaps also a professional, interest in the appalling record of global injustice but who feel unable to do much about the injuries and indignities they observe and sometimes suffer. The point of this book is to move this already existing worldliness, however slowly and unevenly, from interpreting the world toward changing it. To this end, I argue for a translation or transmutation of *cosmopolitanism*, usually understood as a detached, individual view of the global, into the more collective, engaged, and empowered form of worldliness that is often called *internationalism*. But in this effort I assume an understanding of power such that the newly empowered will not feel compelled in good conscience to disavow or abstain from using whatever power they come to possess. Such a disavowal or abstention is the scenario that some cultural styles of worldliness seem to be rehearsing today.

Given the terrible inequalities of power and wealth that continue to structure the world of nations, no version of worldliness—wherever it is located, however close it remains to the grass roots—cannot be accused of depending on and benefiting from these inequalities. The versions associated with human rights, ecology, feminism, and postcolonial studies, which I discuss in the chapters to follow, are not exempt from charges of top-down largesse or neocolonial paternalism. Even human rights activism involves actors of unequal power and mobility and can thus be classified as a form of the "aerial, global view." This is no more true of the inequality between a First and a Third World government than of the inequality between a metropolitan and a Third World nongovernmental organization (NGO). It also distinguishes activists in a Third World capital from the rural population they are trying to help. The differentials of power and privilege are equally dramatic at every scale. No good intentions, no democratic scrupulosity, can wish them away.

But if the same inequalities exist at different scales or sites of progressive action, then it seems unreasonable to allow the fact of inequality to paralyze any of them, even the global scale. In other words, it seems to follow that the global scale is not ethically and politically distinct from other, smaller scales, as the hegemony of the nation-state form has led it to appear. Until the late twentieth

5

century, everything seemed to change, ethically and politically, when one crossed out of the territory of a sovereign state. For some, the state appeared to harbor the more or less beneficent order of law and custom, whereas between states was neither law nor custom, only the eat-or-be-eaten code of the jungle. For others, nationalism was assumed to reign more or less unchecked inside the state, and justice and reason could assert themselves only by escaping the gravitational field of national passion. Often, the case for cosmopolitanism is taken to depend on the latter assumption. My premise, on the contrary, is that the forms of global feeling are continuous with forms of national feeling. This implies that, though the potential for a conflict of loyalties is always present, cosmopolitanism or internationalism does not take its primary meaning or desirability from an absolute and intrinsic opposition to nationalism. Rather, it is an extension outward of the same sorts of potent and dangerous solidarity. So understood, cosmopolitanism or internationalism cannot pretend to embody the interests of humanity itself or of universal reason; hence the word *feeling* in my title and the special motives for investigating particular cultural artifacts, as I do in the chapters to follow.

Let me illustrate this continuity with a counterintuitive but politically pertinent example. In his book *Commissioned Spirits,* Jonathan Arac discusses the meaning of panoramas, panopticons, and other devices of centralized inspection in the nineteenth century, when the ability to see the whole of a city at once was still a rare privilege. Arac argues that "unseen observation" destroyed "the reciprocity of seer and seen" and thus "allowed both for knowledge of individuals as cases and for aggregating such cases into knowledge of populations as statistical wholes" (18). One result, as Michel Foucault has suggested, was the modern pattern of the workhouse, the factory, the prison. But the nineteenth-century experience of overview is also directly linked, Arac argues, to the development of the social welfare state. And cartographic overview, like the social welfare state, is "a hard-won accomplishment of human energies" that should not be surrendered too easily (190). "To find the techniques of overview evil in themselves is a strong metaphysical temptation," Arac concludes, "and to condemn all bureaucracy, administration, organization is an anarchist temptation almost irresistible in our society for the spirit that would be free. The fundamental historical issue, however, remains who is surveying whom and for what purposes."[4]

The versions of internationalism I am interested in can seem opposed to the social welfare state. These days, nationalism is often couched as a defense of the welfare state, which is seen as a prime victim of the forces of capitalist globalization that internationalism is taken to reflect and abet. I suggest, rather, that, like

Marxism itself, both nation-state and internationalism exist in a dialectical relationship with global capitalism. In other words, the globalization that threatens the social welfare state is not the hidden truth of worldliness but at once its proximate cause and the reason worldliness is so necessary—essential to the defense of social welfare. As Arac's argument indicates, there is an unmistakable historical continuity between overview as a component of the welfare state and overview as a component of global feeling. This is how Eric Lott, in a recent issue of *Transition*, can identify the "New Cosmopolitanism" with a particular attitude toward American racial politics, making no reference to any attitudes toward the world outside the United States. Indeed, Lott criticizes the new cosmopolitans not for their transnational rootlessness but for their excessive devotion to their nation.[5]

Cosmopolitanism is more often seen, on the contrary, as the imperative to register the moral and cultural existence of noncitizens and to force that existence on a reluctant and well-defended national consciousness. But national unity, which puts both noncitizens and racial minorities at risk, comes in different modes and degrees of closure, inclusion, and recognition, which have quite different effects on the interests of both groups. And there is no way of articulating the interests of noncitizens and racial minorities—frequently the same people—without allowing national particularities to inflect them. Does anyone believe that taking these interests seriously means deciding that the nation-state is no longer worth fighting for? In this time and place, the proper, if strenuous, position for would-be internationalists might follow the lead of feminists who, while standing up for women everywhere, have also insisted on a need to defend the social welfare state; for the undermining of the welfare state has meant a systematic undermining of the welfare of American women.

From this viewpoint, it is not a surprise or a scandal that any given version of internationalism turns out to be local and conjunctural rather than universal. On the contrary, we should expect it to reflect the particular time and place in which it appears. Internationalism is not a utopian idealism, an infinitely deferred ideal of ultimate justice for all. It is not a synonym for the one universal rationality. There are many versions, and they are all imperfect. Thus, there is no self-contradiction in speaking of an "American internationalism." And there is a high price to be paid for the refusal to work with, as well as against, the particular structures of power available to Americans.

The ideal forms of internationalism to which I offer these worldly, limited, less-than-ideal alternatives are Kantian universalism, like that of Martha Nussbaum (discussed in chapter 8), and socialist internationalism. Socialist internationalism has few champions these days. As Peter Waterman writes, "Proletarian and socialist internationalism—seen as the antidote or antithesis to both the economic internationalization and political nationalism of capitalism—have become embarrassments to contemporary socialists." Neither the low ebb of the political parties that once supported internationalism nor the lack of a visible mass following for the Kantian ethical program is any reason for rejoicing. It is perhaps too soon to conclude, with Waterman, that "if the old internationalism is dead, the internationalisms of the new social movements (women, ecology, peace, human rights) are alive and kicking" (257).[6] What is clear is that internationalism is in distress. Its old forms lack energy and constituency, while its new, culturally particular forms have yet to define a comparable critical edge or capacity for transnational organization. The possibilities of building on, rather than trying to replace, Kantian universalism and socialist internationalism also remain to be proved in practice.

But recent skirmishes over universalism on the American left suggest that some effort at negotiation may be welcome on both the culturalist and the universalist side.[7] The sort of normative pressure that terms such as *internationalism* still bring to bear has its uses for champions of cultural diversity—all the more so in that, as I argue, "cultural diversity" can also serve those very different intellectual circles that are looking for ways to block serious engagement with human rights and related projects of redistributive justice. When culture becomes a refuge for American nationalism, internationalism has to look elsewhere. Who can forget how, at the televised Ohio State University "town meeting" in February 1998, Secretary of State Madeleine Albright and the other representatives of the government's "bomb Iraq" team were so terribly and beautifully embarrassed by a simple demand for transnational comparison, a pause to step back and rise up for a breathtaking overview:

> Does the U.S. intend to respond to other violations of UN resolutions and human rights abuses with military force? For example, Turkey, a U.S. ally, has bombed Kurdish civilians and, along with Saudi Arabia, both have been cited for torturing religious and political dissidents. Israel, the single largest recipient of U.S. foreign aid, has been censured repeatedly by the United Nations for its bombing of Lebanese civilians and brutality toward Palestinians. Why does the U.S. apply different standards of justice to these countries?[8]

It is now March, and the bombs have not fallen. Carried around the world by the unlikely but suddenly handy instrumentality of CNN's global reach, the questions aired at Ohio State certainly did their part to stop the war. Why should I support the bombing, asked President Hosni Mubarak of Egypt, if even the people of Ohio do not? Perhaps there is a message here for intellectuals looking to rethink their ethical obligations and their capacity for global action, their interest in uniting cultural politics with worldly normativity and practical policy making, at a time when their places and privileges in the "new world order" are open to new and profound questioning.

9

INTERNATIONALISM
IN DISTRESS

SUSAN SONTAG ON BOSNIA

In December 1995, Susan Sontag published an article in *The Nation* titled "A Lament for Bosnia: 'There' and 'Here.'" Back in New York in the days after the Bosnian peace agreement in Dayton, Ohio, after her ninth stay in Sarajevo, Sontag finds herself "angry" that "people don't want to know what you know, don't want you to talk about the sufferings, bewilderment, terror, and humiliation of the city you've just left" (818). She is horrified at the "widespread indifference, or lack of solidarity . . . with the victims of an appalling historical crime, nothing less than genocide" (819). But her harshest words are reserved for the intellectuals, who have become "morosely depoliticized." Why didn't they go to Bosnia as George Orwell and Simone Weil went to antifascist

Spain? Their "cynicism" and "nationalist complacencies," their "reluctance to inconvenience themselves for any cause, their devotion to personal safety" are all signs of "a vertiginous decay of the very notion of international solidarity" (820).[1]

Anecdotal evidence suggests that for many readers, Sontag's article occasioned a curious ambivalence. Most were inclined to agree about the tragedy in Bosnia—how much room for disagreement was there? Yet alongside respect for Sontag's extraordinary individual effort, many also reacted with acute exasperation, and sometimes something worse. These mixed feelings are worth inquiring into. They seem likely to reveal something important about the resistance to internationalism, or why, as Sontag says, "only domestic political commitments seem plausible now" (820). They also point to some interesting questions about internationalism itself. How is it that so many versions of internationalism preach in a manner that inadvertently turns even the converted into sullen, gut-level apostates? Is it possible to imagine an internationalist ethic that would be less distressing and more compelling?

The fact that genocide has happened and could happen again is a powerful argument in favor of international solidarity. But for this very reason, it cannot be *representative* of the case for international solidarity. Its power makes it too subject to abuse. The extreme case demands a special tact. When action is absolutely urgent, it is always already too late to indulge much curiosity about the details of the relevant site or to listen to the distracting variety of its voices. Any knowledge beyond the bare, accusing facts of recent atrocity seems beside the point. In Sontag's *Nation* article, for example, actual Bosnians fade into the background; Sontag does not feel any need to quote them, even as survivors or witnesses.[2] Who can blame her? But if this neglect of local perspectives were generalized, "cosmic" urgency would make internationalism itself provincial. The extreme case distorts the rest. Urgency also creates impatience with analogies to not-quite-genocidal situations such as those in Somalia and Haiti, where suffering and injustice were widespread but where the interventions that did happen were problematic in more than one respect. And it discourages memories of a previous moment when Sontag called for international solidarity: with Poland's *Solidarnosc* (Solidarity) in 1982. That appeal included her declaration (self-evident for some, for others notorious) equating communism with fascism.[3] Fascism produced genocide. Does it follow that, in Sontag's eyes, support for Lech Walesa was as morally imperative as support for the Bosnians?

Claiming genocide's moral absoluteness as her authority, Sontag does some sentimental bullying. She strong-arms the reader with an instant and powerfully simplifying exhortation: you must act! Or rather, now that it is too late:

you must *have* acted. *I* have acted, Sontag tells us. I have gone to Sarajevo, not once but nine times. Not trips or visits but "stays"—nine of them. What about you? Were you "almost killed" (820), like Orwell and Weil when they went to Spain?[4] Did you go without a bath for "several weeks" (818)? No, you did not, and there are reasons. Your moral lethargy is proportional to your affluence. You are a creature of "comfortable upper-bourgeois apartments and weekend country houses" (820), and you are loath to leave them. "In the era of shopping, it has to be harder for intellectuals, who are anything but marginal and impoverished, to identify with less fortunate others" (820).

For a prosperous intellectual celebrity, there is a real point here. It does not seem to have occurred to Sontag, however, that though some of her readers may possess luxurious and multiple residences, the majority do not. And very few are likely to enjoy the time, the personal autonomy, and the disposable income necessary for even one or two trips to Sarajevo, let alone nine. To a majority of readers, someone who has been to Sarajevo nine times, even to stage *Waiting for Godot*, is going to look pretty well off—certainly within that range of financial ease that "upper-bourgeois apartments and weekend country houses" indicate. Sontag suggests it is the poor who go and the rich who stay home. But her ethics presupposes a very different sociology: everyone must act, she implies, as if they were as free and as privileged as I am.

Some people suggested that self-interest lay behind Sontag's stand, that her altruistic gesture disguised an opportunistic use of the sufferings of others. The phrase "photo op" came up in conversation with some frequency. Such insinuations tended to offer no evidence and seemed to assume that none was required. Yet they are something more than illustrations of contemporary cynicism. Sontag may be said to invite, if not necessarily to deserve, the mean-spirited, excessively personal treatment she receives. Trying, no doubt, only to put her personal newsworthiness to good use, she pushes herself on her readers as an explicit and unavoidable point of comparison with themselves. But when the moral authority behind Sontag's exacting appeal to others is her account of her own behavior, that account becomes a legitimate and alluring target. Moreover, questioning Sontag's motives is the reader's almost inevitable line of self-defense when the demand for extraordinary sacrifice that Sontag claims to embody includes the risk of the reader's life on behalf of a faraway conflict that little else in that life has prepared the reader to care about.

Such resistance to internationalism is all the more logical and predictable because extraordinary personal sacrifice is not obviously the best solution to the urgencies that Sontag announces. At least as Sontag presents and embodies it, such sacrifice has very little to do with effective action to stop the slaughter.

INTERNATIONALISM IN DISTRESS

Sontag herself is interested in going "there" and in the difficulty of telling us "here" what it feels like to be "there." In other words, she is interested in travel, in self-exposure, and in how both should be narrated to the underexposed nontraveler. But her juicy experience of hardship and danger—an experience that she must walk away from in order to retell it afterward—seems a strange substitute for any analysis of possible or actual interventions. Should the United Nations have a standing army? Should the United States have acted without its NATO allies? How much did it matter that Bosnia in the 1990s, unlike Spain in the 1930s, no longer had a Communist (or Trotskyist or anarchist) movement giving to international solidarity a concrete organizational basis? The inconvenient fact that those who backed the Bosnians with more than empty words did so as Muslims has no place in her argument. Why should they not count as internationalists? Sontag gives no evidence of concern about political action—that is, about the agents, options, modes and costs of an effectual response, one that might make, or might have made, a difference.[5]

Who is supposed to answer Sontag's call for intervention? Sontag doesn't say. She leaves open the possibility that her intended interlocutor is, among others, the U.S. government. But intervening here, the U.S. government might also feel emboldened to intervene elsewhere, perhaps less benevolently. Thus "international solidarity" might do as much to reinvent post–cold war American nationalism as to help Bosnia. (This is by no means the end of the discussion, as I hope my Introduction suggested, but the possibility is worth raising.) There is something a bit sinister about concluding, as Sontag does, with a quotation from Émile Durkheim on the necessary role of idealism in the formation of societies. Sontag does not say that Durkheim lost his son during the First World War—as it happens, fighting in Bosnia. She does not say that though Durkheim spoke in favor of cosmopolitanism (rendered by his English translator as "world patriotism"), he also favored France's entry into that war.[6] Nor does she say that the idealistic intervention of the French state in Bosnia, which cost Durkheim and so many others their sons, betrayed a prior pan-European determination among social democratic parties not to let their respective populations be dragged into what they saw would be a meaningless and prolonged slaughter.[7] Walter Lippmann, another pro-cosmopolitan who supported full participation in the First World War, offers an American parallel. Both figures suggest why a principled call for intervention by the U.S. or French states might be perceived as continuous or complicit with familiar and devastating forms of nationalism.

Instead of channeling her readers toward the dilemmas of appropriate political action, Sontag urges them to compare their everyday routines with her traveling. Her traveling is a process of alienation from ordinary life: an experience, as she says, of "bewilderment, terror, and humiliation." Sontag complains of this, but she also presents it with some pride as rare and revealing. Such experience could have been presented otherwise. In the first chapter of his book *Slaughterhouse*, David Rieff describes his own return from Sarajevo and how he, too, felt "like an alien" in trying to take up his own life again. Yet he notes that he is "not alone in this," that it is the usual case even for "seasoned war correspondents" (25).[8] Sontag's alienation is more likely to be perceived as self-aggrandizement, for it does not merely define her as a special sort of person but reaffirms the specialness for which she was already known. As she tells it, her sojourn in Bosnia becomes a model of avant-garde aesthetic experience. Its aim is the modernist aim of disorientation, defamiliarization, making strange. It is exotic, rare, uncomfortable. Like modernism in general, it is open only to the few, and it takes its aesthetic value—in part at least—from that very inaccessibility, that critical remoteness from the habits of the benumbed multitude. Sontag's contempt for the stay-at-home is the contempt of the coterie tastemaker for the mass of the tasteless or insensitive, those who are incapable of the latest, deepest, most strenuous self-alienation, the most rigorous self-problematizing—those incapable, in short, of modernism's version of aesthetic experience.

In sum, Sontag puts a number of more or less irritating distractions between her American reader and engagement with Bosnia. But are such distractions merely inconsequential flaws in one understandably fervent and perhaps hastily composed text? Or are they and the ambivalence they provoke to some extent constitutive of internationalism itself as a rhetorical and political enterprise—one that oddly joins ethical urgency with aesthetic and geocultural distance, normative pressure with emotional eccentricity, self-privileging with the impulse to expand the geography of democracy?

Each of the points I raise about Sontag—points that help explain the resistance to her version of internationalism—marks an unresolved question, an area in which one cannot simply refuse Sontag's option or espouse its opposite. If her universalism combines with the urgency of action to produce a certain absence of curiosity about the cultural diversity of the world, it is also true that respect for cultural diversity alone provides neither a guide or an incentive to action, on the one hand, nor the sort of common ground that would raise a pluralism of internationalisms above the pluralism of nationalisms that posed the original problem, on the other hand. Sontag's internationalism is based on a problematic domestic sociology, one that adds to already existing tensions between "elites" and "nonelites" as well as tensions within the category of intellectuals. But it also appeals to celebrity intellectuals to follow her example—surely one of the better things that might be done with celebrity. Taking one's distance from Sontag is by no means as easy as it may appear.

GLOBAL CULTURE IS ORDINARY

The term *internationalism* has a number of diverse and overlapping meanings. In its standard international relations sense, it can be defined as the belief, to quote Kjell Goldmann, "that international peace and security benefit if international institutions are strengthened and cooperative ties multiply across borders."[9] As Goldmann notes, this meaning, while widely shared among policy makers and political scientists around the world, is distinct from the most frequent sense in the United States: internationalism as support for an active foreign policy, for the state's foreign entanglements and interventions—that is, "the opposite of isolationism" (2).[10] And both meanings must be distinguished from a more ethical or sentimental, less policy-oriented sense of the word that is also current and that comes closest to Sontag: "concern with far-away peoples in distress" (2).

Each of these meanings has a record of *creating* distress in its domestic addressees. Internationalism in the first, global-governance sense is high on the hate list of the paranoid militias, who associate it with an imminent takeover of the United States by the United Nations or some other agent of transnational conspiracy. But it causes unease in many of the rest of us as well. The American, state-centered sense also tends to sound paternalistic, insensitive to ordinary experience, too oriented—this is the price paid for its privileged intimacy with "real" politics—to the viewpoint of the world's decision makers. Both conceptions of internationalism provoke a hostility among the ruled, in part because they assume the viewpoint of those with the power to dictate action at or beyond the level of the state and fail to address the feelings and values of those who cannot easily or naturally adopt that viewpoint.

In the first two senses, then, internationalism needs help. Thus the ethical and sentimental dimensions that Sontag adds are not a diversion into the luxuries of philanthropy. There may well be a problem of "people knowing so little and feeling so much" (42), as Rieff puts it, but for better or worse, internationalism demands feeling as well as knowing, or feeling combined in some proportion with knowing, if it is going to rouse any support. At minimum, a transnationally shaped and educated sentiment is a necessary means of winning democratic consent for a particular set of policies.[11] This is what Richard Falk had in mind when he noted, apropos of Bosnian intervention in 1993, the "absence of a compassionate ethos—even in relation to Europe itself. . . . Serious intervention presupposes a different political ethic than currently exists in any country, and if leaders attempted to mount such a campaign without a convincing strategic justification, they would encounter overwhelmingly hostile public opinion" (758).[12] Without an internationalist ethic or culture, an internationalist politics will not emerge, or will have little power to diverge creatively or generously from the national interest as the latter is narrowly and strategically construed. Instead of beating Sontag's internationalism over the head for being moral or sentimental—in other words, for not being policy—it is useful to recognize that the moral and sentimental domain is a constituent and precondition of policy and thus to set about discriminating and criticizing the styles or options for internationalism within that domain.

The third sense of internationalism might be called cultural internationalism or cosmopolitanism. The term *cosmopolitanism* is ordinarily taken to differ from internationalism in its emphasis on individuals rather than collectivities, and on aesthetic spectatorship rather than political engagement. For better or worse, it is correspondingly accorded greater independence than internationalism from the system of nation-states, and it is judged to waver between an antinationalist politics, a specifically cultural politics, and no politics at all. These ambiguities are not simply liabilities. They help respond to the further question of whether, by its historical associations, the contrasting term *internationalism* is not too strongly political to describe recognitions and solidarities that are perhaps less organized, more ad hoc than the word *politics* usually implies. The worldliness into which we are now hesitantly venturing mixes the ethical, the political, and the cultural in proportions that are too obscure, too unstable, and too novel to allow any easy escape from such dilemmas. To focus on the hypothesis of a political or protopolitical mobilizing of feeling and effort at the international scale, I use the terms *cosmopolitanism* and *cultural internationalism* here as rough synonyms.

As I have suggested, Sontag's cultural internationalism, too, creates distress nearby while (or by) pointing at the need to relieve it in the distance. Her internationalism can be described as cultural in several senses: first, it is centered on the staging of a play, *Waiting for Godot*, a monument of modern European culture that reaffirms the common membership in that culture of the secular, cosmopolitan Bosnian society that was under attack; second, it uses publicity as its main weapon; third, it addresses morals and sentiments rather than agents and policies. One might argue that, to some extent, it creates distress merely by *being* cultural—in other words, by working in a mode that is visibly severed from other, larger possibilities of remedial or revolutionary action. This is Sontag's own argument against photography: "Photographing is essentially an act of non-intervention. Part of the horror of such memorable coups of contemporary photojournalism as the pictures of the Vietnamese bonze reaching for the gasoline can, of a Bengali guerrilla in the act of bayoneting a trussed-up collaborator, comes from the awareness of how plausible it has become, in situations where the photographer has the choice between a photograph and a life, to choose the photograph."[13] It is also her case against the cosmopolitan hero of her novel *The Volcano Lover,* a cultivated aesthete and collector who fails the crucial test of intervention that Naples's 1798 revolution drops in his lap. The cosmopolitan does not go to Sarajevo.

But in another sense, the point is not that Sontag's internationalism is too cultural but rather that it is inadequately or imperfectly cultural. In this context, culture and aesthetics would seem to diverge. Sontag's modernist aesthetic concedes as little as possible to the diversity and givenness that are also attributes of culture. It tries to make strange, but without adapting to the fact that what is strange to one is familiar to another, and vice versa. Sontag gives no heed to differences of class and circumstance, which dictate that some have more freedom of action than others and thus that various individuals will receive the same appeal for action very differently. Despite Sontag's clear intentions, her modernist aesthetic is also relatively inappropriate for persuading anyone to act; for persuasion entails recognizing and respecting the historically produced characteristics of one's listeners. Sontag is more interested in shocking than in convincing those listeners, thereby putting on a spectacle of significant noncommunication. It does not seem unfair to describe her article as a modernist performance, an exercise in estrangement, intended not to give pleasure but as a deliberate assault on the habits, assumptions, sensibilities of its audience—an assault, that is, on its given culture.[14] Can it be a mere accident of timing that she presents the opportunity for effectual action as belated, lost forever? In effect, she tells her reader: Even if you were to be persuaded by me now, it is already too late to do the only thing that might once have won my respect. Too bad.

In refusing cultural givenness and diversity, Sontag is consistent with one of the best-known clichés about internationalism and cosmopolitanism: namely, that they cannot rival or even acknowledge the emotional power of culture, which is the power of lived particularity. In his book *On Nationality* (one example of the widespread theoretical rehabilitation of nationalism in recent years), David Miller describes cosmopolitanism as "the view that we are citizens of the world, members of a common humanity, and that we should pay no more regard to the claims of our co-nationals than to those of any other human beings regardless of where they happen to reside" (3).[15] Where one happens to reside determines the culture in which one is raised, and with it the loyalties and obligations one naturally and properly feels. The defining principle is "non-neutrality where the national culture is itself at stake" (195). Miller defends a concept of nationality that is "thicker" (188) than civic nationalism or constitutional patriotism because it is more cultural than either.[16] As opposed to these attempts at liberal compromise with nationalism, he wants more respect for the inevitable force of "the inherited culture" (189).

For Miller, culture is always inherited, just as it is always national. Thus culture is not really itself when the word is applied to "the smorgasbord of cultural experiences" with which "the cosmopolitan" offers to replace national identity (186). Smorgasbords may be Swedish, but the examples of cosmopolitan anti-culture are Disney and McDonald's (187).[17] Another of the crop of new and sophisticated defenders of nationalism, Yael Tamir, similarly presents cosmopolitanism as an anticulture, again originating in the United States and again pushing out genuine national cultures, which are inherited: "A postnational age in which national differences are obliterated and all share in one shallow universal culture, watch soap operas and CNN, eat McDonald's, drink Coca-Cola and take children to the local Disneyworld, is more a nightmare than a utopian vision."[18]

The repetitive, not to say obsessive, quality of these examples should be cause for suspicion.[19] The brand names leap to the tongue a bit too readily. What do these familiar tokens of contempt stop us from thinking? I propose that here, as so often in discussions of the cultural consequences of globalization, Disney and McDonald's, Coke and CNN, stand in misleadingly for technological innovation and transnational exchange. Everything we know about and against these particular commodities—there is a lot, of course—becomes an unspoken argument against a larger conception that does not deserve the same instinctive, knee-jerk disavowal: that of culture as neither exclusively inherited nor exclusively national.

Though the concept of culture emerged historically in close connection with nationalism, it does not belong inevitably or definitively on the side of nation, inheritance, or locality. Why, then, has the sense of shared commitments we associate with genuine culture seemed dependent on shared proximity for as long as it has? The reason is simple. Through most of human history, both habitual knowledge of others and habitual opportunities to affect others' lives were very limited in space. But as both social organizations and technologies of communication and transportation have expanded, so too has culture, in the sense of shared habits of connection, mutual responsibility, mutual recognition. As Thomas Haskell has argued, the distance at which humanitarian sentiment is accepted as valid—a distance that is never infinite, always conventional or culturally delimited—depends on the available technologies, which are subject to dramatic change. "New technology—using that word broadly to refer to all means of accomplishing our ends, including new institutions and political organizations that enable us to attain ends otherwise out of reach—can change the moral universe in which we live. Technological innovation can perform this startling feat, because it supplies us with new ways of acting at a distance and new ways of influencing future events and thereby imposes on us new occasions for the attribution of responsibility and guilt" (128-29).[20] Cultures stretch, as humanitarian sentiments stretch, depending (among other things) on possibilities for action and on people's perception of the ease or difficulty of using them.

Consider what Haskell has called "the case of the starving stranger"—an advance commentary (the original essay appeared in 1985) on such internationalist appeals as Sontag's. Knowing for certain that at the moment we are reading, somewhere people are starving to death, why do we not sell our possessions, buy a plane ticket, "fly to Bombay or wherever, seek out at least one of those starving strangers, and save his life"? (127). People do not feel responsibility, Haskell says, for changing something that they cannot affect without stepping entirely outside the routine of their lives:

> The main reason you and I can go about our daily routine and not be overwhelmed with guilt about the stranger's plight is that the only recipe we have for going to his aid is far more exotic and more difficult to implement than the recipes we customarily use in everyday life. It involves a causal connection between his life and ours that is much more indirect, remote, and tenuous than the ones we habitually employ, so we do not regard our failure to act on the recipe as abnormal. None of us habitually liquidates major assets and departs on a moment's notice for the remotest parts of the globe in the pursuit even of selfish ends. (132)

At first glance, this line of argument may appear conservative; it can easily be taken to justify already existing limits on the West's perception of its responsibility for non-Western suffering and oppression. I propose, however, that Haskell's insistence on the already existing is precisely what is needed to break through those limits. He explains what has to happen, and to some extent what *is* happening, in order for the perception of responsibility to be converted from an abstract, utopian ideal that is not even meant to be honored into a common culture that has some small chance of being effectual. What may look like a defense of the nation, then, should rather be seen as an account of how internationalism is theoretically and historically continuous with nationalism, contesting it while extending its style of solidarity and drawing power and legitimacy from the same sources.

Haskell's argument that the scale of humanitarian feelings is a cultural variable, dependent on existing technology and social organizations, parallels Benedict Anderson's account of the origins of nationalism in *Imagined Communities.* Anderson ascribes the advent of nationalism to what he calls "print capitalism." The nation was not born out of the dark, unconscious continuities of inherited culture, he argues, but out of this specific combination of social and technological innovation. These innovations in turn produce a culture that is specifically national. But if Anderson is right, then why should such a process come to a halt once it has produced national culture?[21] As both technologies and social institutions spill over national boundaries, wouldn't we expect the production of culture to do so as well? National print capitalism having given way to global electronic and digital capitalism, the same forces that stretched culture to the scale of the nation are stretching it beyond the scale of the nation. The result is no less genuine, and no less imperfect. The familiar lists of McDonald's and Disney and Coca-Cola—or for that matter, of non-American firms such as Benetton and Body Shop—conceal a certain xenophobia or national self-loathing.[22] No doubt these firms deserve critique, but no more so than producers of humbler cultural commodities reserved for domestic sale. Culture at the international scale is certainly less than ideal, but it is so because of the same inequalities of power and unhappy familiarities that make national cultures less than ideal.

Sontag, who would undoubtedly share the nationalists' distaste for American export culture, unfortunately also shares with them the related assumption that culture is inherited, local, familiar. That is why she fights it, both as a modernist and as an internationalist. There is much that is attractive about her rigorous and elevating project. The case can be made—Julia Kristeva has made it, framing a modernist aesthetic in psychoanalytic terms—that to achieve a genuine cosmopolitanism, people must learn how deeply they are strangers to themselves.[23] Still, the aesthetic of estrangement tends to assume, falsely, that it has to work on people who are as yet *un*estranged. Like Tamir, Miller, and the other defenders of nationalism, this aesthetic imagines culture as the antithesis of defamiliarization. Culture is a (too) happy family; the modernist aesthetic tries to make it unhappier. It does not want to acknowledge the generational and other unhappinesses that are already present, whether within families or within cultures. Assuming that families and cultures are already awash in the warm enjoyment of natural proximity, it refuses to gratify except by offering the acid delights of defamiliarization. Thus the aesthetic of defamiliarization, like the ethic of internationalism, is obliged to make international commitments seem culturally alien, a matter of cold and distant sacrifice rather than an extension of existing interests, affections, and loyalties. This makes its goal seem achievable only by means of a total self-transcendence that is so arduous as to be extremely unlikely.

The realist will answer that this simply describes the sad state of things: internationalism *is* arduous and unlikely. It would be silly to deny the empirical evidence weighing against internationalism. But the choice is not between realism and utopianism; that is no choice at all. A modernist or utopian humanitarianism like Sontag's is merely realism's mirror image. Knowing in advance that it is on the losing side, it is too comfortable in the face of inevitable defeat. It takes the extra credit to be had for speaking in heroic and hopeless isolation, or risks being so perceived. It does not know how to prophesy except in a wilderness where it knows it will not be echoed or answered. It requires such a wilderness and assumes it. But if such an image of heroism is as potent as it seems to be, then the wilderness cannot, after all, be empty. It must be populated with a sizable number of kindred spirits, or at least spirits more open to internationalist appeals such as Sontag's than she would seem to predict. Realism dictates that this population should not be disregarded. Those of us who do our prophesying in the academy, where the temptation to believe in our lonely but collective purity is almost overwhelming, will perhaps recognize the extent to which Sontag's predicament is also our own and begin looking around our self-created wilderness for company.[24]

Those who are ready to hear internationalist appeals include many who do not travel ambitiously to places of atrocity and geopolitical crisis, yet who nevertheless know something of the rest of the world. They know it just as they know something of their nation: by means of the media—for example, by means of photographs, which travel more easily than people. Sontag argues in *On Photography* that photographs, especially atrocity photographs of the sort that might move people to transnational action, do not produce real or genuine experience. They produce only a dangerous semblance of experience, a tourist's detached voyeurism: "Essentially the camera makes everyone a tourist in other people's reality, and eventually in one's own" (57). Thus those who do not go to Sarajevo but instead depend on mere photographs cannot know anything worth knowing about Sarajevo's suffering. This premise seems worthy of doubt. Sontag makes an exception for the photographs of the Holocaust that marked her, quasi-traumatically, as a child. But how are these any different from more recent photographs of Bosnia and Rwanda and their presumed effects on children today? People are being marked, if not always traumatically, even by routine television watching. John Berger, though close to Sontag in his suspicions about photography, suggests, for example, that a guest worker's personal assembly of transnational photographs can be the model of a cosmopolitan experience that is not merely privileged and not merely detached tourism. (I take up this debate between Sontag and Berger in chapter 4.) In a different register, consider TV ads such as those for the 1996 Olympics, which made the "we're all connected" theme into something more than an empty cliché; or the commercially successful Hollywood career of a director such as Steven Spielberg. Spielberg's *Empire of the Sun* features an English boy who identifies with his nation's Japanese enemies. His *E.T.* teaches some things about aliens that the backers of anti-immigrant legislation could not have appreciated. For better or worse, visceral experience of international connectedness is not so very scarce.

This is an ethical as well as an aesthetic point. As internationalist experience cannot be identified with aesthetic estrangement, neither can it be restricted to the risk of life, which will always be rare, nor even to the sacrifice of comfort and convenience. As the price of genuine internationalism, Sontag asks each of her readers to imitate Christ's apostles, abandoning all worldly possessions and loyalties in order to follow her. But internationalism does not always require the dramatic model of apostolic recruitment (which is also self-aggrandizing for the rare apostle-like intellectuals who adopt it and thus another reason for everyone else to resist its exclusive appeal). The number of the apostles was limited.[75] But the rest of the faithful cannot be written off. We need an internationalist ethics of the everyday, one that will not tell us solely what to die or kill for but also how action at a distance can be part of how we live. An internationalist ethic may indeed demand of us some eventual personal sacrifice, perhaps even an extraordinarily brave one. But there is no way such a demand will ever be honored unless the habit of transnational connection has already been established, rooted in routine duties and pleasures as well as in once-in-a-lifetime renunciations, made part of ordinary culture.

THE NEW NATIONALISM AND THE END OF THE CULTURE WARS

Culture valued for its democratic ordinariness as well as for its rarity and exceptional accomplishment, for its newness and power of fresh construction as well as for a tradition inherited from time immemorial—the concept of culture I have been using here has nothing shockingly novel about it. It merely extends into international territory the paradigm of the so-called cultural left, a paradigm that has been the object of aggressive, uncomfortable, and ultimately wearisome controversy through the years of the so-called culture wars.

People are tired of the culture wars, and rightly so. Still, the international dimension of these hostilities merits some separate discussion, especially because it has usually appeared only as malicious innuendo. I offer two seemingly contradictory propositions about the culture wars: first, that they should be seen as part of a larger historical moment or movement, namely, the emergence of a new American nationalism; and second, despite the call to battle that the word *nationalism* seems to sound, that internationalism properly conceived does not require a fight to the death with the new nationalism. I would like to think that the general fatigue of all parties to the culture wars is a sign that nationalists and internationalists have blundered onto some common ground.

My first impulse to use the term *cosmopolitanism* came before an honorably resistant audience at Wake Forest University in March 1991. I had been invited expressly to defend what my hosts considered indefensible: a refusal to honor the great authors of the Western tradition and an insistence instead on flooding the curriculum with writings that merely "represented" oppressed groups, among them writings from the former colonies. Rather than either accept this description of what I and my colleagues were up to or bore everyone by showing, at crushingly conclusive length, that it was *not* what we were up to, I decided at the last minute (during a sleepless night in a superb mansion left to the university by a large tobacco owner) to offer a polemical counterdescription. The academy's controversial interest in diverse and foreign cultures, I told my audience, expressed our commitment to the old Greek ideal of cosmopolitanism, as in Isocrates and the Stoics. It implied an energetic and open-minded curiosity about the world outside our national borders, a healthy willingness to allow our own culture to be challenged by other cultures. It meant nothing more threatening than taking the classics seriously and doing our intellectual and professional duty.[26]

This led to some lively give-and-take at the moment and was finally quite useful, I think, in providing a sympathetic but critical distance on multiculturalism. (See, for example, chapter 2.) Yet the connotations of traditional class privilege that I was self-consciously playing with on that occasion had perhaps already become too dangerous for such playful uses. They were among the crucial targets of an assault that was rapidly gathering force and coherence. Since then, this assault has come close to defining educated common sense for those nonacademics interested in the academy's treatment of culture, class, and nation.

The argument comes in three sections, and from both the right and the left. It holds that contemporary academic critics of culture are (1) privileged elitists, (2) unpatriotic, and (3) detached from political reality. Each element implies the others. The eagerness of the academics to dredge up the antique atrocities of colonialism and to champion the foreign cultures victimized by it merely disguises a new, professional version of an old privilege: the aristocratic privilege of mobility. Imperialism is the favored theme of the academic jet set; such strange and unaccountable topics come naturally to an unaccountable elite. Their concern with culture is irrelevant to the bread-and-butter issues that affect the lives of ordinary Americans. All that talk of identity and difference makes no real difference. Culture is the functional equivalent of foreignness; it is what doesn't count.

So, for example, poet laureate Robert Pinsky accuses champions of cosmopolitanism such as Martha Nussbaum of speaking for "the village of the liberal managerial class."[27] John Patrick Diggins, in a review of Nussbaum's contribution to *For Love of Country* (discussed in chapter 8), makes Nussbaum's "Sixties sensibilities" representative of the "anti-patriotic legacy of the 60s generation" (22).[28] To these charges, Richard Rorty (discussed in chapter 7) adds that the new or "cultural" left is less valuable than the old left precisely because it is too concerned with culture, whereas the old left was primarily concerned with real or electoral politics.[29] Elitists, traitors to the nation, eagerly self-marginalizing, and politically ineffectual, the 1960s left, as seen by its elders, is really no left at all.

One reason for spending as much time as I have on Susan Sontag, a nonacademic intellectual of an older generation, is that each item in this portrait corresponds somewhat unexpectedly to a point that I raised about her above. I cannot see these things in her without knowing that others see them in people like me or worrying that they will be the wisdom about my generation that the still younger generation, for which the Vietnam War is as much ancient history as the Hitler-Stalin pact, will accept. Some self-examination seems called for all around. Academics, who have carried out much of the academy bashing themselves, have also invited national scrutiny by their own expressed concern over their responsibility to extra-academic constituencies. To identify with some version of internationalism is to be willing to push the discussion of constituency further, not to withdraw from it by pointing the finger at our enemies and calling them nationalists.

Consider, for example, what Diggins calls the "anti-patriotic legacy of the 60s generation." One of the distinguishing marks of the new left in the 1960s was its refusal to be defined by the two sides available in the cold war, a refusal that clearly continues to motivate the cultural left today. Today, the same new left complaint about the old left remains implicit: not that the older generation was wrong in choosing to take its distance from the Soviet Union but that it was crippled by the either-or pressures of that choice, unwilling to be adequately critical of so-called Western freedoms—in short, too nationalist. Rorty argues that the cold war, his generation's war, was a good war. But he also makes a characteristic concession to his younger opponents: "Someone prepared to argue . . . that the cold war did more harm than good" would get "support from the Vietnamese and the Salvadorans," he notes, "but none from the Hungarians and the Czechs" (265). Thus he suggests that the generational line between himself and the cultural left is also a geographical or sociopolitical line between accountability to the people of the *Second* World (the Hungarian and Czech victims of the Soviet system) and to the people of the *Third* World (the Vietnamese and Salvadoran victims of the American system).

This is an important concession to an internationalist way of thinking. To bring forward the Vietnamese and Salvadorans along with the Hungarians and Czechs is not to choose a right over a wrong, real electoral politics over unreal cultural politics, or accountability over detachment, or to indulge a necessary ethnocentrism. It is to describe the collision of two equally real, equally concrete rights and vectors of accountability. (Internationalism must admit to its own share of unresolved ambiguities.) This moment of genuine internationalism on Rorty's part calls for a matching concession from the other side. Speaking as someone who came of age in the late 1960s and early 1970s, in the period of national liberation movements and the Vietnam War, I know that I, at least, was much more decisively formed by the atrocities the United States committed and supported in places such as Vietnam and El Salvador (committed and supported in my name and perhaps, but for a bad knee, with my participation) than I was by someone else's totalitarianism in Hungary or the former Czechoslovakia. Yes, a phrase such as "Western freedom" seemed pronounceable only in quotation marks, and I still have trouble doing without them. But our willingness to let the politics of Eastern Europe sit on the back burner was a piece of inverted ethnocentrism. It still put the United States first—if not first in virtue, then first in vice. Our own victims mattered most. In other words, we should have admitted that we, too, were nationalists, after our fashion—and perhaps also that in this sense, at least, it is right and proper to put your own country first.

The internationalism of that student left was also limited and distorted by the relative privileges that many of us possessed, by virtue of our class as well as our education. It seems plausible that, as various commentators have suggested, the antiwar movement was severely weakened by the class divide between those who could successfully avoid military service and those who could not. "Between 1962 and 1972, 29,701 men graduated from Harvard, MIT, and Princeton; only twenty died in Vietnam."[30] And Milton J. Bates argues that, despite the loud hawkishness of George Meany of the American Federation of Labor and Congress of Industrial Organizations (AFL-CIO) and those indelible TV images of construction workers in hard hats bashing antiwar protesters, "antiwar sentiment was stronger in the working class than in the middle class."[31] Working-class hostility to the antiwar movement, Bates argues, "proceeded less from prowar sentiment than from class antipathy" (87). The proportions are hard to measure, but the class antipathy was real and significant, and it has not gone away. The charge of elitism leveled against internationalism now, as then, may well be misdirected, but that does not mean there is nothing to answer.

Elitism is central to the allegory offered up in former labor secretary Robert Reich's *The Work of Nations,* a book that helps put the culture wars into a larger perspective. "As borders become ever more meaningless in economic terms," Reich declares, "those citizens best positioned to thrive in the world market are tempted to slip the bonds of national allegiance, and by so doing disengage themselves from their less favored fellows."[32] In Reich's view, globalization has redrawn the line of class. Class is now national. Instead of separating, say, capitalists from workers, the class line now separates genuinely American interests (the losers) from international and un-American interests (the winners). The losers, who are involved in "routine production," are presumably made up of both workers and capitalists. The winners, who have profited from globalization, are called not capitalists but "symbolic analysts." The word *symbolic* flatters the business elite by enveloping number-crunching skills like those of the corporate consultant in a noncommercial aura. But it can do so only because the word's broader associations are with the cultural—with the *merely* symbolic, as opposed to the real. Thus culture is once again contrasted with reality (in this case, production rather than politics), and once again it is located in international space. Two related versions of the malevolent unreal, the cultural and the global, are again designated as the preserve of an elite.

The ideology of the symbolic analysts, Reich says, is cosmopolitanism. Cosmopolitanism justifies their elite status vis-à-vis the losers as the reward of better adaptation to today's world of economic activity, which is both newly global and newly symbolic. According to "trends already underway," Reich says, "laissez-faire cosmopolitanism" (I say more in a moment about the strangeness of "laissez-faire" here) is now becoming "America's dominant economic and social philosophy" (315). Reich does not utterly condemn cosmopolitanism, but he says it has a "darker side," and his sympathies clearly lie on the other one. "For without strong attachments and loyalties extending beyond family and friends, symbolic analysts may never develop the habits and attitudes of social responsibility. They will be world citizens, but without accepting or even acknowledging any of the obligations that citizenship in a polity normally implies" (309).

This account of cosmopolitanism is crucial to Reich's proposal for what he calls a "positive economic nationalism." In such a nationalism, "each nation's citizens take primary responsibility for enhancing the capacities of their countrymen for full and productive lives, but . . . also work with other nations to ensure that these improvements do not come at others' expense" (311). This benign vision would seem to have no losers at all. But this is a bit too good to be true. By what magic could the crucial qualification appended in that last clause ("not . . . at others' expense") ever come into effect? Reich begins his book by arguing that Americans no longer feel "in the same boat" with other Americans; he ends the book by proposing that other nations, too, need to pull together. How could this proposal fail to produce a rivalry between the different national boats, that is, a substitution of winners and losers—of inequality and hostility—*among* nations for winners and losers *within* nations?[33]

This substitution has often been characteristic of nationalism. It need not be in every case. But in the U.S. case this move is made, let us remember, by what others outside the United States see as a winner nation—a nation that, with 5 percent of the world's population, consumes 30 percent of the world's resources.[34] And Reich's egalitarian demand for corporate responsibility (which is much better than any policy the Clinton administration has been willing to propose) seems aimed at ensuring that this percentage will tilt still further in favor of American consumers. Reich's starting point is the fact that many, and perhaps most, Americans do not see themselves as beneficiaries of a winner nation. What they see around them is increasing inequality: the rich getting much richer, their own hard-won standard of living threatened or already deteriorating, the so-called American Dream more distant than it once seemed. Reich is right to want to do something about this. He is wrong to choose a nationalist solution, displacing discontent away from American capitalism and onto representatives of foreignness.

Taking from some Americans to give to other Americans will work, Reich appears to believe, only if the first group are seen as cosmopolitans, hence not really Americans at all, and if the surplus to be redistributed can come as much as possible from abroad, that is, from maintaining or exacerbating an unjust distribution of global resources. His egalitarian nationalism offers ordinary Americans both a consolidation of their relative advantage in the global economy and (in order to explain growing inequalities within that advantage) a new scapegoat, ambiguously foreign *and* native. The cosmopolitan or symbolic analyst hides the one inequality (the global economic advantage, from which most Americans benefit) while drawing off resentment for the other inequality (the domestic disparity of incomes, from which most Americans do not). Near enough to know and remote enough to hate, the symbolic analysts are convenient targets. But they are not the real casualties. Those who stand to lose most from Reich's scapegoating of the elites are ordinary people who do not happen to be Americans.

Despite his antielitism, then, Reich warmly embraces inequality—on the global scale. He also embraces another key item in the indictment against the symbolic analysts: the symbolic or the cultural itself. Suppose you think you belong in a different, much richer boat. What is to keep you in the poorer, smaller, slower one? David Miller makes the answer explicit: the reason we are so prosperous and others are not is either blind luck, and therefore not to be thought about at all, or, if it must be discussed, located in a domain that severely limits calculations of fairness—the domain of culture. Miller is against extending ethical responsibilities beyond one's fellow nationals. Challenged by the global inequality of resources—for example, between Sweden and Somalia (63)—which seems to undercut this case, he responds as follows:

> I do not wish to defend the present pattern of global inequality, which undoubtedly bears the marks of past exploitation, and the continuing vulnerability of many developing countries to economic decisions taken by the Western states. At the same time, some degree of inequality is inevitable, and not unjust, because it is the direct consequence of a system where independent nations pursue the policies that reflect their cultural values. (192)

Germany is richer than the United Kingdom, Miller innocently goes on, because of its culture. But the initial Somalia/Sweden example takes us in a less innocuous direction. It suggests that the real import of Miller's argument is not cultural comparisons within Europe but rather between Europe and the so-called less developed countries. The Third World is starving, Miller says in effect, not because of "past exploitation" but because of its "cultural values." Respect for national culture means that despite "past exploitation," it is "not unjust" for us Europeans to let it starve, and we may do so with a clear conscience.

INTERNATIONALISM IN DISTRESS

Invoked in defense of national identity, culture naturalizes what we can call, with some understatement, economic inequality.[35] This is what the new liberal nationalism appears to be all about. "For the liberal nationalist," Michael Lind writes in *The Next American Nation,* "the American nation is defined by language and culture, not by race or religion" (8). But by the end of the book, culture has come to mean economics: "the preservation of middle-class living standards in the First World" (323) or defending "the relative status of [our] nation in the world economy," rather than "promoting the absolute well-being of the world as a whole" (375). Our prosperity is the result of our culture. Let's keep the advantages that we have, the new nationalism declares. These advantages may not be fair, but we're not going to let that stop us. Better to throw out any standard of fairness—that is, any universal or transnational mode of thinking.

So stupendous a reversal surely heralds the end of the culture wars. The cultural or multicultural left has been attacked for embracing cultural identity at the expense of rationality and national unity. But those who attack it do so on behalf of the unavowable reality of global economic inequality, which they camouflage as cultural identity—the nation as a culture, which rationality is not allowed to meddle with. (In chapter 7, I make this argument at greater length about Richard Rorty.) If rationality means allowing claims against the United States to be expressed in a transnational language by the rest of the world, then the defenders of national unity are defending not rationality but culture, which sets limits on reason's jurisdiction.

COSMOPOLITANISM, CONSTITUENCY, AND THE WELFARE STATE

Among the various conclusions that might be drawn from this reversal, the most constructive to me is the recognition of a certain common ground between the two sides. If the charges against academic cosmopolitanism turn out to mirror the commitments of the new nationalism, specifically to global inequality and cultural givenness, as I have suggested, it is also true that academic cosmopolitans have something to learn from their opponents about their own commitments, including their unacknowledged commitments to rationality and the nation-state.[36]

The constituency to which Reich and the other liberal nationalists are speaking seems evident. When he courts the good opinion of the labor movement, and even when he cautions the business elite to act more accountable, Reich is appealing to an identifiable self-interest. In contrast, internationalism, like aesthetics, seems to be defined by its *disinterestedness.* (This is why Sontag can so effortlessly combine internationalism and aesthetics.) But no one lives on this high moral ground. Thus Reich seems to be making a safe bet. What is cosmopolitanism's share of the electorate? What voters are going to cast their ballots for foreign profits? Except for arms-exporting industries, does cosmopolitanism have a constituency at all?

The discussion above gestured toward an answer to these questions by proposing that self-interest is not necessarily either simple or national. It is culturally defined, and since culture extends no less naturally beyond the nation than up to the nation's borders, it is to be expected that selves and their interests will do the same. There is nothing inherently shocking, therefore, in the notion that internationalist culture exists—that internationalism is not merely an abstract ideal, a geographical figure signifying the universality of ethics, but a set of interests already visible in the present and awaiting further political organization and mobilization. As the chapters that follow suggest, internationalist culture is already manifest in the lives of many different and overlapping groups, from media watchers to immigrant or diasporic collectivities tied to their countries of origin as well as to their country of residence, and living the resultant mixed and fluid loyalties in an increasingly organized and self-conscious way. These groups include guest workers (discussed in chapter 4), au pairs (the subject of chapter 5), and Third World intellectuals working in the metropolis, such as Edward Said (the subject of chapter 6).

This coin has another side. As internationalism, reconciling itself to culture, acquires constituency, it also surrenders its ideal purity. Unlike culture in its most defensive posture, internationalist culture cannot pretend to be inviolable or incorrigible. And unlike internationalism in most of its versions, it cannot pretend that it is simply the antithesis of nationalism. Such impurities make internationalist culture harder to see (if moral purity is what one is looking for), but they also make it more interesting to look at. For example, ecological internationalism and human rights internationalism, two versions that I refer to in several chapters, combine nationally specific and "selfish" motives with much more self-critical and even self-sacrificing ones. The motives of American unions lobbying against foreign sweatshops are an uncertain mixture of the desire to hold corporations accountable, to protect American jobs against capital flight (even at the expense of foreign jobs), and to protect the living and working conditions of workers everywhere. American human rights activists who work to impose higher standards on child labor in Bangladesh or Honduras, at the same time perhaps undermining America's foreign competitors, cannot be decisively labeled either selfish or altruistic, internationalist or nationalist. The same holds for ecological activists struggling, with an inevitable unevenness and inconsistency, against the consequences for existing American lifestyles of damage to natural resources elsewhere as well as for others of America's unwillingness to drop its consumerist lifestyles. And it is not merely activists but also the much larger population, whose moral and financial support keeps the activists going, who embody these internationalist ambiguities.

As Reich says, the constituency of cosmopolitanism also includes the symbolic analysts. Given the transnational scope of today's markets and cultural flows, the interest symbolic analysts have in an enlarged cosmopolitan perspective does not call for much explanation. But what is the political valence of that interest? Is it their only interest? Reich describes cosmopolitanism as a free trader's simple and unambiguous desire for the unregulated mobility of global capital. In his view, the archetypal representative of cosmopolitanism would be an antigovernment, "laissez-faire" figure like Newt Gingrich:

> On the one side are zero-sum nationalists, typically representing the views of routine producers and in-person servers, urging that government advance America's economic interest—even at the expense of others around the globe. . . . On the other side are laissez-faire cosmopolitans, usually representing the views of symbolic analysts, arguing that government should simply stay out. In their view, profit-seeking individuals and firms are far better able to decide what gets produced where; governments only mess things up. (311)

Is Newt Gingrich really the paradigmatic cosmopolitan? Do cosmopolitans characteristically think that "governments only mess things up"? Reich's winners in the world market include management consultants but also academics and intellectuals like Reich himself. Academics and intellectuals depend heavily on government support for their services. Where would the 80 percent of the nation's students who go to public universities be without the government's sponsorship? Those who teach them would be out of a job, along with a great number of other cultural workers who staff publicly funded institutions such as museums and libraries or who benefit indirectly from other grants and subsidies. This is self-interest of a pretty straightforward sort. How, then, can Reich jump to the blatantly spurious conclusion that cosmopolitanism automatically aligns one with laissez-faire economics and smaller, weaker government?

He, along with many others, can do so in part because academics in general, and the cultural left in particular, have not always been willing to admit their structural alignment with the social welfare state. At least in the humanities, which work at some distance from policy, being an academic has seemed to require ritualized expressions of alienation from the state. Taking a distance from the federal government's authority and its calculating, instrumental rationality has seemed to be precisely what "culture" meant. Even in its more progressive manifestations, such as the New Deal, the Great Society, and the limited but real backing for the Civil Rights movement, the state could thus be assumed to be good for nothing but criticism. Thus internationalism might be accused of functioning, like culture in its traditional definitions, as merely a new excuse for the humanities' self-legitimating estrangement. This is the risk we ought to be able to hear in Susan Sontag and take warning from. To the extent that internationalism remains stuck in this antistatist professional deformation, it will have limited political resonance outside it.

Transnational culture offers possibilities for expression and organization that are less threatening than direct political demands yet are quietly influential. The adjacent and overlapping topography of "international civil society," where activist NGOs have recently been throwing more weight around, is also worthy of enthusiastic efforts. Still, internationalism can be assured the political impact it merits only if it does not confine itself to the domain of culture or civil society—that is, if it does not set itself simply and definitively against the nation-state. This strategy is not without risks, yet it is truer than most versions to internationalism as an impure historical phenomenon. If national and international culture are, respectively, a smaller and a larger result of the same processes of sociotechnological bonding, as I argue above, then it is a mistake to think of them as opposed in some fundamental and definitional way. Despite what international relations jargon calls the "Anarchy Model"—the assumption that an unbridgeable abyss exists between the relative moral order within states and the anarchy between them—there is the same lack of fundamental opposition between national and international politics as between national and international culture.[37]

Cosmopolitans are sometimes accused of hypocrisy when they adopt an oppositional stance toward the nation-state. Their critics find them unwilling to admit their dependence on the relative prosperity and stability of well-ordered states.[38] This dependence is provisional, and it does not entail uncritical loyalty, but it is real and can be admitted without shame. Consider, for example, Martha Nussbaum's argument against Peter Unger's proposal that people redistribute their income and possessions among agencies that combat world hunger. If people did give a large portion of their incomes to Oxfam and the United Nations Children's Fund (UNICEF), as Unger recommends, then "national and local governments" would no longer find themselves "able to maintain such welfare efforts as they now fund," Nussbaum objects, "since so much property would have been given away. Within a few years, governments from India to Britain would be in disarray, as Oxfam became the owner of increasing

INTERNATIONALISM IN DISTRESS

amounts of everything."[39] Hunger would get worse, and fewer political remedies for it would be available. Even for someone trying to mobilize support for an extremely radical redistribution of global resources, it is not good politics to take the state as such as the enemy. Using the machinery of the nation-state to try to control the predatoriness of global capital is a clear example, and a crucial one, of a necessary tactic that may be simultaneously nationalist and internationalist. There will be moments of choice between the two, but there will also be many moments when what is called for are subtle operations of steering, emphasis, and enlargement within a project that is neither simply one nor the other.

The cultural left's silence about its partial but significant conjunction of interests with the state is one reason that the picture of global capital as "multiculturalism's silent partner"[40]—the former tearing at the state from without, the latter from within—has been allowed to stand uncontested. But there are various things wrong with this picture. On the one hand, like the Civil Rights movement, multiculturalism has depended from the outset on soliciting the direct and indirect pressure of the federal government on its behalf. On the other hand, the undermining of the welfare state is by no means a simple effect of globalization, any more than multiculturalism is.

Does the global market necessarily sabotage state sovereignty, thereby producing McWorld? How does this apply vis-à-vis the economies of East Asia, which Benjamin Barber himself brings up in *Jihad vs. McWorld* (14–15)? Their dramatic success in the world market (at least, while it lasted) seems only to have reinforced the powers of the state. This should be no surprise. There are many situations when the interests of capital demand a stronger, rather than a weaker, state. Well-policed borders, for example, help discipline the workforce, holding wages down and making sure that capital remains more mobile than labor. As Michael Mann argues, the extent of "breathless transnationalism" has been overstated (117).[41] Financial transnationalism (much more developed, Mann says, than transnationalism in production or commerce) does cut down the ability of the nation-state to control interest rates and currency valuation (118). But this has been a relatively unused power. The welfare state in the more developed countries has been in retreat for other, more conjunctural reasons, Mann writes, including economic stagnation and its impact on state finances. Neoliberal economic policies and the scapegoating of women, children, and minorities were not forced on the major political parties by the necessities of an implacable, uncontrollable planetary process. They were contingent choices, though made within a pregiven framework. And the fact that there has recently been a swing back in the other direction—for example, toward restoring welfare benefits to some of those expelled from the rolls—shows that other choices were and are possible.

Globalization has not been the cause of culture wars, in other words, but only a convenient excuse for them. Thanks to this malevolent quasi deity, the real decline in American living standards could be blamed not on American decision makers, corporate and governmental, but on foreign agents: on globalization abroad and on the cultural divisiveness at home that was supposedly its mere reflection. The new nationalists have been tempted by this xenophobic escapism. That is why someone like Michael Lind cries first and loudest for drastic limits on immigration and mentions control over capital only in a weak afterthought. But xenophobia is not the full story of the new nationalism.

A more generous and, I think, more accurate interpretation of the new nationalism would put equal emphasis on the urgent effort to protect what remains of the U.S. welfare state. That is the example many of its proponents reach for first, and they have a point. When David Miller argues "that a proper account of ethics should give weight to national boundaries," he is also arguing "that in particular there is no objection to ethical schemes—such as welfare states—that are designed to deliver benefits exclusively to those who fall within the same boundaries as ourselves" (11). "The building of the welfare state," which emerged from "decidedly nationalist movements" such as the New Deal and the Great Society, is a crucial exhibit in David Hollinger's case for liberal nationalism in *Postethnic America*.[42] Whatever qualms one may feel about such arguments, today the threat to the welfare state is real, and the aim of gathering a progressive majority around the defense of the welfare state is one that academic internationalists have every reason to join in. At least in the short term, one of our political tasks must be a return to what Michael Mann calls "the diffuse popular solidarism of the nation-state, especially the relations between the majority and the poor—the latter being disproportionately the unskilled, the sick, ethnic minorities, female-headed households, the elderly and the young" (119). Feminist internationalists (discussed in chapters 3 and 5) have led the way in this delicate negotiation. While experiences such as the 1995 Beijing conference on women's rights have demonstrated that "feeling global" is neither a masculine fantasy nor a prerogative of the privileged, feminists have also urged measured support for the welfare state in the knowledge that its weakening is an enormous blow struck against women around the world. The labor movement, too, has been trying to fight on both fronts simultaneously. If it is not anachronistic to speak of a "left," then the common task for that left, in the short run, seems clear. As Fredric Jameson writes in his "Five Theses on Actually Existing Marxism," "the Left is . . . today placed in the position of having to defend big

INTERNATIONALISM IN DISTRESS

government and the welfare state, something its elaborate and sophisticated traditions of the critique of social democracy make it embarrassing to do" (4).[43] Embarrassing or not, this means cautiously making common cause with those who call themselves liberal nationalists.

This task is all the more imperative for American intellectuals, and all the more embarrassing, because we depend on the social welfare state not merely for financial support but also for legitimacy. Historically, the social welfare state has been a cross-class project, the result of popular demands for public services, entitlements, and protection combined with the rising social influence of expertise. For all its imperfections, then, the social welfare state is the closest thing we have yet seen to a synthesis in which the different interests of the poor and needy, on the one hand, and elite experts, on the other, could be resolved. In short, for the moment it is the best answer to the charge of elitism that intellectuals have.

This is not to say that there are no other answers, or that there will be no differences between nationalists and internationalists—for instance, over immigration and the rights of noncitizens. But those differences do not define an absolute contradiction between the welfare state as fortress and a borderless, unattached humanitarianism. On the one hand, mobilization on behalf of the social welfare state need not take virulently nationalist form. On the other hand, internationalism cannot claim to incarnate that miracle of a humanitarian politics without others or enemies that would permit it to claim intrinsic moral superiority to a constitutively exclusive nationalism. Though Richard Rorty and others tend to set commitment to the welfare state against commitments to noncitizens, as if the one excluded the other, the relations between the two, while difficult, would seem to allow more room for maneuver. From one perspective, the welfare state can be seen as a necessary means of embodying and extending cosmopolitanism. According to Étienne Balibar, citizenship and nationality came together in the first place only because of the concrete social benefits offered. In other words, it was the social welfare state, rather than belligerent ethnic nationalism, that gave national citizenship such emotional power as it has come to possess.[44] It seems plausible, then, that transnational citizenship or cosmopolitanism will need to be deepened or thickened in much the same way, by concrete social entitlements, if it is going to become part of that effectual internationalist ethic that Sontag's appeal demanded. In this sense, the success of the social welfare state at the national level should be seen as necessary preparation for that ethic, rather than its antithesis. The point would be both to defend the social welfare state and, as much as possible, to extend it outward—for example, toward residents who are noncitizens.

Still, a perfect fit between the two projects is not to be expected. This perhaps explains the somewhat unstable emphasis in the chapters to follow. Most of them were written with the double aim of (1) developing an internationalist viewpoint that would avoid some of the distress produced by existing models, and (2) in defense of the welfare state, encouraging some provisional reconciliation with the more progressive champions of the new nationalism. Within that double intention, the balance has varied. This is one reason for being wary of this somewhat awkward enterprise, and there are others. Still, it would be some satisfaction if people on either side could take it as an opportunity to think through some of the difficulties and perhaps come up with other areas of common initiative.

SOME VERSIONS OF
U.S. INTERNATIONALISM

This is a rough and provisional report on some ways in which American cultural critics have recently been conceiving and practicing what Edward Said calls, encouragingly, "adversarial internationalization."[1] Said's phrase is clearly not meant as a tautology, as if, in the domain of knowledge, any move from the local toward the global scale were necessarily deparochializing, destabilizing, and therefore desirable. It should be understood, rather, as a necessary provocation, a challenge to inquire whether, to what extent, and on what terms any versions of international knowledge production might truly be considered adversarial in relation to the hegemonic internationalization of the capitalist market and the now largely uncontested political and military supremacy of the United States. As with the still more oxymoronic phrase "U.S. internationalism," the double assumption here is (1) that there can be no American-style or American-situated internationalism that will not reflect, on some level, American assumptions and interests, and (2) that this is not utterly damning. There are good reasons for discriminating among the sorts of Americanness that the different versions offer and among their meanings and consequences, for they bring with them political opportunities as well as risks and threats.

In pursuit of some polemical oversimplification, this chapter looks, for starters, at four journals: *Diaspora, boundary 2, Social Text,* and *Public Culture.* Each has broken new ground in stimulating and supporting work in the international area—the nonspecialist area beyond area studies—and each has seen the work it published as in some sense adversarial.[2] Still, to display the arbitrariness and inevitable injustice of my procedure, I have not only neglected all the many other journals that have been publishing similar kinds of work (*Third Text, positions, Transition, Millenium, Identities, differences, Cultural Studies, Race and Class, Dissent, New Left Review, Oxford Literary Review,* and more), but I have also narrowed the focus to only one issue for each of the chosen four: specifically, the Spring 1994 issue. It is clear that no one issue is likely to be representative, that none of these journals even approaches unity in its editorial policy or publication record, and that there is considerable overlap from one journal to another. The reader is encouraged to take these categorizations as an irreverent incitement to reflect on arguments or tendencies that point in very different directions from the four I detail here.

In that spirit, then, here are four keywords corresponding to four sorts or styles of internationalism: in *Diaspora,* "diaspora"; in *boundary 2,* "global capitalism"; in *Social Text,* "popular culture"; and in *Public Culture,* "civil society."

First of all, *diaspora*. The backlash against multiculturalism in the United States, which is continually discussed in the past tense, as if it had finally exhausted itself, and just as continually pops up again in some new and virulent form, has perhaps obscured what is arguably the strongest version of U.S. internationalism now current: that which identifies internationalism with domestic multiculturalism and with the tradition of American pluralism and heterogeneity—in short, with genuine Americanism. I associate this version, somewhat unjustly, with *Diaspora,* the journal of the four I have chosen that has gone furthest—though never without qualification—toward celebrating transnational mobility and the hybridity that results from it as simple and sufficient goods in themselves. Only such a celebration could, for example, generalize Bharati Mukherjee's immigration to a flatteringly portrayed North American metropolis as (in the unambiguously enthusiastic words of one *Diaspora* essay) "relocation as a positive act."[3]

The sense in which this can become an excuse for a reckless American expansionism may be obvious, but if it isn't, the Spring 1994 issue of *Diaspora* clarifies the policy implications. Yossi Shain, in an essay called "Marketing the Democratic Creed Abroad: U.S. Diasporic Politics in the Era of Multiculturalism," notes with pleasure that "the United States is finding that it has an opportunity to mold an international system more in harmony with its professed values, those of democracy and pluralism" (85). The essay concludes as follows: "The fear of U.S. domestic balkanization should be mitigated by the realization that both the actual and potential openness of American government to the influence of ethnicity may guide diasporic groups to champion the creed of political democracy and human rights around the globe" (108).[4]

Under present circumstances, this willingness to identify with the point of view of the "American government" seems to invite the charge of political naivete. After all, what grounds do we have for giving up the oft-substantiated fear that, whatever the input from "diasporic groups," the United States's "opportunity to mold an international system" in harmony with "political democracy and human rights" will again be used, as it has in the past, to defend or expand a partisan view of its national interest abroad? And even if there were grounds for believing that the government would listen to and learn from its hyphenated citizens or residents, the idea that the hyphenated as such make reliable guides to the politics of their distant homelands (more reliable, at any rate, than those who remained there) seems an excessively generous tribute either to exile or to the unique civilizing influence of North American life, as Shain apparently perceives it. Why should anyone be ready to believe that diasporic residence in the United States, or indeed, anywhere else, consistently or characteristically produces political clairvoyance or engagement on the side of virtue? More interesting than the sense of political virtue produced by contrast with an implicit, perhaps fictitious state of stay-at-home homogeneity, then— and indeed, perhaps crucial for the future of *Diaspora* as a journal—is the question of diaspora's actual and potential vices.[5]

From this angle, *Diaspora* can serve to represent a sort of ethically idealized internationalization, projecting American pluralism outward in such a way as to guarantee the supposed multicultural impartiality behind future American interventions around the world. The purest antithesis to this politically complacent internationalism would perhaps come from the strenuously dissatisfied internationalism of *boundary 2*—a journal that finds it difficult even to print the word *internationalism* without strong and immediate reservations. In the Spring 1994 number, a special issue titled "Asia/Pacific as Space of Cultural Production," edited by Arif Dirlik and Rob Wilson, Christopher Connery speaks derisively and characteristically of "left-liberal humanist internationalism" (33) as "an affordable luxury to an imperial power." "As E. H. Carr has noted," Connery goes on, "internationalism is the British credo in times of British hegemony, the French credo in times of French hegemony, and the U.S. credo in times of U.S. hegemony" (34).[6] Thus cold war internationalism had its origins in the "institutions of U.S. finance capital that stood to benefit from an international economy free of trade barriers, anchored by strong regional economic powers" (37).[7] Internationalism is equated with the U.S. national interest, which is equated, in turn, with the interests of *global capitalism.*

The opposition to *Diaspora,* at least as I have just described it, could not be starker. Rather than transnational diaspora, *boundary 2* puts a positive value on the local. *The local* is a national or subnational term (the ambiguity is worth exploring, since it can work either for or against the nation-state) that is offered as the determinate, stay-at-home negation of global capitalism's mobile expansiveness. In their introduction to the issue, the editors note that "the move toward mapping 'mega-trends in the Asia-Pacific' as a locus of economic surge and trans-Pacific promise often entails ignoring the cultural micropolitics of the region as a source of dynamic opposition and local difference worthy of international recognition" (5).[8] They speak up, therefore, for "emerging counter-hegemonic practices and flows that would remain staunchly 'local' in orientation and resistant in political design" (7). "Flows" that "remain staunchly 'local' " are not easy to imagine. And within one page, the flows have been dammed or bottled up: the political message, according to the editors, is "to resist ingestion into a global fantasy by an assertion of historical experiences and local enclaves of resistance, survival, and cultural critique" (7–8). Instead of flows, here we have enclaves, which seems a more precise term for the sort of "historical experiences" that are to be allowed as resistant.[9] Their slogan is given in italics: *"The global deforms and molests the local"* (8).

Here the local, as such, is assumed to be the different, and the different is assumed to be adversarial. Each of these assumptions is extremely questionable, and in both cases, the question turns back toward the assumed antagonist Dirlik and Wilson call "transnational capital" (8). Diaspora becomes adversarial only if one assumes an initial state of oppressive, or at any rate undesired, purity and immobility; the local becomes adversarial only if one assumes that the global deforms and molests it, and does *only* that—if one assumes, in other words, that no genuine and desired expressiveness, no improvement or supplement of cultural or political self-determination, can come to the local from the global.

What must transnational capital be, other than a set of heedlessly profit-maximizing and therefore exploitative economic practices, for Dirlik and Wilson's description to hold? One answer is that it must be a self-sufficient and functionally all-inclusive system—a system that would not be frail or incomplete enough to need, as J. K. Gibson-Graham reminds us, "the protection and fostering of the state" (15);[10] for what it is being asked to represent is universality itself. Since *boundary 2*, unlike *Diaspora,* did not come into existence only in the last few years, it is worth noting the curious historical twist by which what had been a Heideggerian journal, pioneering in the celebration of a fervently antihumanist postmodernism, has turned toward a left-wing politics willing to espouse, rather than trying to subvert, the diagnostic powers of "Western rationality"; and yet has done so, at least intermittently, by way of a specific turn to Asia and the Pacific. It is as if "Asia/Pacific" represented two very different things at once: on the one hand, a geographical region whose neglect and distortion serve to reprimand the transcendent universalizing of Eurocentric categories, but on the other hand, a means of saving and reinvigorating the universal value of Marxism, which itself has been attacked as Eurocentric, since only some sort of totalizing reason could diagnose the totalizing system of capitalist oppression.[11] Even if one approves this act of salvage (and there are reasons to do so), one must note that from this perspective, "Asia/Pacific" is not local in the strong sense at all but rather a move in a game Euro-American reason is playing with itself.

Is the local truly a winner in this game? By defining the global as it does, *boundary 2* romanticizes the local as difference to be preserved for its own sake, thereby making the same move Fredric Jameson made in his controversial *Social Text* essay on "Third World literature."[12] Standing against the encroachment of global capital, difference becomes adversarial as such, in advance of any actual evidence. But by the same token, difference is also homogenized; any actual particulars that might depart from this adversarial scenario are eliminated. In effect, there can be no significant differences *except* differences from capitalism, all of which are, in this crucial sense, alike. The local is given nothing more creative to do or to be, by this script, than to refuse to be violated—or wait to be violated—by capitalist historicity.[13]

In short, *boundary 2*'s reversal of *Diaspora* is too symmetrical. For *boundary 2*, as for *Diaspora*, transnational mobility means Americanism in disguise—the disguise of apparently rootless, borderless capital. For *Diaspora*, this is a desirable cultural heterogeneity; for *boundary 2*, it is an undesirable overriding of cultural difference by the homogenizing force of global capital. But neither journal appears to interrogate the equation itself. Neither speculates about the most salient anomaly in the global/local division: the riddle of the global as local, or the local as global, whose traditional answer is the synthesis of global capitalism with the national interest of the United States, that is, global capital as the United States. Neither tries to explore the real or potential separation of these two terms, whether by acknowledging the complicating presence of German and Japanese national capitals, for example, or by examining them in the light of the Republican assault on the U.S. state since November 1994, which suggests at the very least that U.S. capital is now of two minds about its own state apparatus. Even in the act of accusing the United States, *boundary 2* thus allows it to remain a unified center. No degree of self-blame can offset the monopolization of mobility, the excessive ascription of agency, creativity, and power, that centrality carries with it. And by the same token, there can be no internationalism of the local; no version of internationalism can ever be a rallying cry if the only true internationalism is the malevolent, seemingly omnipotent internationalism of U.S. capitalism.[14]

Social Text seems to offer an interesting alternative both to *Diaspora*'s largely celebratory attitude toward diaspora and to *boundary 2*'s version of the local/global opposition, and this despite the fact that the Jameson piece that can be said to have launched the *boundary 2* position was first published in *Social Text*'s pages. Like *boundary 2, Social Text* has devoted less of its attention to transnational matters than have the other two journals. When it has done so, however, it has, like *boundary 2*, been suspicious of the North American interests hidden away in moves toward the global. I am thinking, for example, of the critiques of the term *postcolonial* offered by Anne McClintock and Ella Shohat in number 31/32 (1992), as well as George Yúdice's emphatic essay "We Are *Not* the World" in the same issue. To quote Yúdice: "The impulse to recognize the diversity that constitutes the United States overshoots its mark and self-servingly celebrates 'American' multiculturalism as isomorphic with the world" (202).[15]

Unlike *boundary 2,* however, *Social Text* has characteristically refused the local as the prime site of resistance, in part because of the reasoning of which I have just given a sample: because to champion the local as anti-imperialist is to preserve, if indirectly, the United States's "pretensions of being the world" (Yúdice, 215). This was the brunt of Aijaz Ahmad's important critique of Fredric Jameson, which objected (among other things) to the devious Americano-centric nationalism envy that was assumed by Jameson's otherwise attractive anti-imperialism.[16] In contrast, Ahmad's version of an earlier socialist internationalism was so uncharacteristic, both of *Social Text* and of most other left-wing discourse on these topics in the United States, including that of *boundary 2*, that it was often misread as a piece of Third Worldist cultural nationalism, a protest in the name of cultural specificity (which was, indeed, one element in it).[17] But Ahmad's internationalism also overlaps with a continuing

Social Text emphasis at another and more definitive point: it repeats and extends *Social Text*'s insistence on a politics of *popular culture*.

The concept of popular culture turns its political edge in at least two distinct directions: (1) as one instance of what has been called culturalism, it tries to colonize and assimilate authoritative discourses that claim *not* to be culture by identifying them as cultural constructs and revealing the social interests hidden behind them, as the titular notion of the social as text suggests; (2) as specifically *popular* culture, it turns against hierarchy, whether embodied in domestic cultural elites or in foreign political elites, in a quest to uncover, explicate, and validate the cultural constructions of nonelite social actors and interests. The latter emphasis, though not the former, shares with Ahmad's socialism an insistence on class division within any version of the national. It also shares with Ahmad a refusal of any simple demonizing of the colonizer that would allow the colonizer to remain the definitive point of reference, thus swallowing up any autonomous or even semiautonomous history of conflicts internal to the colonized.[18]

This is my segue, finally, to the Spring 1994 issue of *Social Text*. In this issue, two pieces seem especially characteristic of an internationalizing move whose (entirely unacknowledged) center is popular culture. The lead essay, by Katherine Verdery, tries to account for the intensity of nationalism in Eastern Europe in terms of the particular relations between intellectuals and the Eastern European state. It sees Eastern European nationalism, that is, as essentially an elite rather than a popular formation. And the effect of thus dividing the nation is to save the popular as at least a potential site for internationalism.[19] The hypothesis here would be the existence of a popular cosmopolitanism, exemplified, perhaps, by what Faye Ginsburg calls, with a certain reserve, "the indigenous photographer as a kind of bush cosmopolitan" (562).[20]

This somewhat inchoate, still largely negative or incipient internationalism is somewhat fleshed out, however, by the dossier on Puerto Rico in the same issue, and in particular in an essay by the late María Milagros López. In López's essay, the antiproductivism of *Social Text* cofounder Stanley Aronowitz, which has since helped Aronowitz switch from socialism to the more "popular" umbrella of radical democracy, is reflected in an appreciation of "post-work" attitudes in Puerto Rico under conditions of vast un- and underemployment. "Post-work" belongs to postmodernism, a popular cultural style that can be claimed outside the metropolitan centers. López shows unusual honesty in articulating culturalism's refusal to evaluate the political implications of these "post-work" and postmodern attitudes, and its willingness to remain politically agnostic about a popular culture that seems delinked from the given institutional forms and objectives of any particular struggle:

Whether these aspirations represent forms of transgression or accommodation, the carnivalesque and its populist utopia or Nietzsche's politics of *ressentiment,* is uncertain. But I subscribe to them, whether they stand for the "good" forms of resistance, leading categorically to a more democratic and just society, or the "bad" forms of disorganized, short-term victories through negativity (the morality of the slave). . . . It is the triumph of impermeability, silence, indifference, and sabotage, challenging our notions of contestatory practices and questioning the common sense erected around rational, "straightforward" conceptions of struggle. (130)[21]

Thanks to a delinking of nationalism from the state, accompanied by a delinking of popular culture from politics at the level of the state, national versions of popular culture like Puerto Rico's, in this argument, can leapfrog over the overrationalized statist ambitions of local elites and, in so doing, rejoin the avant-garde that is redefining the contestatory in the metropolis. In effect, these versions can aspire to be "contestatory" both locally and globally.[22]

This sort of postmodern (multi) cultural international seems to aspire to no more than to be, at least for the moment, an international on the level of culture alone. It is one thing to be agnostic about the eventual political meaning or utility of an internationalized popular culture. But if that means being too comfortable with a flaccid, overstretched concept of the political, I, for one, am not totally comfortable about saying so and leaving it at that. The drawbacks of a culturalist politics have to be weighed and measured not only against an inevitable uncertainty, as López says, about the effective political forms of the future but also against the other options immediately available to those who practice it, limited and situated as they—or rather, we—find ourselves.[23] Because of its militant popular culturalism, *Social Text* has had little engagement with options such as international politics at the level of nation-states (what used to be called international relations or geopolitics). More surprising still, it has been actively or neglectfully uninterested in one manifestly imperfect but genuinely popular form that internationalist feeling has taken outside "culture" in the academic sense, and indeed, outside the academy: namely, the discourse of human rights centered in institutions such as the United Nations.

Where the forms of "adversarial internationalization" are concerned, the clearest contrast between *Social Text* and *Public Culture* would seem to be between *Social Text*'s qualified championing of popular culture on an international scale and *Public Culture*'s more explicit, if uneasy, foregrounding of international *civil society*—a concept that produces just that dangerous but serviceable proximity to the state that is lacking in culturalism. The article that seems most characteristic here, again from the Spring 1994 issue, is Michael Shapiro's "Moral Geographies and the Ethics of Post-Sovereignty." Shapiro argues that ethical imperatives have been attached to and modeled on the sovereign state, even when they have seemed to be international. If one accepts the premise that the state as such is the most necessary and urgent antagonist and target of an internationalist adversarial politics—a premise that I find problematic, especially since the Republicans captured Congress in 1994—then an ethics is necessary that will be international without modeling itself on the state.

As Jean-François Lyotard and other poststructuralists have suggested, to return to ethics is not necessarily to repudiate the postmodern critique of universalism.[24] Yet it does entail some edging back from the domain of cultural difference toward the state's limited but internally universalizing authority. In other words, if Shapiro tries to remove us from the state, he does not, after all, remove us very far from the state. However controversial, his is a call for an ethics at the level of civil society—a concept that, since the vigorous controversy initiated by Charles Taylor and Partha Chatterjee in 1990, *Public Culture* has never ceased to put forward and worry over, largely because of its uncertain relation to the state.[25] Indeed, civil society—in the words of Jean Cohen and Andrew Arato, "a sphere of social interaction between economy and state"—seems to be largely defined by just this double gesture of insistent approach to and cautious avoidance of the state.[26]

And this mid-distance has its (often unrecognized) advantages. To begin with, it allows civil society, in turn, to define for *Public Culture* the peculiar object or field designated by its title phrase: culture that, at least in the strong sense, is not merely culture. Claiming to be public, in ways that make certain sorts of culture seem relatively private, this object or field seems to encourage more enthusiasm for universalizing protocols of rational debate than humanists are sometimes comfortable with. It is more conducive to a Habermasian ideal of undistorted communication, and perhaps also, therefore, to dialogue with journalists, policymakers, and other nonacademics or nonhumanists.[27] At the same time, it directs the researcher toward areas of "give," or leeway, that, whether described as cultures or as public spheres, evade the strict determinations of the nation-state while remaining in interesting proximity to them. If, like culture, it values alternative or subversive practices wherever they exist, even within enclaves of self-expressive otherness, it also goes beyond culture in giving priority to practices that achieve the satisfaction of palpable friction as they push and are pushed by state power.

On the international level, the political advantages of a discourse of civil society include, as Shapiro shows, some purchase over the negotiations between nation-states and nonnational groupings, such as the nongovernmental organizations (NGOs). In pursuit of broad transnational consensus, or at least alliance, the NGOs have no choice but to speak the universalistic, statist language of international civil society; their internationalism usually declines or downplays assertions of cultural distinctiveness. Yet this neglect of cultural difference can bring with it more direct address to global inequalities of power, including inequalities that have major cultural impact. One thinks, for example, of the "southern" and Asian NGOs whose increased role at the UN Vienna, Cairo, and Beijing conferences provided sudden new creativity and legitimation to international agreements on population policy and human rights, especially the rights of women.[28]

Of course, the divisiveness of power continues to work in and through this now more promising international arena, just as it does within civil society on the domestic scale.[29] There are rich, elite NGOs, as Gayatri Spivak has been pointing out, funded by international agencies and thus tied to the agendas of the latter, that claim representative status at the expense of poor NGOs, which often cannot afford to send representatives to crucial meetings. The United States recently decided to channel a higher percentage of its foreign aid through NGOs than through foreign governments, a clear sign that NGOs are perceived as less able or likely to resist U.S. influence. And the discourse of "international civil society" has now been picked up by the World Bank.[30]

The most obvious problem of civil society, internationally speaking, is the danger of an invidious drawing of lines so as to flatter the developed and democratic nations of the West, as already supposed possessors of an independent civil society, at the expense of the rest, which are then seen as needing to follow where the West has led, needing to sow or graft onto their own a civil society not native to their territory and to cultivate it assiduously, thus (and only thus) growing out of the dilemmas of undemocratic underdevelopment.[31] Cohen and Arato include Latin America in their *Civil Society and Political Theory* but exclude the rest of the non-European world. As the subtitle of his otherwise equally universalistic *Civil Society and the State,* John Keane specifies "New *European* Perspectives" (emphasis mine).[32] Given the almost inconceivable disparities of suffering and well-being between North and South that so axiologically imbalanced a vocabulary inevitably ratifies or rationalizes, there are good reasons for Partha Chatterjee's desire "to send back the concept of civil society to where I think it properly belongs—the provincialism of European social philosophy."[33]

It has been argued, in much the same spirit, that the discourse of civil society inevitably produces for itself an uncivil other to which it cannot do justice. "Civil-society theory," Jeffrey Alexander argues, "despite the extraordinary self-consciousness of philosophers like Cohen and Walzer, seems unable to theorize empirically the demonic, anti-civil forces of cultural life that it normatively proscribes. . . . While the analytic concept of civil society must by all means be recovered from the heroic age of democratic revolution, it should be de-idealized so that 'anti-civil-society'—the countervailing processes of decivilization, polarization, and violence—can be seen also as typically 'modern' results" (100–101). At the present moment, Alexander suggests, this "anti–civil society" can be identified specifically as nationalism. "Nationalism is the name intellectuals and publics are now increasingly giving to the negative antinomies of civil society" (93).[34] This caution against triumphalist Western antinationalism is well founded. But note that each of the other versions of internationalism we have been discussing could find itself targeted equally well by the same logic. Chatterjee's own version of the argument, for example, suggests that the uncivil negation that civil society discourse produces can be called by the name *culture*.

"The crucial break in the history of anticolonial nationalism," according to Chatterjee, "comes when the colonized refuse to accept membership in this civil society of subjects. . . . They do not have the option of [constructing their national identity] within the domain of bourgeois civil-social institutions. They create, consequently, a very different domain—a cultural domain. . . . The inner domain of culture is declared the sovereign territory of the nation, to which the colonial state is not allowed entry" (130–31). Culture, in Chatterjee's sense, is not naturally nationalistic. Only the ironic fact that the new cultural community is "again violently interrupted" by the new state, after independence, forces culture to take a nationalist form: it can give itself "a historically valid justification only by claiming an alternative nationhood with rights to an alternative state" (131).

The notion that there might exist, in contradistinction to international civil society, a nationalism that is specifically cultural, and thus not really nationalist at all in the strong sense, is articulated in Arjun Appadurai's "Patriotism and Its Futures." Appadurai argues that "many oppressed minorities . . . have suffered displacement and forced diaspora without articulating a strong wish for a nation-state of their own: Armenians in Turkey, Hutu refugees from Burundi who live in urban Tanzania, and Kashmiri Hindus in exile in Delhi. . . . Territorial nationalism is the alibi of these movements and not necessarily their basic motive or final goal" (418).[35] It is a relatively short step, on the one hand, from these transnational patriotisms to *Diaspora*'s celebration of diasporic identity, which renounces nationalism's demand for a perfect correspondence of one eth-nos to one state—but which also flatters the specific multicultural nationalism of the United States. It is an only slightly longer step, on the other hand, from this cultural transnationalism to a cultural internationalism (imagining, that is, a solidarity at once more organized and more dispersed), an idea that intersects interestingly with the nonstatist project of *Social Text* as described above. And as with both of those projects, political questions are again pressing, almost by definition. The very attempt to conceive an emotion as strong as patriotism that would not aim at seizing or defending the power of a given nation-state threat-ens to disengage the mind from any real adversarial situation, and perhaps from political reality itself.

If civil-society discourse's ambivalence toward the state thus sends us back to the unanswered question of the politics of culture, the same is perhaps true of a similar ambivalence linking the discourse of civil society to capitalism. One of the founding gestures of *Public Culture* was a refusal of any simple correspon-dence between culture and capitalism, a refusal articulated, for example, in as-sociate editor Arjun Appadurai's much-anthologized essay "Disjuncture and Difference in the Global Cultural Economy."[36] But capitalism, like the nation-state, continues to haunt the discourse of international civil society. Indeed, along with its continuity with or separation from the state, this is a second cru-cial ambiguity of the concept of civil society: Is the economy within civil soci-ety or separate from it? Apologists for international capital who imagine world-wide transitions to democracy happening through the extension of the free market are naturally prone to place the economy at the very heart of civil soci-ety. Progressives committed to salvaging the concept's critical, idealizing force just as naturally tend to hold the two as far apart as possible. So Cohen and Arato argue in *Civil Society and Political Theory,* for example, that "only a con-cept of civil society that is properly differentiated from the economy (and there-fore from 'bourgeois society') could become the center of a critical political and social theory in societies where the market economy has already developed, or is in the process of developing, its own autonomous logic" (viii).

On the whole, *Public Culture* has refused these purist alternatives. This is the point, I take it, of Charles Taylor's discussion of the "L-stream" and "M-stream" modes of civil society: the "L," or Locke, mode centered on the econ-omy and the "M," or Montesquieu, mode related more directly to the state. Taylor freely admits his preference for a Tocquevillian variant of the latter, in which civil society, made up of "self-governing associations," "is not so much a sphere outside political power; rather, it penetrates deeply into this power, fragments and decentralizes it" (117). Yet, Taylor concludes, "we can't just opt for the M- against the L-stream" (117), for the systematic power that must be penetrated and fragmented, it seems, belongs at least as much to capitalism as to the state, and with fractions of each now so visibly at loggerheads, there is no longer any excuse for conflating them. But what, then, is the proper place of the international L-stream—that is, civil discourse tied to the incivilities of global capital—in the imagining of adversarial internationalization? Must we, can we, think of the two as related by something other than a simple opposition?

The suspicion that internationalist or cosmopolitan tendencies may be nothing but the ideological reflections of global capital has been eloquently updated by Masao Miyoshi in an article in *Critical Inquiry*. Transnational corporations, Miyoshi notes, have been expanding astronomically in recent years, and as they do, they "will increasingly require from all workers loyalty to the corporate identity rather than to their own national identities . . . employees of various nationalities and ethnicities must be able to communicate with each other. In that sense, TNCs [Transnational Corporations] are at least officially and superficially trained to be color-blind and multicultural" (741). The political rewards of multiculturalism, Miyoshi argues, are no more than superficial distractions. The primary effect of international civil society World Bank style is political disorientation. In the age of TNCs, "intellectuals and professionals" who earlier had been "led to think of themselves as free and conscientious critics and interpreters" are less liberated than confused by their new conditions, for the same extranational standpoint they have learned to associate with critique is now willingly conceded to them by the very social force they have learned to see as their antagonist: "Transnational corporatism is by definition unprovincial and global, that is, supposedly free from insular and idiosyncratic constrictions." "Are the intellectuals of the world willing to participate in transnational corporatism," Miyoshi therefore asks, "and be its apologists? How to situate oneself in this neo–Daniel Bell configuration of transnational power and culture without being trapped by a deadend nativism seems to be the most important question that faces every critic and theorist the world over at this moment" (742).[37]

The logic pointing beyond this impasse would seem to be that, in the absence of any international adversary matching international capital on its own scale, and rightly wary of any claim on their own part to constitute such an adversary, intellectuals and professionals should go back to the nation-state, or back to their own nation-state; for "the state did, and still does, perform certain functions, for which there is as of now no substitute" (744). They should identify with and organize their activities within the only unit presently capable of offering capital serious resistance—yet should so so, somehow, without falling back into a "dead-end nativism."

A dead-end nativism is no idle threat. It is no secret that the end of the cold war has reinvigorated nationalism in the United States, as well as elsewhere, or that nationalism is as much a temptation for the left as for the right. Here is John Judis (before his move to the right and the *New Republic*) writing in *In These Times*: "The left should reclaim from the right the cause of nationalism—nationalism as opposed to sectionalism and individualism. The left should stand for policies and programs that put the national interest before that of private corporations or Washington interest groups. The left should be at the forefront of those urging the economic revitalization of the country, and it should be vigilant about protecting America's interests against those of foreign governments and corporations and the new globalists of Wall Street and Washington."[38] What this would mean not for "foreign governments and corporations but for foreign *people*, who have already suffered quite enough from the unstinting protection of "America's interests," is anyone's guess.

And yet, as I suggested in chapter 1, recent and spirited efforts to dismantle the welfare state have given extra force to the logic I am imputing to Miyoshi. In the United States today, it is arguable that the only responsible politics for a more-than-academic left, the highest feasible goal under present unpropitious conditions, would involve overcoming the militant antistatism of American voters and trying to give the United States something like the developed social welfare system characteristic of other highly industrialized nations. Again, the social welfare state is also a site where the self-interest of "intellectuals and professionals" can be shown to coincide, at least provisionally, with the interests of the most disenfranchised members of American society. It is thus the site of a progressive agenda that is both significant and seemingly viable.

The benefits of recognizing an identification between cultural workers and the nation-state might even include, paradoxically, a certain deprovincializing of the American cultural left or the flowering of a particular internationalism (all internationalisms are, of course, particular) that the cultural left has hitherto neglected at its own expense. "Practitioners of a hermeneutics of suspicion," Meaghan Morris writes, offering her experiences of Australia's relatively approachable state to her less fortunate foreign readers, have been left "muttering uselessly on the sidelines of most fields of contestation, open to the charge of indulging a purist and publicly-funded politics of self-marginalisation."[39] This is much the same point that anthropologist Benjamin Lee makes when he complains that American cultural politics are useless or meaningless in what he calls "state-saturated societies," for example, in China.[40] The hypothesis presents itself that the need to engage constructively with the state may provide common ground for a sort of serialized internationalism—a series of national projects joined at least by the consciousness of parallelism, if not yet by active cooperation in any transnational goals.

Or would this simply mean, practically speaking, a move to replace the anti-imperialism that once linked the First and *Third* Worlds (admittedly, often without sufficient regard for other locations of injustice) with a new post–cold war convergence between intellectuals of the First and *Second* Worlds, now that the latter are caught between a residually authoritarian state and the emergent ravages of the open market? Such an internationalism would be less new to the American right than to the American left. More precisely, it would pull the generation of the new left, formed by the 1960s and the Vietnam War, toward the older and culturally distinct left formed during the cold war. Motivated in large part by the need for a provisional alliance in defense of the welfare state between the cultural left and people like Richard Rorty, who are liberals in an other than free market sense, this project would seem necessarily to entail some concession to liberal complacencies about the superiority of "the American way of life."

However desirable it might be as a way of putting some spine into the looser sorts of "politics" talk, such an alliance would not come cheap. And whether or not the price is finally judged too high, something is to be learned from the items we are thereby asked to sell off: specifically, investments in the Third World and, in interesting conjunction with them, investments in culture. Politically speaking, culture has meant a stretching of what counts as reality in "the political sphere." But this stretching does not just include ordinary language and everyday social activities—what Rorty satirizes, not without some justification, as "that ubiquitous, insensibly corrupting, bourgeois ideology" (487). It also includes "real actions and events" *beyond the nation's borders.* In other words, culture seems to have been a sort of Trojan horse by which solidarity with and accountability to distant others could be smuggled into America's notions of pertinent political reality and the public sphere—notions that Rorty and others are willing to confine within the nation and our patriotic duties to it.[41]

This sheds some light on the otherwise strange alliance between the cultural left and the "southern" or Third World constituencies in whose name it has frequently chosen (not without audible representational agonies) to speak. I hope it also helps us see the cultural left as a distinctly internationalist formation that gets some political results in exchange for its apparent political indirectness. But it is not a satisfactory argument in favor of the cultural left's culturalism. Such an argument would have to prove its force by taking up the immense challenge of discovering how to *use* the circuits of internationalist solidarity thereby held open.

If making up with the liberals means shifting the working vocabulary away from "culture" and in the direction of "civil society," while also restricting the definition of "the public" to the scale of the nation-state, then for better or worse, none of the periodicals under discussion here seems actively interested.[42] Yet some willingness to reconsider their relations with liberalism can perhaps be inferred from their marked, if uneven, turn toward the lexicon and institutions of "the public," especially—though not exclusively—on an international scale. A turn away from the valuing of difference for its own sake, or at least a commitment not to stop with a discovery of difference, this concern with the forms of publicness also modifies these periodicals' shared commitment to culture in a more provocative way: it refuses to define culture against the market. That is, it refuses to rest culture's implicit claim to be public, which has sustained it throughout the "culture and society" tradition—from Ralph Waldo Emerson and Matthew Arnold through to the New York intellectuals—on an implicit opposition to the privacy of the market.

This marks a serious change in the conceptualizing of the public sphere. For Jürgen Habermas, the economy is emphatically not part of the public sphere. Habermas's normative, anticommercial view of the public sphere has swallowed up many contemporary treatments of civil society as well, which similarly exclude economics out of a desire to sustain the purity of civil society's ideal or critical function. Though *Public Culture* retains much allegiance to Habermas, however, its version of civil society has left room to renegotiate with the familiar otherness of political economy that Appadurai brilliantly circumvented in "Disjuncture and Difference"—room to rethink not the *dis*juncture between culture and capitalism but their *con*junctures. Craig Calhoun argues, for example, that "the crucial early contribution of markets to the idea of civil society was as a *demonstration* of the possibility of self-organization. Markets led thinkers like Adam Ferguson and Adam Smith to the idea that the activity of ordinary people could regulate itself without the intervention of government" (271).[43] Is this a disposable example that should henceforth be avoided, leaving us to look for organization only outside or against the market? Or, on the contrary, does it continue to serve as a paradigm of how cultures or publics can maintain significant and even adversarial autonomy within, and perhaps by means of, the market?

In its Fall 1994 issue on "The Black Public Sphere," *Public Culture*'s editorial appears to adopt the latter, anti-Habermasian position.

> The Black public sphere is post-Black-nationalism, and includes the
> diaspora among its primary audiences. As the international market

counters constantly demonstrate, the transnational migration of signs and wares, narratives and archives generates Black life globally, and in many registers. . . . The commodities transport both nationality and racial signs: yet their value for a Black diaspora is in the possibility of a public sphere articulated around the circulation and possession of Black things. . . . The Black public sphere is thus not always a resistance aesthetic which defies modernity and finds comfort in the politics of identity and difference. To think the Black public sphere we have to be willing to rethink the relationship between markets and freedom, commodity and identity, property and pleasure.[44]

This offers a strong contrast to the linking of capitalism and Black culture in Hortense Spillers's recent treatment of Black intellectuals in *boundary 2*. Spillers usefully tries to liberate Black intellectuals from the guilt of their "relative success," within an economy of knowledge production that remains formally capitalist, whatever its content, as well as from the heavy burden of organically representing their Black constituency. "This paralysis of understanding, brought on by guilt over one's relative success and profound delusion about one's capacity to lead the masses (of which, one supposes, it is certain that she is not one!) out of their Babylon, disables the intellectual on the very material ground where he/she now stands" (73). The desire to model oneself on "the black preacher," which she finds in Cornel West (83), or on any other version of the "organic intellectual" is "a symptom of nostalgic yearning" (92). The relative autonomy of intellectual work can be defended, Spillers rightly suggests, without any obligation to show that it is "public" in the strongest or most nostalgic sense. Yet Spillers can restore Black intellectuals to a pragmatic sense of their proper business, it seems, only by returning to the still more nostalgic language by which humanism has always established itself: by defining culture and criticism in opposition to "business civilization." "We risk banality in saying that today's academy, by trivializing and degrading its *critical* function in the society, has shot itself in the foot: administratively top-heavy, bogged down in the 'business' of making money, 'busy' with 'image,' 'name,' 'rep,' 'public relations,' . . . today's academy has broken faith with its own most sacred duty, if we may call it that—to feed the mind-life of the civilization entrusted to it" (112).[45]

Instead of this alignment of culture against commerce, which Spillers's Marxist humanism shares with Habermas, *Social Text* lines up more readily with Habermas's critics Oscar Negt and Alexander Kluge, as Miriam Hansen delineates their position: "While Habermas and, for that matter, theorists of civil society such as Charles Taylor, see the political function of the public sphere primarily in its ability to challenge, 'determine or inflect the course of state policy,' Negt and Kluge deemphasize that function and extend the notion of politics to all social sites of production and reproduction."[46] Reproduction here includes the spheres of commerce and consumption. Attending to the processes of reproduction entails taking seriously such "sites of production and reproduction" as consumerism. And in some circumstances it means not just analyzing seriously the cultural work accomplished in capitalist exchange but finding virtues in it.[47]

Thus Spillers's critique of Cornel West in *boundary 2* can be fruitfully compared with Eric Lott's critique in *Social Text*—both journals, by the way, with which West has been energetically and constructively engaged. Taking issue with West's diagnosis of "nihilism" in "the Los Angeles uprising of April 1992," Lott writes, "West misses the active (if leaderless) political character of the 'riots' because he doesn't fully believe people make their own history. They suffer conditions, and these must be remedied mostly by the state" (40). But Lott does not simply snipe at West from his left flank. Ascribing more causal and ethical power than West to the people, Lott also, and perhaps unexpectedly, ascribes less causal and ethical power to "U.S. capitalism" (41): "a little attention to the 'market morality' West so often moralizes away might be instructive. Surprising things happen in the culture industry West several times decries, like 1992's most uncompromising rap single, ex–Geto Boy Willie D's 'Fuck Rodney King.' . . . Willie D's political analysis is in many ways more incisive than West's" (41–42).[48]

Hip-hop, a genre full of savvy popular voices permitted and, in part, fashioned by the "market morality" of "the culture industry," makes it hard and, perhaps, futile to distinguish between the creativity of the streets and the creativity of the corporate boardroom—both of them far from ideal, but both in some incontrovertible sense public spaces. The rap artist is an exemplary expression of one who would otherwise more likely be abandoned by capitalism than directly exploited by it, and for whom exploitation is not self-evidently the less desirable choice. As Hans Magnus Enzensberger writes, "In New York as well as in Zaire, in the industrial cities as well as in the poorest countries, more and more people are being permanently excluded from the economic system because it no longer pays to exploit them . . . there is only one thing worse than being exploited by the multinationals, and that is not being exploited by them" (35–36).[49] If this is the case, then to think we can take our political bearings directly and negatively from the economic system is a dangerous illusion and a piece of moralistic self-indulgence.

The provisional conclusion here seems to be that global or transnational interconnectedness must never be allowed to serve as a surrogate universality, a means of reinscribing moralism's sweeping strokes in place of multilevel, multidirectional political commitments and the quick empirical curiosity such commitments require. In the Winter 1994 issue of *Social Text*, Andrew Ross's "Earth to Gore, Earth to Gore" strikes a useful note of caution about the moralistic temptations of an ecological internationalism. The danger, Ross says, is playing into the hands of "a military-industrial-environmental complex" that "will come into being as a way of securing and completing the globalist ideologies of the new world order." Its appeal, incorporating an apparent reverence for nature into the usual muscular *Realpolitik,* will increasingly be to "environmental security" (5).

Like the discourse of human rights and, for that matter, the more complacent globalism based on information and telecommunications, ecological internationalism is working its way gradually into popular consciousness. As Ross notes in *Strange Weather*, the public that is hearing again and again how "the motion of a butterfly's wings in Peru can cause tornadoes in Iowa" is getting accustomed to the global image of "shared dependency."[50] There is something here to build on. The danger is that, amid the general and growing appreciation of interconnectedness, *some* connections will be urged to stand in for *all* connections. Speaking at a 1990 Earth Day rally, Paul Erlich declared, "A cow breaks wind in Indonesia, and your grandchildren could die in food riots in the United States" (193). A better example, Ross comments, would have been the global effect of North American automobile emissions: "The corollary of Erlich's story is one in which actions and events in North America have immeasurably more effect on people and social life in Indonesia (or Peru, for that matter) than vice versa" (195). Yet those environmentalists who ask North Americans to accept responsibility for such effects, Ross argues, produce the wrong sort of global popular consciousness. Among the "cultural costs to be borne in transforming people into global citizens" is "the tendency, already well advanced, of passing on to individuals the deeply moralistic sense of assuming responsibility themselves for the very largest ecological problems that ought to be borne primarily by corporate executives and their stockholders" (219–20).

Ross's particular target, most recently in *The Chicago Gangster Theory of Life,* is the ecological discourse of "scarcity," which he describes as "a political tool, skillfully manipulated by the powerful whenever it suits their purpose."

In Judeo-Christian ethics, scarcity, voluntary poverty, and asceticism are prized as virtues. Unquestionably this tradition has reinforced a fierce evangelical tendency among environmentalists to cast us all as ecological sinners in a fallen world. . . . As capital goes through its latest cycle of binge and purge, scarcity, eco-style, has become one of the new discourses of regulation, directed with the force of religious guilt at the level of the individual conscience. The result is an acquittal, on the one hand, of corporate responsibility, and an evasion, on the other, of the hedonism that environmentalist politics so desperately needs for it to be populist and libertarian. (16–17)[51]

Yet some doubt remains as to whether "the level of the individual conscience" can be bypassed, even (or especially) in pursuit of a new internationalism. A libertarian hedonism is indeed one key to the deep or unorthodox desires of ordinary Americans—desires that the American cultural left may be said to have defined itself, domestically speaking, by holding tight to. It may be, as James Livingston has been suggesting, that a renewed socialist politics in the United States in an "age of surplus" can come about only if more attention is paid to the cultural revolution that has been quietly happening within corporations and consumption.[52] But even that intriguing prospect should not blind us to all that it leaves unchanged, internationally speaking. The difficulty remains of finding some other interface—not merely a more equitable interface but an actively and affirmatively compensatory one—between domestic progressiveness and the crushing, confusing weight of objective daily scarcity in the world beyond our borders, where there is no reason to predict that what William James called "pacific cosmopolitan industrialism" will arrive any time soon.[53] The challenge remains of passing from enclaves or flows of autonomous culture to enclaves or flows of economic sustainability. At present, and perhaps for the foreseeable future, to evoke surplus and postscarcity as political slogans will probably have to remain the prerogative of the techno-utopians of digital information, who happily equate one sort of abundance with another.[54] Whatever hedonism's proper hold on domestic popular consciousness, it inevitably assumes a North-versus-South geography (or perhaps Northwest versus South and East) in which "our" abundance continues to produce and ignore "their" scarcity.

This is not to insist that any new internationalism must take the guilt-ridden, regulatory form of revolutionary asceticism, an ethic and aesthetic of belt-tightening and anticonsumerism at home. There may be another way of doing something effective about the profound, continuing misery of the Third and Second Worlds. But it remains to be seen how any internationalism that does not put an ethical and even a quasi-religious fervor into an assault on "overdevelopment" can ever conceive of winning broad U.S. support for that radical redistribution of global resources that has already been postponed for far too long.

3

THE WEIRD HEIGHTS

IMPERIAL EYES, UNIVERSALITY, AND HUMAN RIGHTS

[Political economy] develops a *cosmopolitan,* universal energy which breaks through every limitation and bond and sets itself up as the *only* policy, the *only* universality, the *only* limitation and the *only* bond.

Karl Marx[1]

Neither leisured foreigner seized the weird heights with a counterfeit seismograph.

Anonymous (pedagogical)

In the last chapter of her book *Imperial Eyes,* Mary Louise Pratt offers a contrast to what she has been calling "the monarch-of-all-I-survey scene," the male European traveler's view of the non-European world from the superior vantage point of a promontory or, later, a hotel balcony. Pratt finds perspectives that she prefers in the travel writing of a European woman, Mary Kingsley, and an African American man, Richard Wright.[2] For both Kingsley and Wright, the contrasting scenes tend to take place "in the night, when the alienation of the seer/seen relations is suspended" (222). Further, female explorers like Kingsley, Pratt observes, "do not spend a lot of time on promontories. Nor are they entitled to" (213). Kingsley's preference is for swamps, which she discovers "not by looking down at them or even walking around them, but by sloshing zestfully through them in a boat or up to her neck in water and slime" (213).

The opposition between the white male explorer on his promontory or balcony (the "view from nowhere") and the black or female traveler in the night or in a swamp (a "view from somewhere") might be described as an opposition between false universal and real particular. Yet the familiar passage from the first to the second might also be described, a bit tendentiously perhaps, as an unacknowledged narrative of epistemological progress. If we agree to "expose," as Nancy Hartsock urges, "the falseness of the view from the top" and subsequently embrace "an account of the world as seen from the margins," we are assuming a norm or *telos* of marginality in relation to which the abandonment of "the view from the top" can and will appear as an improvement—even if the notion of improvement seems carefully precluded by the topographical incompatibility between "margins" and "top."[3] This disguised progressiveness, an instance of what Amanda Anderson calls "cryptonormativism," lurks in every account that purports to come from the margins, and in every imperative that enjoins us to speak (or measure our distance) from them.[4] Criticism today, Vivek Dhareshwar writes, must "examine its own location and site of production." To the extent that this directive has even been acknowledged, let alone obeyed, it is assumed that "the view from the top" can one day be recataloged as a relic of the past, a casualty of some actual or potential version of progress.[5]

By hinting not very subtly that the repudiation of universalism belongs to a contemporary narrative of progress that is itself usually taken as an instance of universalism, I am not trying to arrive, via a logical quibble, at a defense of universalism. I am suggesting that defenses of universalism, like attacks on it, are increasingly a trivial pursuit, for it is no longer clear whether there is anyone home on either end. "When multiculturalism and postmodernism . . . came on the scene," the conservative historian Gertrude Himmelfarb wrote recently, "they confronted not an absolutist, universalist history, but an already relativized and pluralized history."[6] The supposed universalists are no longer to be found manning the same old ramparts. But if no one actually holds to the arrogantly absolutist version of rationality that many of us have defined ourselves against, then what does it mean to think of ourselves as antiuniversalists? This question is all the more urgent if, at the same time, we admit that we, too, are inescapably caught up in some moment or degree or version of rational, normative discourse. What follows if this universalism, to paraphrase Luce Irigaray, is not one?

If it is too soon to say that we are all antiuniversalists now, it is certainly not too soon to give up the comfortable assumption that either universalism or antiuniversalism takes a heroic stand against a set of entrenched, dogmatic adversaries fully and necessarily committed to the contrary—in other words, that either does work that urgently needs to be done.[7] What does need to be done, I think, in the interest of the anti-imperialism that Pratt and I share, is to shake loose terms such as *cosmopolitanism* and *internationalism* from the rationalist universality with which each has been entangled since Kant, and thus to perform the delicate work of defining, nurturing, revising, and propagating a cosmopolitan or internationalist politics that will be more self-limiting and more efficacious than any we have yet seen.[8] The mild paradox of progress toward antiprogressivism suggests that such a politics can never fully escape from the universalisms with which it has so often been guiltily associated or damningly identified. My hypothesis here, however, is that it can perhaps negotiate for itself an affiliation with universalism on more advantageous—that is, looser and more self-conscious—terms.

Imperial Eyes usefully initiates this task of negotiation—to begin with, by recognizing its own inescapable complicity with various modes of universalism. Pratt's unusual intellectual boldness is immediately manifest in her refusal to adopt the version of the "view from nowhere" that so many rejections of "the view from nowhere" unreflexively assume: namely, a refusal to critique the male European traveler (who, in so many less rigorous commentaries, is simply assumed to get everything wrong) without also offering up some counterexamples of how description of the alien landscape might have been done right, or at least done better. And she also explains *why* it could have been done better. Both the how and the why are, of course, invocations of a normative, universalizing discourse to which lesser, more circumspect critics have learned to avoid all allusions, however such universalizing may be silently implicated in their negative critiques.

As an explanatory context for Kingsley's dark swamp, Pratt contrasts the commanding view from the promontory or hotel balcony with two alternative sources or principles of traveling identity. The first is "hyphenation," as exemplified by the "Afro-American" Richard Wright (221) and "the Franco-Algerian Albert Camus" (223). To be an "extraordinary hyphenated subject of empire" (223) like Camus or Wright, Pratt suggests, offers one way of being a mobile outsider without falling into the ordinary errors of the white male perspective.

To say this, however, is to invite the objection that almost anyone could avoid these errors—or at least, any American could. In the United States, self-conscious hyphenation is less the exception than the rule. It thus runs the risk of replacing the male European traveler as universal figure of the wrong way to look at the rest of the world with the American traveler (of either gender, perhaps) as the equally universal figure of the right way. And recourse to this new American universalism would have political consequences. In a 1994 article, Yossi Shain, quoting Louis Gerson's 1964 book on "the hyphenate" in American politics and diplomacy, used "the actual and potential openness of American government to the influence of ethnicity" as a sign that it can be induced by "diasporic groups to champion the creed of political democracy and human rights around the globe" (108).[9] But when "the impulse to recognize the diversity that constitutes the United States overshoots its mark and self-servingly celebrates 'American' multiculturalism as isomorphic with the world" (202), as George Yúdice points out in an essay titled "We Are *Not* the World," the more likely result is a new and dangerous form of American nationalism.[10] Yúdice's compelling example is the 1991 mobilization against Iraq: "The U.S. army, that global defender—or, more accurately, mercenary—of free trade in the interests of transnational capital, was projected as the epitome of multiculturalism by the televisual charade that promoted the Gulf War to markets around the world" (213).

The second principle that Pratt counterposes to "the monarch-of-all-I-survey scene" is, more surprising perhaps, what Yúdice calls "the interests of transnational capital." Pratt writes, "An imperialist but passionate anti-colonialist, [Kingsley] used her fame as a writer and explorer to lobby hard for the free market view that expansionism and frontier relations were best left in the hands of traders. Colonial administrations, missionary operations, and big companies were all oppressive, destructive, and impractical" (215). In other words, behind Kingsley's project to recover "European innocence," behind her "particular way of being a European in Africa," lay a commitment to "the possibility of economic expansion without domination and exploitation" (215).

Pratt draws attention to the fact that Kingsley's proposal, which "seems expressly designed to respond to the agonies of the European who has landed in a swamp after falling from his promontory, constitutes her own form of mastery" even as it also tries "to separate mastery from domination" (215). In insisting that "the relation of *mastery* predicated between the seer and the seen" (204) is not the only kind of mastery, and that mastery of one sort or another is an indispensable part of critique, Pratt bravely refuses the tempting but illusory purity of a position outside power, or outside the desire for power. It is only a short step from this exemplary refusal, however, to the conclusion that Pratt's appreciation for Kingsley's swamp is inseparable from the alternative source of masterful but not dominative power that Kingsley thought she had found in the operations of the market. It is hard not to infer, in other words, that Kingsley's sensual relation to swamps is not a simple expression of her gender, irrelevant to or in contradiction with her espousal of free-trade imperialism, but rather is consistent both with her gender and with free trade. The swamp is a figure of feminine subjectivity and, at the same time, a figure of a market-induced leveling or liquefaction. Indeed, one might take it as a topographical exhibition of the process by which, to misquote slightly from the *Communist Manifesto,* all that is solid dissolves. (Dissolution is one of Pratt's favorite figures.) In a swamp, the line between solid and liquid is both close at hand and out of sight. Antihierarchical, collapsing high and low into obscure intimacy, characterized not by fixity but by indeterminacy, capitalism finds a better image for itself in a swamp than on a promontory. Like Kingsley herself, it promotes a kind of mastery that avoids the offensively visual model of domination from above.

Slavoj Žižek supports this identification of market and swamp by arguing, just as surprisingly, that Hegel's lord/bondsman pair, one above and one below, is precisely *not* characteristic of capitalist society. The rule of the market, he says, means the fetishism of commodities, and the fetishism of commodities is incompatible with a fetishism of human relations. According to Žižek, "In societies in which commodity fetishism reigns, the 'relations between men' are totally defetishized, while in societies in which there is fetishism in 'relations between men'—in pre-capitalist societies—commodity fetishism is not yet developed." The transition to capitalism, then, meant the end of the sort of direct, transparent domination of one person by another that Pratt embodies in the monarch-of-all-I-survey trope. "The place of fetishism has . . . shifted from intersubjective relations to relations 'between things': the crucial social relations, those of production, are no longer immediately transparent in the form of interpersonal relations of domination and servitude (or the Lord and his serfs, and so on); they disguise themselves—to use Marx's accurate formula—'under the shape of social relations between things, between the products of labor.' "[11]

If the market, as Žižek suggests, marks the end of Hegelian domination, then it would seem that master/slave allegory is itself an example of the sort of Hegelian or "bad" universalizing that supposedly anti-Hegelian antiuniversalists have been doing a great deal of.[12] In this sense, Pratt's allegory of the female swamp and the male promontory is self-subverting, for the opposition between the two visual metaphors is swept away by the swampish indistinction that accompanies the universalizing of market relations. The analogy also demands to be carried into the present. If mastery is to domination as the free market is to colonial rule, then Pratt's preference for Kingsley (which is by no means unqualified) seems to align her with America's neoimperial hegemony in the period since decolonization and formal independence, which similarly makes possible mastery without domination. Her own argument, it then appears, depends not just on a gentle, unavoidable homogenization of women and Blacks but also on the invisible working of two late-twentieth-century North American crypto-universals—hyphenation and the market—and it builds on them a recognizably North American vision of "progress."

My point here is not that anti-imperialist universalism, like the imperialist universalism it opposes, is inevitably reducible to the interests of its local point of origin. To make the nation the inescapable horizon of internationalism in this way would merely be to move, as Ernesto Laclau and Chantal Mouffe warn, "from an essentialism of the totality to an essentialism of the elements."[13] I only suggest that if the critique of universalism is inextricably bound up in universalism of one sort or another, and if (as Diana Fuss has argued about essentialism) the universals whose power of determination we are inevitably accepting pass without scrutiny because the critique of universalism blinds us to them, then we need to switch our most scrupulous attention away from the universalism/antiuniversalism debate to focus instead on the universals which it has undoubtedly been hiding—not so as to do away with them but so as to debate, instead, the equally hidden criteria for discriminating among them.

To take the example raised above, we clearly need to take another look at the universalism of the market—a universalism that tends to pass unnoticed because it is seen as anything but a desirable ideal, but which is no less effectively universal for all that. Even fervent antiuniversalists find it difficult to do without some notion of a genuinely universal capitalist market, as soon as they want to account for the real inequalities that false universalisms disguise. Yet Žižek's account of how capitalism displaces Hegelian tableaux of dominator and dominated can be disputed on the grounds that whether or not such twosomes are missing from capitalist relations of production, they are certainly not missing from the relations of gender, race, and neoimperialism. Slogans such as "micropolitics" and "The personal is the political," whatever their insufficiencies, have made that much clear. Amid much anti-Eurocentric, anti-Hegelian rhetoric, Hegel's master/slave dialectic remains a central figure for First World/Third World confrontations like the ones Pratt is discussing. In the course of denouncing the opposition between universalism and (national) particularism, Naoki Sakai writes, "The relationship between the West and the non-West seems to follow the old and familiar formula of master/slave."[14]

But if this is so, then we are wrong to treat "the market" or global capitalism as an effective universal. The assumption that capitalism is indeed universal, in the sense of dominating every aspect of social life, has probably done more than anything else to reinvent the issue of universalism for our time. Nicholas Garnham writes, for example, "If we accept that the economic system is indeed global in scope and at the same time crucially determining over large areas of social action, the Enlightenment project of democracy requires us to make the Pascalian bet on universal rationality. For without it the emancipatory project of the Enlightenment is unrealizable and we will in large part remain enslaved by a system outside our control."[15] For Garnham, global capitalism is a universal fact, and in response it necessitates ethical and epistemological universalism. Beginning at much the same place—what he calls the "real universality" of the new global interconnectedness—Étienne Balibar offers a more subtle discrimination of "fictive" and "ideal" universalities.[16] He also speaks pertinently to the question of how to imagine a capitalism that does not do away with domination. Nation formation, he argues, is "bound up not with the abstraction of the capitalist market, but with its concrete form: that of a 'world-economy' which is always already hierarchically organized into a 'core' and a 'periphery' . . . between which relations of unequal exchange and domination are established."[17] The question remains, however, whether this is a single system that turns different faces to the core and periphery (e.g., commodity fetishism at the core, personal domination at the periphery) or whether it is, perhaps, only the *appearance* of a single system. What about those whom global capital may have picked up and then dropped, or those in whose exploitation it never had more than minimal interest? Are we sure that, as the telephone company tells us, we are all connected?

Paradoxically, the project of salvaging cosmopolitanism may take some encouragement from the possibility that we are less connected than we thought we were. According to Neil Lazarus, among others, when cosmopolitans at the core condemn nationalism at the periphery, they are acting in unreflective accord with the interests of world capitalism; for "the further capitalism has been able to consolidate itself as a world-system over the course of the past 50 years, the more insurgent nationalisms have come, to bourgeois metropolitan eyes, to loom preeminently as barriers of expansion and accumulation."[18] It is this equation between cosmopolitanism and global capitalism that *Imperial Eyes* upsets. In Mary Kingsley, as Pratt describes her, support of "expansion and accumulation" stands behind not cosmopolitan spectatorship but its opposite—not the clear heights of the promontory but the moist, dark indeterminacy of the swamp. This suggests, reading the logic backward, that the perspectival superiority that Pratt associates with cosmopolitan mobility may not, after all, correspond to the market in any simple or straightforward way, or to the geographic universalism of the cosmopolitan traveler, but rather to a style of personalized domination that is not essential to or characteristic of the modern epoch. Following the course of this suggestion, one might conclude that Kingsley's free-market perspective need not result in a position against Third World demands for national independence—indeed, depending on the cooperativeness of the relevant elites, it could well work in complicity with such demands. And one might conclude that in a given situation, even cosmopolitanism of the heavily symbolic, top-down variety might work not for but against the interests of world capital.

The sort of disconnection I have in mind, and the sort of space it makes within and against an unscrutinized universalism, can be illustrated by Lazarus's own superb critique of Frantz Fanon on the Algerian Revolution. Lazarus writes, "It is impossible, in Fanon's reading, to account for the wholesale demobilization and disenfranchizement of 'the people' in the years following the acquisition of independence in Algeria in 1962. . . . Such a development cannot be reconciled with Fanon's evocation of a disciplined and progressively unified population coming closer and closer to self-knowledge as the struggle against the French colonial forces intensified."[19] "The truth, rather, would seem to be that as a class the Algerian peasantry was *never* committed to the vision of the FLN [Front de Libération Nationale], even when it was fighting under the FLN's leadership" (77–78).

Fanon's mistake, according to Lazarus, was to confuse dominance with hegemony. In *Black Skin, White Masks,* if not in *The Wretched of the Earth,* Fanon seemed to assume "the decisiveness of the transformation wrought by colonialism" (76). In fact, however,

> inherited subaltern cultural forms (language, dance, music, storytelling) were able to retain both their traditionality and their autonomy from most forms of elite culture (colonial and 'national'). . . . For a majority of the colonized, above all those (mostly peasant) members of the subaltern classes living at some remove from the administrative and increasingly urban centers of colonial power, colonialism was experienced primarily in terms of dominance, that is, along the lines of material, physical, and economic exaction: conquest, taxation, conscription, forced labor, eviction, dispossession, etc. There was comparatively little attempt on the part of the colonial establishment to seek *hegemony* among these subaltern classes, that is, to win their ideological, moral, cultural and intellectual support for colonialism. (77)

The sort of postcolonial identity that was forged in the (Hegelian) struggle between colonizer and colonized—an identity that remains both dependent on and resistant to the European colonizer—has thus been falsely universalized, along with its will and authority to obstruct the internationalism that is its equally universalistic potential ally. According to Lazarus—though he does not explicitly draw this conclusion—such an identity would, in fact, belong only to the minority urban elites who led the struggle. This opens the way to a schematic hypothesis for which there is increasing evidence, in areas of the world as far apart as China and Eastern Europe: namely, that the much-publicized new nationalist fundamentalism is, above all, an elite, urban phenomenon, most pronounced among those in most direct friction with "the West," and that there exist elsewhere, thanks to the continuing unevenness and incompleteness of capitalist development, a series of partial, popular cosmopolitanisms of the sort that Amitav Ghosh finds among the Egyptian workers of *In an Antique Land.*[20] If so, and if we are thus encouraged to break with the holism shared by any number of Hegelian-Freudian models of postcolonial otherness, we may discover that the biggest obstacle to some sort of reinvigoration of internationalism is not the crude nationalism of stay-at-home Third (or First) World majorities but the mobile, sophisticated, less accessible nationalism of literate elites like ourselves.

This inference from the premise of an incompletely connected world strikes at one of the more obscure but widespread obstacles to internationalism: the assumption that all psychology is national psychology, that all feeling is national feeling. In Pratt, for example, the cosmopolitan mobility that is caught in the monarch-of-all-I-survey tableau is associated with a refusal of the erotic. In Pratt's account of Albert Camus's writings about Algeria, another of her counterexamples, the story "The Adulterous Woman" "culminates with a climactic nocturnal scene . . . when, alone in the dead of night, the [French] woman experiences an orgasmic momentary fusion with the 'desert kingdom' that 'can never be hers'" (224). In the Richard Wright–in–Africa passage, the darkness brings "a serene receptivity and intense eroticism" (222). It is as if eroticism could only thrive with the eyes closed, as if affective intensity and the faculty of sight were mutually exclusive.[21] Sight means possession, and possession means power. The point of the implied syllogism seems to be that the erotic is also irreconcilable with power.

Again, laundered but recognizable versions of this logic are familiar wherever tales of transnational mobility are told. This is what Richard Rorty was suggesting, in the now notorious op-ed piece in the *New York Times,* when he accused U.S. academic multiculturalists of spurning "the emotion of national pride."[22] And it is what accompanies Benedict Anderson's lyrical description of the nation as a "deep, horizontal comradeship" (16). The would-be internationalist who looks down from a commanding height must live without the comforts of erotic and emotional contact, for deep or true feeling is "horizontal," that is, national. The nation takes the place of religion, becoming "the most universally legitimate value in the political life of our time" (12), Anderson says, because people are willing to die for it. "Who," he then asks pointedly, "will willingly die for Comecon or the EEC [the European Economic Community]?" (55).[23] With perhaps a trace of self-contempt, Anderson thus disposes of the Abraham Lincoln Brigade, Amnesty International, and Médecins sans Frontières (Doctors without Borders), allowing the internationalist or cosmopolitan to become a sub- or inhuman subject unwilling to die for anything—floating, without material base or emotional attachment to others, insubstantial.

If culture is the domain of feeling, then for Anderson there is no culture of cosmopolitanism, only an elegant, decorous absence of feeling. But as I argued in chapter 1, this does not, in fact, follow from Anderson's premises. Feelings are produced within a bounded administrative unit on a national scale, but it is not the bounds themselves that do the affective producing; the same sorts of feeling are also produced, if not to the same degree, by the sorts of connections now increasingly common on a transnational scale. If people can get as emotional as Anderson says they do about relations with fellow nationals they never see face to face, then why not with those who are not fellow nationals, people bound by some other sort of fellowship?[24] If there can be an "emotion of national pride," then why not emotions of international pride, based on a horizontal comradeship across the formal equality of nations? Why is it that Martha Nussbaum is forced to affirm so energetically that "the life of the cosmopolitan . . . need not be boring, flat, or lacking in love"?[25]

One answer to these questions emerges from Étienne Balibar's description of the cosmopolitanism exported by the *philosophes* in the era of the French Revolution. In a distant echo of Freud's joke about the woman in labor who cries out first in French, then in German, but requires her doctor's services only when she gets to Yiddish, Balibar identifies cosmopolitanism with an acquired, nonnational language, one that rules out deep, authentic feeling:

> "Cosmopolitanism"—as it appeared in the eighteenth century in the "Republic of Letters," for which it was a point of honor—is only the *alienated* figure of humanism and universality. Far from announcing the overcoming of national rivalries, it is their ideological manifestation, whose truth lies in what is *done* in its name and not in what is *said*. Now what is done is, on the one hand, the imposition of French as a "universal language" on the philosophy and language of all peoples, and on the other hand the institution of a split between the lower classes, the masses, and the "cultivated class" of all nations, the two processes being obviously related. A double alienation, both for the intellectuals (*Gelehrten*) and for the people: the former feel nothing of what they express in a foreign language (their concepts are empty), the latter have no rational knowledge of what they feel (their intuitions are blind) and thus become foreign to their own thought.[26]

Feeling, it appears, is a coded reference to constituency; the cosmopolitan's supposed absence of feeling means that the masses aren't following.[27] But how can we be so sure that they are not following—or even leading? In fact, Balibar's scheme need not necessarily exclude such a possibility. Like Pratt's *Imperial Eyes* and other recent examples of anti-cosmopolitanism aimed at the global domination of the United States, his gesture of national self-critique (vis-à-vis the era of French cultural predominance in Europe) assigns a rhetorically convenient but causally excessive agency to the malevolence of the imperial power.

Cosmopolitanism, he suggests, is a device by which the imperial power dominates its national rivals, by dividing them internally. That is, the "alienation" of the intellectuals from feeling and from the people (the two alienations are actually one) is produced, decisively if not exclusively, by the intrusion of the French language. Without the foreignness of the French language, there would be no gap between intellectuals and people—as there should be no gap, the implication goes, in France itself. There, it would seem, the people should be able to think, and the intellectuals should be able to feel. Without the divisive but aberrant intrusion of the colonizer's nationality, the colonized nation would be a whole person, perfectly able to combine feeling with thought.

Identifying himself, as a Frenchman, with the alien source of cosmopolitanism, Balibar seems willing to suggest that if such alienness could be expunged, national harmony would reign again, transcending internal class divisions that are finally inessential. In other words, cosmopolitanism does for anti-imperialism just what racism, in Balibar's own analysis, does for nationalism. In "Racism as Universalism," Balibar argues that, faced with the task of overcoming "class antagonisms and struggles," national institutions and ideologies *almost succeed, but not quite . . .* this situation unleashes a permanent process of displacement and escape. You need more nationalism. You need a nationalism which is, so to speak, more nationalistic than nationalism itself: what I would call . . . in the language of Derrida a *supplement* of nationalism *within* nationalism." Racism, Balibar concludes, "simply *is* this supplement."[28] Balibar's view of cosmopolitanism offers a fascinatingly masochistic parallel. Here, the damning identification of cosmopolitanism with elitism supplies the decisive supplement—a supplement not to nationalism but to anti-imperialism—for it eliminates the divisiveness of class from anti-imperialism just as, in Balibar's analysis, racism eliminates the divisiveness of class from nationalism. The class privilege ascribed to the cosmopolitan would have to be invented if it did not exist, for it provides an ideal solution to nationalism's internal problems. By means of such an ascription, class division is exorcised, projected onto a group that seems both internal and external, indigenous and alien. This group can be racialized (the Jews) or sexualized (homosexuals), as it so often has been, but it can also serve its purpose without race or sexuality. These days, when it is generally believed that racial and sexual sensitivities are running dangerously high, there is obviously some usefulness in a national scapegoat category—the cosmopolitan—that can avoid both.

As Rorty's outburst made clear, logic like this is a pressingly unpleasant problem for the cultural left in the United States. Whatever the supposed intimacy between cosmopolitanism and capitalism, cosmopolitanism is under attack today from many quarters that are emphatically not interested in attacking capitalism. And though these attacks often come from the right, the preferred assault weapon is a populist, antielitist discourse that censures a supposedly excessive interest in non-European, noncanonical cultures by associating it with arrogant hierarchy and economic privilege at home. The cultural left sometimes cooperates with this domestic discrediting of the transnational, as when it lingers self-laceratingly on the class affiliations of Third World practitioners of postcolonial discourse in the metropolis, even when the latter make visible efforts to free their thinking from such affiliations.[29]

Self-defense would seem to require both refutation and concession. On the one hand, there is some truth in the picture painted by anticosmopolitans. The task of educating our students and ourselves to make connections with cultures at a distance will not get any easier until the cultural left reconsiders some of its own missed connections on the domestic level. On the other hand, the place to begin making those missed connections may be the questioning of one crucial step in the logic that scapegoats cosmopolitanism, namely, that "where the feeling is" means "where the people are," and where the people are, affectively speaking, is with and inside the nation. But who says that where the people are, in the United States, for example, is so deeply and exclusively national? Consider the discourse of human rights centered in institutions such as the United Nations. Whether one thinks about the U.S. public's tortured fascination with Bosnia, with Chinese prisons, or with the 1994 Michael Fay "caning" case in Singapore (about which polls disclosed that, unlike the president, a majority of Americans did not respond with nationalist outrage at the punishment of an American boy by Asian policemen), it is clear that the vocabulary of human rights expresses widespread, warmhearted, and, in a sense, internationalist emotion. Imperfect as it may be, it comes as close as any vocabulary to what people feel is "fair"; it is one massively and passionately felt form that internationalism has taken outside the academy. The feeling is there; the people are there. But where are the intellectuals? This is an internationalist discourse that the cultural left in the academy, which is otherwise so strenuously transnational, has had little dialogue with, to say the least.

There are various reasons for this, but I think it is especially important to distinguish between two that are easily confused. One obvious reason for the cultural left's neglect of human rights discourse is the cultural left's attachment to culture in an antiuniversalistic sense. Culture as difference has lately been one, perhaps even the major, rationale for knowledge production in the humanities, and the universalizing discourse of human rights seems to set itself straightforwardly against this rationale. Thus the opposition between culture and human rights, or between culture and any universalizing standard, takes the form of a devotion to differences that can be described in what Charles Taylor calls the "incorrigibility thesis." On this thesis, cultures are supposed to be seen only from their own point of view and in their own terms, Taylor says; then they can never be "wrong, confused or deluded" (123).[30]

The cultural left has continued to merit that name (increasingly problematic but as yet irreplaceable) by never having fully accepted the incorrigibility thesis. "To apply abstract Enlightenment values in a rigidly intolerant legal way is to undermine the system's own claim to universality," Françoise Lionnet writes, discussing the debate over female genital mutilation in France, "since it thereby condemns practices . . . upon which rests the global equilibrium of a *different* culture."[31] This makes cultural difference sound incorrigible. But Lionnet allows for Enlightenment values to be applied in a way that would not be "rigidly intolerant." "What does appear to be 'universal'," she concludes, "is the way in which *different* cultures, for better or for worse, impose *similar* constraints on the bodies of their members, especially when those bodies are already marked by the sign of the feminine" (111). One need not affirm that equality exists outside the domain of differences (Naomi Schor has made the case decisively) to hold that the respect for differences must always run into limits of one sort or another — in short, that no culture is incorrigible.[32]

The second reason for the cultural left's indifference to a universalizing human rights discourse is a judgment of the latter's true relations to power and justice. Rey Chow writes, "From the days of England's gunboat diplomacy to the present day, the question of human rights, when it is raised in China in relation to the West, has never been separable from the privilege of extraterritoriality demanded by the Western diplomat, trader, or missionary." In other words, "nationals and subjects of the 'treaty powers' were subject to the civil and criminal laws of their own countries and not to Chinese law" (85).[33] The reverse, of course, was not true; exemption from local jurisdiction worked in only one direction. Notice, however, that Chow's protest against this classic double standard is not a protest on behalf of cultural difference or against universalizing standards as such. Rather, it is a protest against the abuse of power, and it is perfectly compatible with a version of universalism, at least in principle.

How much difference does it make when universalism is disputed in terms of power rather than in terms of culture? In a recent article in *The Nation* titled "Globocop?" C. Douglas Lummis quoted the opening statement by UN secretary-general Boutros Boutros-Ghali at the World Conference on Human Rights in 1993 in Vienna: " 'Human rights,' he says, are 'absolutely universal.' At the same time, 'human rights . . . reflect a power relationship.' . . . For Boutros-Ghali, 'human rights' serve the same function that 'divine right' did in the seventeenth century: As absolute injunctions, they generate an authority higher than any other" (303–4). The prospect of UN-sponsored war-crimes trials in

THE WEIRD HEIGHTS: *IMPERIAL EYES*

the former Yugoslavia, on the precedent of the Nuremberg and Tokyo trials, brings the following reflection: "Any international tribunal established by the U.N. in the context of its present power structure is not going to go after the really big international criminals," for example, those who bombed Iraq or those who manufacture nuclear weapons (304, 306):

> What is being founded here is not, after all, a new world superstate but a front for New World Order politics—in other words, G7 rule. We can be confident that only the borders of middling and small countries will show a "new legal permeability." These are the same countries whose borders were always "permeable" throughout the age of colonialism and European continental imperialism: the countries of the Third World and eastern Europe. However much good might be achieved by, say, Norwegian or Nigerian peacekeepers protecting human rights in Los Angeles or Detroit, it's not something we are likely soon to see. (306)[34]

As I write (in October 1994), it happens that Maurice Glèlè-Ahenhanzo of Benin, a Special Rapporteur on Contemporary Forms of Slavery appointed by the UN Commission on Human Rights, is visiting the United States to investigate problems of racial discrimination that NGOs and others have alleged. This is an event; it marks the first time that a human rights mechanism of the United Nations has been allowed by the U.S. government into the United States to monitor the situation. While the event is not exactly "Nigerian peacekeepers protecting human rights in Los Angeles," it is not a negligible step in that direction. And it forces us to consider human rights as an instrument whose power cannot be wholly or permanently circumscribed and contained by a double standard—a dangerous instrument in the hands of the G7, certainly, but also an instrument that can be turned against the G7.

To think politically about the provisional universalism of human rights is perhaps to begin with the following simplistic axioms. Universal standards represent provisional agreements arrived at by particular agents. They are produced in a situation of unequal power, and they are applied in a situation of unequal power. Thus they are always applied unequally, and the result is always some degree of injustice. The same is true, however, of any discursive instrument or agent that might serve to upset the status quo, for it has been produced and will be applied within the status quo. To discredit such instruments and agents in advance, as Lummis does on that basis, is to vote to leave the status quo as it is. This is the problem, for example, with David J. Depew's view of cosmopolitanism. All macronarratives of world unity invariably break down, Depew writes, and are seen merely as "projections of particular interests, in which some nation, class, or cultural totality would appear as hero . . . while other nations, classes, or cultures appeared as objects rather than as subjects of history" (359). For if "the idea of historical unity receives too concrete an articulation—in which the historian or the community of historians advocates world-historical unification *on some definite plan and under the aegis of some definite power or agent*—it loses its cognitive worth, becoming merely an ideological accessory to the acquisition and exercise of power."[35] The point here is that there can never be a universalism that is not "under the aegis of some definite power or agent." To disqualify it on those grounds, in the hopes of eventually finding a "clean" universalism independent of all partial powers and agents, is to condemn oneself to an indefinite wait— and, in effect, to withdraw from the project of political change.

In short, all universalisms are dirty. And it is only dirty universalisms that will help us against the powers and agents of still dirtier ones. There is no room for purism here—which is not to say that important distinctions don't have to be made. In criticizing human rights as a tool of the G7 nations, Lummis implicitly speaks in the name of nations other than the G7, especially those nations of the "Third World" or "South" that have often been denounced in human rights language. In a discussion of the 1992 Rio summit, Tom Athanasiou casts some doubt on the implicitly nationalistic (one might also say holistic or Hegelian) model of "domination" behind this choice: "Even Greenpeace, which should know better, told its members in a Rio follow up that the South had 'little choice but abandon any nobler planetary visions and demand a bigger piece of the disintegrating global pie.'" But, says Athanasiou, "this view excuses far too much. In lumping southern corporations, governments, and people together, it paints even vile actions as the inevitable consequences of northern domination, and verges on just the kind of third worldism that helped destroy the new left. Malaysia illustrates the point all too well, for it was, if anything, the ideological leader of the South at Rio, and its ruling elites have made a mission of justifying both social repression and environmental destruction as the costs of 'development.'"[36] Why the "strange sympathy with corporations and governments that routinely harrass and arrest indigenous and environmental activists" (83)?

If one decides, with Athanasiou, that it is a bit late in the day to throw oneself behind anything as politically suspect and variegated as the "corporations and governments" of "the South," this does not mean one is thrown back onto what Christopher Hitchens calls the "arid name" of "international *norms*" such as "human rights and self-determination and democratic procedure."[37] If the abstraction of universal principles without particular agents, as empty of emotion, is indeed arid, these principles have recently become much less so. This is thanks to what Hitchens calls "the larger role and capacity of non-state organizations on the periphery of the UN" (23)—that is, the nongovernmental organizations (NGOs) of and to whom Athanasiou is speaking. "Over the past few years," Hitchens goes on, "an unusual volume of NGO activity has been pressing the UN to live up to its charter. There was the 1993 Human Rights Conference in Vienna and also the International Women's Conference, both of which were able to mobilize thousands of activists world-wide to lobby UN delegations concerning long-unkept promises on human rights and gender equality" (40–41).

NGOs had no voice at the United Nations before 1970. But at the Vienna conference in 1993 that provoked Lummis's fears of the United Nations as "globocop," the force that broke the stalemate between First World universalists and Third World relativists was the NGOs, especially NGOs that had a strong Third World voice but did not identify wholeheartedly with the interests of Third World nation-states. (I discuss this episode in more detail in chapter 7.) They insisted that while the terrible and growing economic disparity between North and South should guide human rights debates more than it has done, it was not a reason to obstruct such debates or to label as imperialist the tools that issued from them. The human rights vocabulary was a necessary ally in these NGOs' own struggles—struggles aimed simultaneously within and beyond their respective countries. The result of this new array of nongovernmental Third World voices was tangible gains for international feminism and, more generally, a greater legitimacy for the new, provisional human rights consensus: a partial but working (that is, at least partially empowered) version of universalism.

There are many reasons for delaying any uncritical celebration of this new accord. As Laura Flanders points out, women paid a price for their much-noted victories in Vienna: "Of the recommendations from the Women's Caucus, those that addressed violence mostly got accepted. Those that dealt with poverty and development did not. . . . The anti-permissive, pro-control, pro-action-now approach of the new Victorian feminists seems suited to the dominant current in international affairs. Its one-woman-equals-all, for-us-or-against-us ideology translates well into potentially global codes—far better than the feminism that emphasizes education above control and social mobilization over social regulation" (177).[38] To think of NGOs as helping to constitute a new "public sphere" or burgeoning international version of "civil society," in contradistinction to the system of nation-states, may be to neglect progressive possibilities that states retain. It can serve to downplay, for example, the continuing struggle for social welfare at the state level.[39] Under no circumstances presently imaginable could NGOs constitute an alternative cosmopolis. The fact that the language of international civil society is now being used by the World Bank is disquieting, among other reasons because the World Bank includes in "civil society" economic forces that work, like the bank itself, in secrecy rather than in public. And as Gayatri Spivak has pointed out, it is always necessary to ask who provides "elite collaborative" NGOs with their power and funds, and with what effects on the state and its grassroots accountability.[40]

Still, something would be gained if the argument about universalism could be shifted from the terrain of culture to the terrain of power, as I have been suggesting, and if its energies could be shifted to the work of discriminating among the partial, imperfect agents and struggles that I briefly engage in above. Thinking about universals in terms of unequal power, rather than solely in terms of cultural difference, makes visible the common or universalizing ground that we already occupy—whatever our necessary insistence on difference—from the moment that we protest against any injustice. And it is an invitation to learn how to exercise power, rather than simply to protest its exercise by others, and to do so at altitudes that may seem uncongenial. To learn to act as well as think on the transnational scale, at which so much of our political fate is increasingly decided, is, of course, a weird idea (weird comes from the Old English for "fate" or "enchanted power"). It is easier to leave the weirdness of these heights to others.

Reflecting on the ambiguities in Mary Louise Pratt's discussion of privileged travelers and elevated viewpoints at the end of Imperial Eyes, I was reminded of a memorable spelling example from elementary school: "Neither leisured foreigner seized the weird heights with a counterfeit seismograph." Initially, I assumed that many others had encountered the same sentence in school, but the experience of circulating drafts of this chapter has suggested otherwise. The first and last lesson to be taken from it, then, is still a suspicion of the apparent universal. But there are other lessons. A way of remembering the order of i's and e's—that is, of taking on the appearance of an educated person by learning to reproduce the universal standard of orthography—this mnemonic device becomes, in this context, a lesson about eyes and ease. It suggests that we cannot equate the weird heights of cosmopolitanism with foreigners of the leisure classes—that these heights are weird because what they lay before one's eyes is not a simple reflection or prerogative of the ease that allows one to be there. (Ease, etymology reminds us, comes from the old French for "elbow room"; it is nothing more overprivileged than the minimal space required for action.) And it suggests that to detect the quakings of the social foundations that signal the operation of power, to know where to place ourselves in relation to that power, we need truer, more sensitive seismographs than allegories of the seer and the seen, the mobile and the fixed, universalism and antiuniversalism.

4

FEELING GLOBAL

JOHN BERGER AND EXPERIENCE

Much of John Berger's writing since 1975 has had to do with peasants. What Berger calls "peasant experience" is the explicit subject of the short fictions of *Pig Earth* (1979); it is the point of departure and social counterweight of his essay on European migrant workers, *A Seventh Man* (1975); it provides the privileged field of instances drawn on by the art criticism of *About Looking* (1980) and the unclassifiable volume of and about photographic narration, *Another Way of Telling* (1982)—like *A Seventh Man,* a collaboration with the photographer Jean Mohr. Peasant experience insinuates itself less directly into the urban volumes of the "Into Their Labors" trilogy, *Once in Europa* (1987) and *Lilac and Flag* (1990).[1] Considering this choice of subject matter in the light of Berger's own experience—for many years, he has lived in and shared the labors of a peasant village in Haute-Savoie—reviewers have wondered "whether his notion of peasants isn't an idealized abstraction of rough-hewn nineteenth-century souls who aren't alienated from their labor"[2] and have suggested that his "turning to the margins," whether idealized or not, can hardly be anything other than "an attempt to escape the hopelessness he finds in our culture by entering a world still heavy with the density of Being."[3]

The first pages of *Pig Earth* offer evidence both for and against the charge of pastoral simplification. They describe, in unsettling detail, the slaughter of a cow. The abrupt unpleasantness of the scene seems intended as an initial guarantee that unpleasant specifics will not, as in the simplified pastoral, be rounded out. In contrast, the animal's death might be read as a bid to dissolve peasant specifics in a "human" universal. Since it is a universal truth that *Homo sapiens* kills animals, the humanist can always use the killing of animals to slip the reader past the actual diversity of historical men and woman to the putative species-being of a universal "Man." Berger's implicit argument, then, would be that the experience of peasants slaughtering a cow is representative of human experience itself. The fingers of the ordinary urban shopper are not permitted to touch the meat of life. The peasant alone can "experience" the universals of "Experience." And in so doing, Berger suggests, peasants also handle their own deaths. Repeatedly, the book parallels the deaths of animals and the deaths of those who care for them. City dwellers, whose life is mediated through advertising and industrial abattoirs, cannot grasp life's defining extremities. "Publicity, situated in a future continually deferred, excludes the present and so eliminates all becoming, all development. Experience is impossible within it" (*WS*, 153). In their spontaneous, present-tense fronting of the essentials of life, Berger's peasants preserve "Experience" and thus form a pastoral refuge for the truly human.

Berger's work demystifies rural stereotypes, observes a scrupulous self-consciousness, experiments freshly with forms of narrative and authorship; it also commemorates the good old days, once again, in an uncorrupted countryside. So tardy a version of pastoral cannot expect to be greeted as the latest thing. Nevertheless, what is most interesting about this writing is precisely its engagement with our impalpable postmodernity. Granted that peasant culture "is hardly an option" for us now,[4] the reader of the end of the twentieth century has more choices than simply to take or leave the Frankfurt School–ish pessimism about all things contemporary that trails in Berger's wake. More than half a century has gone by since Bertolt Brecht told his friend Walter Benjamin to start with not the good old things but the bad new ones. What this phrase means now requires fresh attention. Whether or not we can usefully read Berger's peasants may depend on how well we can read our bad new things.

Literary modernism and academic departments of literature took shape in roughly the same period, and there are reasons for suspecting a complicity between them—between, say, the ejection of history simultaneously from certain modernist texts and from the New Critical apparatus that canonized them.[5] If this suspicion is justified, then the awkward compound *postmodernism* can be understood both as the literary disturbance that produced Thomas Pynchon, Robert Creeley, and others and as a disturbance in the institutions of criticism. At least for those of us who study and teach the so-called humanities, postmodernity seems to present itself in large part as an unease with the humanistic principles that so recently brought our disciplines into being and so powerfully continue to shape our practice. One source of this unease may be the naturalization of Marxist thought, which has slowly passed from the status of an exotic foreign dogma to an assured, if limited, place within a humanist "common sense" that tries to assess the effects on humanity of something called "globalization." This unease also seems to stem from the working vocabulary and operational procedures that Marxism and humanism have thus come to share.

It is at this conjuncture that John Berger commands further attention. As a "permanent Red"—in 1979 he reissued his collection of twenty-five-year-old art criticism under the same defiant title—and a man of letters in the old Arnoldian sense, writing outside the shelter of the university, he has tried, for a long and accomplished career, to negotiate between a broadly Marxist view of the world and a broad nonacademic readership. He has as good a claim as anyone to have fought for and added to a new Marxist-humanist "common sense." And if he is thus implicated in its strains, compromises, and incoherences, by the same token his work is a valuable indicator of its latent powers and directions.

In the "Historical Afterword" to *Pig Earth,* Berger defends his interest in peasants as an effort to retrieve and preserve their neglected experience: "To dismiss peasant experience as belonging only to the past, as having no relevance to modern life, to imagine that the thousands of years of peasant culture leave no heritage for the future, . . . to continue to maintain, as has been maintained for centuries, that peasant experience is marginal to civilization, is to deny the value of too much history and too many lives" (*PE*, 211–12). The issue here is the value of experience. Adopting the vocabulary of humanism, Berger adopts along with it the assumption that writers like himself are enjoined by a sort of Hippocratic Oath to "save lives"—to recover and protect the "heritage" of experience for its own sake, out of respect for life itself—or perhaps more precisely, to extend humanism's protection to those more marginal lives that would once have been neglected. The argument has immediate power. Who will dare admit to disrespect for life? However, this view of scholarship, in which a generous, democratic indiscriminateness seems to guarantee ideological neutrality, does not correspond to the inevitable selectivity of actual and potential practice. Worse, it sustains the mirage of a disinterested, nonideological tradition that would merely pay homage to what has happened: if not what the best have known and said, then what the rest have been through. Reverence for experience thus becomes a tool of mystification.

Berger also follows out a more convincing line of thought. The famous conservativism of the peasant is that of a "culture of survival," he suggests, and therefore is particularly well suited to the present, when hopes of revolutionary progress have given way to a scramble to avoid various threats of extinction. Commanding respect as the prime mover of twentieth-century revolutions in the Third World, the peasant is now also a guide to conservationism and disarmament. This is a version of humanist practice in its most frequent Marxist inflection: the experience that needs to be salvaged, raised to canonical status, and propagated is assumed to be that of the proletariat, which is the focus of humanity's struggle to liberate itself and, consequently, of the creation of new values. But this position, too, is subject to the critique of experience and of its place in the human sciences that is one of the more important developments of recent years. "Experience, though noone auctoritee / Were in this world, is right ynogh for me," said Chaucer's Wife of Bath. But in a number of different fields, it has been noted that experience is no longer an opponent of authority; it has become authority itself. James Clifford has pointed out the powers and presuppositions hidden away in the participant-observer's innocent "I was there."[6] When Louis Althusser admonished Jean-Paul Sartre that "Marxism is not a humanism," he was suggesting, among other things, that human experience might be seen as a history of errors and illusions. This proposition undermines a cornerstone of the humanities: the assumption that past experience is loaded with values that are worthy of being extracted and brought forward in canons and traditions to guide the present. A challenge to experience is a challenge to the fundamental practices of salvage and tradition building that, in disciplines such as literary criticism and historiography, have allowed Marxists and humanists to come together. Long vulnerable to various theoretical attacks, experience now assumes a new importance as the center of debate about revised and up-to-date humanist practice. In the present context, this debate would have to include the specifically *national* limits imposed by experience.

The editor of History Workshop's *People's History and Socialist Theory* (1981) devotes a preface to the defense of its project: "the recovery of subjective experience." He concedes, however, that "the notion of 'real life experience' is certainly in need of critical scrutiny."[7] One full-scale scrutiny appears in Perry Anderson's *Arguments within English Marxism* (1980), where reliance on an undertheorized concept of experience is taken as a crucial weakness of E. P. Thompson's national history of the working class and of Marxist-humanist history in general. For Thompson, Anderson writes, "experience is the privileged medium in which consciousness of reality awakens and creative response to it stirs." But this account "is irreconcilable with the blinkering from reality and the depth of disaster which such salient experiences as religious faith or national loyalty have brought upon those in their grip. Althusser wrongly identifies experience only with such illusions: Thompson inverts this error, identifying experience essentially with insight and learning."[8] Thompson uses the word *experience* in two senses: in the minimal, neutral sense of "subjective reaction . . . to objective events" but also in the more loaded sense of "a *lesson*" that those who live through history learn from it—in other words, *knowledge*. Experience means both merely being there with one's eyes open and the firmly grounded, reliable knowledge supposedly carried away from being there. Everyone has the first, but the second, especially with regard to "social relations," may well be rare. Anderson accuses Thompson's humanist rhetoric of "unconsciously transferring the virtues and powers of the (more restricted) second type to the (more general) first type of experience. The efficacy of the one is fused with the universality of the other." The result is an exaggeration of the extent to which people are conscious, creative agents of history.[9]

In the field of literary criticism, Anderson's critique of Thompson is paralleled by Terry Eagleton's critique of Raymond Williams. In Williams's work, Eagleton writes, "the insistence on experience, this passionate premium placed upon the 'lived' . . . supplies at once the formidable power and the drastic limitation."[10] Eagleton traces this theme back to the humanist heritage of English critic F. R. Leavis: "To combat 'ideology,' *Scrutiny* [the critical journal launched by Leavis and his wife] pointed to 'experience'—as though that, precisely, were not ideology's homeland." In what Eagleton calls the "Left Leavisism" of Williams, experience again draws a veil over ideological determinations, programmatically refusing the notion "that 'ordinary people' were not, after all, the true creators of 'meaning and values.'"[11] This is the vulnerable spot of the taken for granted where Williams is also prodded by the interlocutors of *Politics and Letters*. Experience, they observe, "must be the only word you use recurrently that is not given an entry in *Keywords*." They suggest to Williams that "the epistemological privilege of experience" in his work implies a "domain of direct truth," "a kind of pristine contact between the subject and the reality in which this subject is immersed." Williams concedes, in his words, "the impossibility of understanding contemporary society from experience," as well as the conclusions his interviewers draw about the disciplinary limits of literary criticism: "It is not possible to work back from texts to structures of feeling to experiences to social structures. There is a deep disjunction between the literary text from which an experience can be reconstituted and the total historical process at the time."[12]

This concession disconnects literary criticism from a major source of its power: the claim to serve as a repository that safeguards what is true and valuable in the national past. Without the authority of experience, it is not clear how criticism could ever have helped Williams become a national figure. In a magisterial attempt to mediate between humanist and Althusserian attitudes, Richard Johnson concludes that critics of culture and ideology have arrived at an "impasse." If the humanist "move into the experiential" tends to ignore determining factors located "behind men's backs," it can at least speak about the troubles men and women see in front of them. And its critics, in contrast, seem to achieve a more comprehensive or cosmopolitan view "at the cost of any real connection with a popular politics."[13] Somewhat less lucidly, Terry Eagleton's *Walter Benjamin, or Towards a Revolutionary Criticism* (1981) leaves the reader in a similar bind. The book opens by discovering in Benjamin a protodeconstructionist whose version of the seventeenth century (in the *Origin of German Tragic Drama*) serves as an antidote to the agrarian "unified sensibility" projected there by T. S. Eliot and Leavis. However, the book also uses Benjamin, no less strangely, as the excuse for an enthusiastic critique of deconstruction, and in particular of its pretensions as a guide to revolutionary practice. Deconstruction, which helps purge the left of its residual Leavisite humanism, seems unable to duplicate or rival humanism's hold over feelings or actions. The bad new days start here: with the need to replace a humanist vocabulary that has been discredited, along with the parties that have used it, and the equal need for a theoretical clarity that in interpreting the world will not renounce the drive to change it.

"Stranded between social democracy and Stalinism, his political options were narrow indeed. There was little left to him but 'experience'."[14] Eagleton's tactical unbending toward Benjamin's "idealism" might also be stretched to cover John Berger, who shares Benjamin's ambivalence about modernity and has borrowed freely both from the open nostalgia of Benjamin's "The Storyteller" and from the embrace of the media in "The Work of Art in the Age of Mechanical Reproduction." Benjamin can be forgiven because, in a time of limited political options, his retreat into experience also expanded and discriminated its categories. Does not Berger do the same? Clearly, the criticisms addressed to Williams and Thompson are pertinent to his work as well. He speaks both of and to ordinary experience. His writing is shamelessly empathetic, an effort to articulate how others construct the world. The ideological limits of experience are built into the literary form of his project. However, this writing also reflects Berger's own experience, which has not been ordinary. In particular, it has been extraordinarily *international*—a key term in the experience discussion.

The absence of the international, Perry Anderson argues, is one crippling consequence of E. P. Thompson's privileging of experience in *The Making of the English Working Class*: "international dimensions of English working-class history" are missing, he says, since "social revolutions abroad," for example, "cannot be entered as self-activity of the working class of England."[15] The interviewers of *Politics and Letters* point out a parallel lack of "foreign or overseas developments" in Raymond Williams's account of the 1840s. "The Parisian insurrections of 1848" could not be measured as an influence "because 1848 was not a national experience in the direct sense"; nor was the Irish famine. "If we consult the two maps of either the official ideology of the period or the recorded subjective experience of its novels, neither of them extended to include this catastrophe right on their doorstep, causally connected to socio-political processes in England." On the basis of their experience alone, which was almost exclusively national and European, British novelists of the 1840s could do very little with the facts of the British Empire, though the Irish famine was happening right next door and ties to Ireland, India, and the other colonies were directly and indirectly determining so much of daily life. Even an unusually deep and broad national experience does not guarantee that one will know much, finally, about those transnational forces that determine the fate of the nation. As Williams admits, we cannot expect that the all-important knowledge of how to act within "an integrated world economy" will turn up in the nets of literary criticism, for the movements of the world economy, for the most part, could not register in everyday consciousness and thus—this is the rule that gives exceptions like Joseph Conrad and Pynchon their special interest—could not leave a literary record.[16]

John Berger is another exception. He has made experience's international border zone into his chosen territory. In a number of ways, global movement has become an unusually large and conscious part of his experience. International ownership and exhibition of art objects and the existence of an international canon make an art critic such as Berger *structurally* a cosmopolitan—unlike the literary critic, whose reproducible objects do not require the critic's change of place and who, in any case, is free to choose a respectable provinciality. In addition, the canonizing activities of the art critic are more directly exposed than those of the literary critic to pressure from the worldwide fluctuations of the market. Without prying any deeper into Berger's biography, it is safe to say that by profession alone he has had more direct experience of international determinants than is ordinary. More to the point, this experience appears in the literature he has produced, whether as a central theme (as in *A Seventh Man*) or as a peculiar perturbation in the margins of the novels, the film scripts, even the art criticism. The same writing that can be read as a humanist's

FEELING GLOBAL: JOHN BERGER

attempt to save the brand of experience he knows, endangered as it is by the modern world, by finding refuge for it in a knowable (peasant) community, can also be read, more interestingly perhaps, as a series of preparatory inroads into the obscure, uniquely modern no-man's-land of global experience—that is, not as a reduction but as an expansion of experience, in which sections of the impalpable but determining realm of the international begin to solidify and become sensuously present. Reading Berger, we can recognize that we have not yet learned how to "feel global."

To begin with, it is important to see how much of Berger's work does not simply retreat into the local. In a review of *Pig Earth*, Terry Eagleton complains of Berger's respectful fidelity to the "inevitably partial consciousness" of his peasant subjects—in other words, to the categories of their experience. But as Eagleton himself sees, this is a strange remark to make "to the author of *The Moment of Cubism*."[17] As a champion of the cubists, Berger was celebrating paintings whose figures, "when found . . . may have little connection with the sensuous experience of a body" (*SFP*, 59). His description of cubism in terms of "interjacency" and "interaction" insists on the act of making visible a relationship which is not ordinarily available to the senses in the way an object is. To bridge the gap between cubism and common sense, he repeatedly evokes the phrase "action at a distance"—the "traditional terms" in which Michael Faraday had posed the problem whose solution would be the "field of force" (*SFP*, 67, 99). The phrase is worth pausing over. Challenging experience with the apparent anomaly of determination without visible agency, "action at a distance" might almost be the emblem of the international problematic Berger introduces into everyday national consciousness.

Behind the cosmopolitan best-seller that tries to milk exotic politics and international terrorism for every ounce of sensation, there is at least one genuine problem of twentieth-century consciousness: how to measure the domestic weight of foreign revolution. This might be expressed as a problem of rhetoric. To what extent does each metaphor (the structurally similar event happening elsewhere) become a metonymy (effectively connected with processes underway here)? Berger's writings, which are as cosmopolitan as those of the international thriller, are perhaps more useful in formulating such questions. Should his translation of Aimé Césaire's *Cahier d'un retour au pays natal* (Return to my native land) and his fondness for Césaire's phrase "unique people" be understood as a wishful identification with a *négritude* he cannot possess? Or, on the contrary— coming out at a time (1969) when the later history of the national liberation movements was already beginning to reveal the impossibility of any "return" to traditional cultural identity—should it be understood as a bitter embrace of Césaire's knowledge that there are no "home" cultures, only "unique" ones? To the

European or American reader, Césaire's Martinique has more force in the latter reading.

In Berger's novel *A Painter of Our Time* (1958), a suave, hateful art collector and diplomat named Sir Gerald Banks—as cosmopolitan as the capital his name suggests—is played off against the naive but positive provinciality of a neighborhood painter-butcher. The intended flow of sympathy is clear. At the same time, the reader is expected to feel as loyal to Lavin, the painter and exiled revolutionary of the title, as Lavin himself remains to the political hopes of his distant homeland—and to its remembered organic life. (Characteristically, Berger conflates revolution and experience.) The local is celebrated both here and elsewhere. Where is the reader supposed to be located? This question disturbs the celebration. The celebration of the local is also disrupted by Lavin's English wife. When he leaves eventless England at the end of the novel, to return to where the action is (Hungary in 1956), he also leaves her. Poor in passionate political experience of her own (as Berger has made to seem inevitable in England), she has fallen in love with his. Both Lavin and Berger appear to despise this vicarious, secondhand fastening onto another's commitment. But of course, the reader—like "John," the narrator—is precisely in the position of the wife, obliged, at least for the moment, to invest libidinal energies from afar in someone else's revolution.

Lavin is both a "native" and (for almost the entire novel) an exile. In consequence, the reader who shares his consciousness might be said to suffer an international dislocation. Is it possible that all Berger's natives are also exiles? If so, then the reader is confronting not exotic others whose difference might discourage her own activity but *semblables* (likenesses) who invite her to see all action in its new and difficult global terms. In this case, we can no longer describe Berger's literary project as "realist" in any simple sense.

There is something elusive, for example, about even the most solid object of Berger's supposed realism—"peasant experience." Discussing "[Jean-François] Millet's ambition to paint previously unpainted experience," Berger uses *experience* as a synonym for "subject-matter" (*AL*, 71). But when he explains "the writer's relationship with the place and the people he writes about" in *Pig Earth*, it is astonishingly hard to tell whether the experience he refers to is theirs or his own:

> The act of writing is nothing except the act of approaching the experience written about. . . . To approach experience, however, is not like approaching a house. . . . Experience is indivisible and continuous, at least within a single lifetime and perhaps over many lifetimes. I have never had the impression that my experience is entirely my own, and it

often seems to me that it preceded me. In any case, experience folds upon itself, refers backwards and forwards to itself. . . . And so the act of approaching a given moment of experience involves both scrutiny (closeness) and the capacity to connect (distance).

When he says, a few lines later, "My writing about peasants separates me from them and brings me close to them" (*PE*, 6–7), it seems that he has been speaking about peasant experience all along. But for most of the passage, experience belongs to anyone—or no one.

This vagueness as to its exact location permits the odd inference that peasants do not, in fact, possess experience. And when Berger asserts that the "life" of the village is itself a fiction, like his own fictions, the ostensible object of his subjective naturalism dissolves into thin air: "What distinguishes the life of a village is that it is also a *living portrait of itself* . . . constructed . . . out of opinions, stories, eye-witness reports, legends, comments, and hearsay. . . . Without such a portrait . . . the village would have been forced to doubt its own existence" (*PE*, 9). In allowing for the fictionality of peasant life, Berger stresses its vulnerability, the possibility of its nonexistence. "Should [this communal portrait] cease, the village would disintegrate" (*PE*, 11). It is almost as if the threatened "historical elimination" of the peasantry (the last words of the book) had worked its way into experience itself, that which was to be rescued from elimination.

"Writing," Berger says, "has no territory of its own" (*PE*, 6). Is this also the case, then, for peasant storytelling? The suggestion is made. Peasant experience, a "question of place," seems inseparable from spatial and temporal continuity, from the fact that the peasant "has no choice of locality": "It is very rare for a peasant to remain a peasant and be able to move" (*PE*, 11). But there is a good deal of movement in *Pig Earth*. The last and longest story, which occupies almost half the volume, revolves elliptically around the foci of its two main characters' moves beyond the village. And yet it is this story, in Berger's opinion, that goes most "deeply into the subjectivity of the lives" it narrates (*PE*, 13). Here, peasant experience has become that of emigration and displacement. Like the peasantry itself, in a time when the uneven and combined development of the world economy has forced us to use *underdevelop* as a transitive verb, the "life" of the peasant seems less a residual plenitude than a fragile modern construct.

Another Way of Telling makes the same point, in effect, when it asks the reader to participate in the process of construction. Like Benjamin, Berger has sensed a threat to experience in the free-floating polysignification of the photograph. "It is because the photographs carry no certain meaning in themselves, because they are like images in the memory of a total stranger, that they lend themselves to any use" (*AL*, 53). In the text of *Another Way of Telling*, this danger is extended to journalism. "A magazine sends photographer X to city Y to bring back pictures. Many of the finest photographs taken belong to this category. But the story told is finally about what the photographer saw at Y. It is not directly about the experience of those living the event at Y" (*AWT*, 279). The implication is that Berger and Mohr have avoided this surrender of experience to a "total stranger" by anchoring their photographs in the imaginary history of an old peasant woman. But once again, the text is strangely fuzzy about whose experience the narrative is faithful to. "Photographs so placed are restored to a living context: not of course to the original temporal context from which they were taken—that is impossible—but to a context of experience. And there, *their ambiguity at last becomes true*" (*AWT*, 289). Behind the screen of true ambiguity, the reader, invited to use her or his memory to arrange and rearrange the captionless photographs from a number of different countries, has supplanted the experience of the peasants themselves, which is presumably no longer strong enough to hold the fragments together. What is left of peasant experience but, in Berger's powerful expression, "images in the memory of a total stranger"?

This striking metaphor for the absence of experience reappears in *A Seventh Man*, where it subverts one of the book's main premises. The subtitle, "A Book of Images and Words about the Experience of Migrant Workers in Europe," places experience so as to parry the blow of analytic consciousness that falls on the peasant workers. It creates an equilibrium between their subjectivity and the global meaning of migration. This meaning "can only be fully recognized," Berger says, "if an objective economic system is related to the subjective experience of those trapped within it" (*ASM*, 7). In fact, he has tilted the balance still further in the direction of experience. It is a paradigmatic individual experience of migration ("Departure," "Work," "Return"), rather than migration's historical roots, analogues, repercussions, or possibilities of development, that shapes the book and dictates crucial choices of emphasis.

At the same time, the book begins by referring to its subject as a "dream/nightmare." "By what right," it goes on, "can we call the lived experience of others a dream/nightmare?" (*ASM*, 7). The redundancy "lived experience" brings into sudden existence the logical alternatives of "unlived experience" or "lived inexperience," and these are precisely what Berger proceeds to evoke. "In a dream the dreamer wills, acts, reacts, speaks, and yet submits to the unfolding of a story which he scarcely influences. The dream happens to him." The dreamer not only cannot influence his story, but he also cannot understand it. Later in the book, Berger uses the metaphor in a still more intense form:

His migration is like an event in a dream dreamt by another. As a figure in a dream dreamt by an unknown dreamer, he appears to act autonomously, at times unexpectedly; but everything he does—unless he revolts—is determined by the needs of the dreamer's mind. Abandon the metaphor. The migrant's intentionality is permeated by historical necessities of which neither he nor anybody he meets is aware. That is why he acts as if his life were being dreamt by another. (*ASM*, 43)

Though Berger continues to insist that "the full measure of the violence being done to [the migrant] is revealed by what happens within him" (*ASM*, 166), he has shown that the meaning of the phenomenon largely exceeds what appears in the migrant's consciousness. Like the photographs of *Another Way of Telling*, the peasant-migrant's experience now belongs to—makes sense in—the consciousness of another. At this remove, it is perhaps no longer accurate to speak of "experience" at all.

At the end of the book, the word seems to have begun its own immigration to the metropolis. Berger has been suggesting that migrant labor in the metropolis abolishes experience, whether because it sacrifices the present to hopes for the future or because, in so doing, it is determined by forces it cannot comprehend. He has also been suggesting that experience can be restored only by revolt or return. "To re-become a man (husband, father, citizen, patriot) a migrant has to return home" (*ASM*, 58). But having returned to his native village, the (obviously male) migrant discovers that "an assured place for him no longer exists," that he is now "homeless," because "his different experience is not applicable" there, because he is "a man of different experience" (221). It would seem to follow that experience in and of the metropolis does, after all, exist. Is this experience only in the minimal, universal sense of what one lives through? Or does the restricted sense of valuable knowledge also apply? A great deal hangs on the word. To the extent that Berger has been obliged to allow the latter sense in reference to the urban destination, he avoids falling into a total rejection of modernity; accepts the lived inexperience of emigration and global determination as a new, if repugnant, norm; and begins assembling the materials out of which a new mode of "global feeling" can be constructed.[18]

What are the elements of a hypothetical "posthumanist" experience toward which Berger might help move us along? Money is unlikely to disappear as a result of any conceivable revolution other than that of computer technology, which is not a genuine alternative to it. Berger sometimes speaks as if a change that did not abolish money would be no change at all, as if it stood between humanity and the experiential ground zero of Being, fatally abstracting us from the sensuous, qualitative immediacy of use value and daily impoverishing subjectivity. This is not the attitude of Marx, who did not confuse money with capital and had a healthy appreciation for the necessity of symbolic action.[19]

The celebration of a self-sufficient peasantry entails an equal hostility to emigration and to money, and Berger often brings the three elements together in a dense metaphoric cluster that shapes arguments on various subjects. *The Success and Failure of Picasso* (1965), for example, can be read as a parable of emigration as a fall from peasant plenitude into the abstract emptiness of money. Picasso's "success" is that of a "vertical invader" (*SFP*, 40) from semifeudal Spain, where "the consciousness of the average Spanish peasant" still included the wish "to destroy all money" (19), and where life—even among Picasso's middle class—had not yet been "depersonalized and made anonymous by the power of money" (21). Picasso's "failure" is the consequence, on the one hand, of the emigration to France that cut him off from this premonetary society and, on the other hand, of his legendary "earning power and wealth" (4). "The truth has become a little like the fable of Midas. Whatever Midas touched, turned into gold. Whatever Picasso puts a line around, can become his. But the fable was a tragic-comic one; Midas nearly starved because he couldn't eat gold" (3–4). Money, like emigration, is opposed to experience, the synonym of subject matter. Exile has brought money but no new experience to digest. "What he has lacked are subjects" (140). As emigrant, the wealthy artist perishes of experiential emptiness.

Does this mean that neither money nor emigration can be the source of new experience? An essay called "Hals and Bankruptcy" in *About Looking* teases a different answer out of the same metaphors. Describing a Frans Hals portrait, Berger finds a "metaphysic of money" that has released "a new energy" and has relativized "all traditional values." In effect, it is a portrait of money. "What distinguishes this portrait from all earlier portraits of wealthy or powerful men is its instability. Nothing is secure in its place. You have the feeling of looking at a man in a ship's cabin in a gale. . . . At the same time the portrait in no way suggests decay or disintegration. There may be a gale but the ship is sailing fast and confidently" (*AL*, 163–64). This portrait of money is, once again, a portrait of travel and displacement. But here, experience is its fruit rather than its opposite.

When Berger maintains the opposition between experience, on the one hand, and emigration and money, on the other, he is paradoxically obliged to deny experience precisely where his evidence tells us we would find it. The emigrant leaves and works, as the inhabitants of his place of destination complain, "in order to earn and save the maximum amount of money in the shortest time" (*ASM*, 163). This is an initiative he takes—"the only initiative still open to the migrant"—"for the sake of a transformed future—or his attempt to transform his future" (164). Berger's point, here and elsewhere, is that this involves "negligence of the present." "To make present sacrifice for the sake of the future," he nonetheless concedes, "is an essentially human act." Is it possible that experience supports rather than condemns the migrant, that he alone escapes the devaluation of the present that results from the absence of a future? Backtracking, Berger insists only "that the value of his present sacrifice is denied" by the society around him (188). And if, by some chance, the value of that sacrifice were acknowledged? To keep the act of emigration, which vitalizes the present by adding to it a future, from becoming the very paradigm of human experience, Berger must refuse this contingency. The wager cannot be allowed to succeed.

Of those emigrants who have managed to stay on in Europe, resisting the various tides of anti-immigrant nationalism, and of the lines of collective action open to the ethnic mix now discovering its permanence and its power, Berger has little to say. Commenting on the paintings of Ralph Fasanella, he offers a view of New York that amputates the city of immigrants at the past point when they arrived, thereby cutting off their future and our present:

> Just as capital is compelled continually to reproduce itself, so its culture is one of unending anticipation. What-is-to-come, what-is-to-be-gained empties what-is. The immigrant proletariat, unable to return home, suffering from being who they were, yearned to become, or for their children to become, American. They saw no hope but to exchange themselves for the future. And although the desperation of the wager was specifically immigrant, the mechanism has become more and more typical of developed capitalism. (*AL*, 101)

Ironically, here it is Berger who, fixated on what has been, creates the atmosphere of "bereavement" in which, as he explains, no new experience is possible (*ASM*, 177–79).

After the saving of money, the migrant's major symbolic activity is the collection of photographs. In his exile, he—like Berger—arranges images. On his walls, family snapshots coexist with nudes, icons, portraits of politicians and athletes, advertising—all amply documented in the photographs of *A Seventh Man*. Cannot this promiscuous mosaic be seen as the migrant's construction, like the book's, of a new, exiled experience? If Berger acknowledges a parallel between his writing and the stories of the village, can he avoid seeing one here?

Berger's humanism reveals its outer limits in comparison with that of Susan Sontag, whose *On Photography* (1977), like Berger's writing on the subject, is largely inspired by Walter Benjamin.[20] For Sontag, photographs are another agent of capitalism's impoverishment of direct, spontaneous experience. "As a way of certifying experience, taking photographs is also a way of refusing it . . .

by converting experience into an image, a souvenir" (*OP,* 9). Because it is "essentially an act of non-intervention" (11), because "aesthetic distance seems built into" it (21), photography tends "to subtract feeling from something we experience at first hand" (168). The caption, which Benjamin hoped would make the wayward photograph politically responsible, "cannot prevent any argument or moral plea which a photograph (or a series of photographs) is intended to support from being undermined by the plurality of meanings that every photograph carries, or from being qualified by the acquisitive mentality implicit in all picture-taking—and picture-collecting—and by the aesthetic relation to their subject which all photographs inevitably propose" (109).

Plurality of meaning, observation that is also a relation of power, action that is mediated and indirect—in convicting photography of these crimes, Sontag dismisses out of hand the ineluctable conditions of action in the modern world. Her naive technologism rejects the modern world in the name of a prephotographic world when action was direct, meaning was singular, aesthetics was innocent, and experience was immediate because ideology had not already distorted the image of what was seen. Despite the glitter of avant-garde style and allusion, and despite the frontal assault on "humanism," this is humanism of a particularly antique and despairing sort. Next to it, Berger's "experience" acquires hidden virtues.

Compare Berger's and Sontag's comments, for example, on the famous "Family of Man" exhibition organized by Edward Steichen in 1955. Sontag takes Roland Barthes's early critique of the exhibition's "myth of human 'community'" and translates it into typically American terms, so that the exhibition's false universality, like photography for her in general, is now accused in particular of aiding and abetting U.S. imperialism's global reach.[21] It is "the last sign of the Whitmanesque erotic embrace of the nation, but universalized and stripped of all demands" (*OP,* 31). Its "sentimental humanism" assumes "a human condition or a human nature shared by everybody," suppressing "historically embedded differences, injustices, and conflicts" in order to make its international viewers into "citizens of World Photography all" (32–33).

Berger, who also rejects the word *humanism* explicitly, takes much the same position, though with a nuance of difference that seems significant both of what he has kept of the humanist legacy and of the eventual possibilities for a posthumanist discourse. He cannot entirely dismiss the idea of "treating the existing class-divided world as if it were a family" (*AL,* 56). "Steichen's intuition was absolutely correct: the private use of photographs can be exemplary for their public use." In the arrangement of photographs "as though they formed a universal family album," Berger finds both sentimental complacency and, equally important, "an alternative photographic practice":

Photographs are relics of the past, traces of what has happened. If the living take that past upon themselves, if the past becomes an integral part of the process of people making their own history, then all photographs would reacquire a living context, they would continue to exist in time, instead of being arrested moments. It is just possible that photography is the prophecy of a human memory yet to be socially and politically achieved. Such a memory would encompass any image of the past, however tragic, however guilty, within its own continuity. The distinction between the private and the public uses of photography would be transcended. The Family of Man would exist. (57)

Though it has the frailty of prophetic abstraction, this statement is also a source of practical strength. For Sontag, experience is a past plenitude from which we have been sundered by the proliferation of photographic images, and there is little to do now but "apply the conservationist remedy" (*OP,* 180), that is, allow as few of them as possible. For Berger, however, these images also invite the new practice that would give them a "living context." In the mind of the "total stranger" in today's "class-divided world," they induce familiarity and make possible a new, global experience.

In Berger's humanism, experience is always also a field where alternative practices, like weeds, feed on the same ideological fertilizers as the crops they were meant to nourish. For this reason, it is inadequate to see the treatment of subjectivity in Berger's novels as naively realistic. If Berger does not routinely lay bare the working of ideology in individual experience, it is in part because he does not *record* experience at all. The much-remarked violence of his metaphors, which never bend submissively to the characters' subjectivities but rather hang awkwardly outside, is a sign that subjectivity is being wrenched out of its normal channels. By this violence (which can also be read as indecorous authorial intrusion or simply as overwrought prose), ordinary experience is cultivated and made to yield up moments of apocalyptic disturbance. Sex, sports, and work become exemplary of messianic truth. Reading experience against itself, without sacrificing its authority, Berger manages to politicize it.

Berger himself would probably not see his attitude to experience in this way. With regard to photography, he prefers to view the furnishing of an "adequate context" as a move backward—"back into the context of experience" (*AL,* 61)—rather than forward. "Logically," he says, the boards to which people pin personal snapshots "should replace museums" (*WS,* 30). But this logic does not carry him to the recognition that other exiles can collect photographs, as he does, in an effort to seize and hold the new world of interlocking events that occur, as he often repeats, "on a global scale." For Berger, the eyes of the migrant can only be trained on his lost home. Thus the photographs of *A Seventh Man* are said to work "in the opposite way" from those of the migrants they display. "Seen in this book when reading it, the image conjures up the vivid presence of the unknown boy. To his father it would define the boy's absence" (*ASM*, 17). Migrants must be assumed not to require fresh information, for they are assumed not to be able to act any differently if they had it.

Like Sontag, Berger has difficulty imagining a public, international context of experience—that is, of action. When Sontag attacks photography's "false sense of ubiquity" and connects its "overview" to "our very notion of the world—the capitalist twentieth century's 'one world' " (*OP*, 174), she assumes that action on a global scale is the prerogative of cosmopolitan capital and imperialist power. Michel Foucault's paradigmatic suspicion of the "universal intellectual" would seem to take the same set of facts into consideration.[22] A case could also be made for Berger's peasants as a Foucauldian strategic retreat to local margins. Berger is literally, as Paul Bové recommends, cultivating his own garden.[23] For Berger, too, all total and universal images are tainted by the powers that operate at their level. The globes that fill the paintings of the Renaissance are icons of conquest and possession, and even the photographs of worldwide atrocity to which we have become so accustomed work, for the moment at least, against rather than for experience. Since there is nothing adequate to do about what one sees, Berger argues, it would be better not to see it at all. The supposed stimulation, in fact, wears down human concern, turns it inward, squanders it:

> The most extreme examples . . . show moments of agony in order to extort the maximum concern. Such moments, whether photographed or not, are discontinuous with all other moments. But the reader who has been arrested by the photograph may tend to feel this discontinuity as his own personal moral inadequacy. *And as soon as this happens even his sense of shock is dispersed*: his own moral inadequacy may now shock him as much as the crimes being committed in the war.

Hence "the issue of the war which has caused the moment," Berger goes on, "is effectively depoliticized" (*AL*, 39–40). Berger wishes to curtail atrocity photos for the same reason Matthew Arnold said he suppressed "Empedocles on Etna" from *Poems* (1853): because they "find no vent in action," because "there is everything to be suffered, nothing to be done." But this argument could also be taken as a plea for the "vent in action," the global contextualizing that would use these images and thus make "global feeling" possible. If Berger cannot provide, and does not promise, such a new experience, he certainly makes us desire it. To say this is to say something for his humanist heritage.

5

UPWARD MOBILITY IN THE POSTCOLONIAL ERA

KINCAID, MUKHERJEE, AND THE COSMOPOLITAN AU PAIR

Défiez-vous de ces cosmopolites qui vont chercher au loin . . . des devoirs qu'ils dédaignent de remplir autour d'eux.

Jean-Jacques Rousseau

I was not a man; I was a young woman from the fringes of the world, and when I left my home I had wrapped around my shoulders the mantle of a servant.

Jamaica Kincaid

E. J. Hobsbawm opens his book *Nations and Nationalism since 1780* with an anecdote about "an intergalactic historian" who lands after a nuclear war and, going through the archives, concludes that "the last two centuries of the human history of planet Earth are incomprehensible without some understanding of the term 'nation' and the vocabulary derived from it."[1] I take Hobsbawm's appeal to this not otherwise very entertaining anecdote as an illustration of how contradictory the general understanding of nationalism has become. If he has to ascend into outer space in search of an observer who will look at nations and nationalism with an alien eye, it is presumably because everyone on earth during the nineteenth and twentieth centuries has been so much inside them, incapable of breaking free from their categories and assumptions. So ubiquitous and deep-rooted is the nation, Hobsbawm implies, that no perspective that is truly alien to it can be discovered any closer to home.

The central argument of *Nations and Nationalism*, however, seems to suggest just the opposite. Appearances to the contrary, nationalism is no longer nearly as important as it once was, Hobsbawm argues, for—to speak schematically— the globalization of multinational capitalism in the postmodern era has undermined it.[2] Nationhood can now be bestowed on even the tiniest, unlikeliest claimants, in much the same way that (as Wlad Godzich has remarked) the status of "culture" can suddenly be shared equally between the "high" and the "low," because neither term is crucial any longer to the projects of capitalist development. It seems to follow, then, that a skeptical, distanced view of nationalism, something like Hobsbawm's own Olympian perspective—a perspective for which the "intergalactic historian" is a rather transparent disguise—would be common to a great many observers all over the planet. (Empirically, this seems indeed to be the case.) But if so, then why does the extranationalist perspective have to be incarnated by an extraterrestrial? Why does Hobsbawm imply, on the one hand, that nearly everyone stands outside nationalism and, on the other, that nearly no one does?

If this paradox can be reformulated as a riddle—Who is it that represents nearly everyone and nearly no one?—then its answer may lie unexpectedly near to hand: in that figure of modernity whose self-appointed mission has been to speak for the many but whose social situation has been that of a privileged few. Taking our cue from the suspicious redundancy of the space-traveling researcher, we can perhaps read Hobsbawm's hesitation between a ubiquitous and a nonexistent nonnationalism as a report on the structural contradictions of the metropolitan intellectual. Intellectuals, Hobsbawm seems to suggest, must be and yet cannot be, cannot be and yet must be, cosmopolitans. The Dreyfus Affair of the 1890s, which is often cited as the origin of the term *intellectual*, exposed the category's immediate vulnerability to charges both of class pride and privilege vis-à-vis "ordinary people" and of treason to the nation. The latter charge has frequently been reversed since the era of national liberation struggles and decolonization: while cosmopolitan intellectuals are still accused of serving their own interests, they are now accused not of betraying their nation but of serving their nation, and the West, all too well. But intellectuals themselves are often the first to make both accusations—and this fact offers striking evidence of their contradictory relation to nationalism. For where do such accusations originate, if not from an implicit claim to cosmopolitan detachment from the nation?

Linked to both social hierarchy and the guilty history of Eurocentric universalizing, cosmopolitanism has been out of fashion. Metropolitan intellectuals, feeling newly accountable to a public sphere stretching beyond the NATO alliance, have urged themselves to rediscover their own particularity, their situatedness in terms of gender, race, class, and of course nation. It has been widely assumed, accordingly, that a truly extranationalist or even extranational viewpoint—the extent of the difference remains controversial—can exist only as a piece of science fiction, a disembodied fantasy of quasi-divine ubiquity and omniscience. Yet at the same time, I would argue, this state of galactic alienation remains inscribed in the protocols of even the most multicultural discourse. In part, this is a paradoxical but necessary result of the same sense of accountability to a newly expanded, less Eurocentric public opinion. For metropolitan intellectuals, Eurocentric universalizing has been an unconscious way of "speaking as," speaking from within our best-defended perimeters of belonging. That is precisely why a *conscious* way of "speaking as," a mode of address that anticipates and recognizes the diversity of readers and colleagues, demands a degree of self-alienation. Despite all the lip service paid to the humble acceptance of location and all the sarcasm lavished on fantasies of disembodied mobility, therefore, the fantasy or convention of geographical self-distancing is one that academics and other intellectuals implicitly identify with and act out, on a daily basis, through the whole range of their routine choices of viewpoint and attitude, comparison and evaluation.

To be sure, genuine changes in the politics of scholarship have occurred since the age of Matthew Arnold and Max Weber. It is clear that nationalism is often a deep (and sometimes a necessary) inspiration for intellectual work; if Julien Benda thought intellectuals were distinctively and constitutively supranational, Weber described them as "predestined to propagate the 'national idea.' "[3] Yet the abstraction of the self from the nation remains a fantasy or convention without which the form and even the content of intellectual life as we know it would be unrecognizable.[4] In our heart of hearts, do we really believe there can be a historian worthy of the name who is *not* extraterrestrial?

Unluckily, this is not merely a puzzle for intellectuals. Both points of this contradiction have become weapons in the continuing attacks on U.S. teachers and other cultural workers—especially, though not exclusively, from the right—that have been called the "culture wars." The double charge is "Third Worldism" on the one hand, "elitism" on the other. The right has presented its opponents as traitors to European civilization, a new set of misguided palefaces rapt with admiration before Third World redskins; it has also presented them as coddled children of the 1960s, elitists out of touch with American values, "tenured radicals." There is just enough truth in both charges to give extra sting when they are consolidated by the right's paradoxical appropriation of "class" as a weapon against the left. Both charges are also translatable into lack of concern for the national welfare, and both lend themselves to a growing backlash, in

UPWARD MOBILITY: KINCAID, MUKHERJEE, AND THE AU PAIR

favor of teaching and against research, posed in the seductive terms of *national responsibility* and *democracy*. In the interest of self-defense as well as self-knowledge, then, intellectuals seem called on to rethink their narratives of where they come from and to propose some alternative account of their undeniable yet perpetually denied cosmopolitanism—an account that will help negotiate between the charge of elitism (one of postmodernism's accusations against modernism) and the charge of nomadic, touristic delectation of distant cultures (modernism's corresponding accusation against postmodernism).

Once alerted to this state of contradiction, it is suddenly possible to appreciate that a certain amount of intellectual effort has already gone into trying, however obliquely, to resolve it. For example, ever-proliferating scholarship about nationalism offers the occasional slender insight—most often implicit and in passing yet therefore all the more valuable—into the history of that which is *not* nationalism, the apparently oxymoronic and troublingly reflexive question of where cosmopolitanism might come from. (I offer two examples at the end of this chapter.) There has also been a more explicit move to salvage the concept from its associations with class and Western privilege by demonstrating the existence of a sort of popular, non-Western or nonelite cosmopolitanism. James Clifford has emphasized the traveling that is always already part of the non-European cultures investigated by European ethnography; for Clifford, the phrase "different cultures" can thus be replaced by the phrase "discrepant cosmopolitanisms."[5] Paul Gilroy's *The Black Atlantic* reveals the hidden circuits of transnational cultural circulation that have gone into the constituting of a hybrid, diasporic black identity.[6] In two interlocking stories—one about himself as a Hindu anthropologist working among Muslim peasants in Egypt, the other about the unsuspectedly rich bonds of commerce and culture that linked India and the Mediterranean in the prenationalist period of the twelfth century—Amitav Ghosh's *In an Antique Land* paints a beautifully bittersweet picture of a lost cosmopolitanism, a cosmopolitanism that his own travels and those of contemporary Egyptian workers to and from Iraq cannot quite reconstitute.[7] Summing up a distinct theme, evident in new journals such as *Public Culture* and *Diaspora* as well as in the older *Transition*, the South African critic Benita Parry writes, "There is a recognition that the 'global flows' of transnational cultural traffic have issued in 'public cultures' productive of an emergent *postcolonial* cosmopolitanism" (41).[8] Thus extended both geographically and socially, the term *cosmopolitanism* now includes an Indian slave sent by a Jewish merchant to transact business around the Persian Gulf in the Middle Ages, African servants of British travelers in the 1800s, African American travelers in modernist Europe, and European, Caribbean, and Asian au pairs in the contemporary

United States, as well as the more obvious Third World intellectuals operating out of metropolitan centers, such as Ngugi wa Thiong'o, Edward W. Said, and Gayatri Chakravorty Spivak.

To bring together the last two groups—Third World intellectuals and au pairs—is to raise the more restricted question I explore in the remainder of this chapter: namely, what to make of a cosmopolitanism whose agents or participants are non-Western but whose movement is toward the "advanced" or "developed" West and can thus be described as a form of upward mobility. Critics such as Parry, Tim Brennan, Aijaz Ahmad, and Gayatri Spivak, among others, have wondered, with varying degrees of alarm, whether Third World fictions and careers (including careers in the making and reading of fictions) that aimed at and were embraced by the metropolis could ultimately signify anything other than an opportunistic affirmation of the metropolis. Spivak makes a pointed parallel between the current First World enthusiasm for Third World writers and the earlier divide-and-conquer strategy of colonialism, which simultaneously served the interests of the colonial power and of a native-born "aspiring elite." Do we see here again, she asks, "the old scenario of empowering a privileged group or a group susceptible to upward mobility as the authentic inhabitants of the margin"?[9] Any critic writing in the metropolis today seems obliged to reflect on this, as well as on some further questions. Is it possible that this diagnosis might itself repeat earlier charges against "rootless cosmopolitanism" (such as Rousseau's, in the epigraph to this chapter)? Does cosmopolitanism from the margins neatly duplicate that of the center? Does it leave the metropolitan center precisely as it was? What does it tell us about the center that it produces both narratives of upward mobility and impatient critiques of those narratives, including our own? Is it possible or desirable to produce political criticism that does not refer to some narrative of upward mobility, feasible progress, personal and collective development?

The double focus of these questions, referring at once to literary texts and to critical careers, finds one revealing object of investigation in the budding, pre-Nannygate subgenre I call *au pair narrative*, as in Bharati Mukherjee's short story (and novel) titled "Jasmine" and Jamaica Kincaid's novel *Lucy*.[10] I propose to investigate the genre, in a preliminary and provisional way, through the suggestive problematic offered by Spivak's essay "Three Women's Texts and a Critique of Imperialism."[11] In that essay, Spivak interprets Charlotte Brontë's *Jane Eyre* as a double allegory: an allegory of the role of empire in the canonical literature of the nineteenth century, and an allegory of the twentieth-century "bourgeois feminist" critic. Spivak suggests that Jane's upward mobility, marked by her final replacement of Bertha/Antoinette as the rightful "Mrs. Rochester," is achieved only by economically exploiting and symbolically destroying figures

UPWARD MOBILITY: KINCAID, MUKHERJEE, AND THE AU PAIR

who represent Europe's colonial possessions. Jane's mobility, moreover, has been mobilized in turn by recent feminist readers in the metropolis, who find in it a legitimizing myth of feminist criticism's parallel rise to institutional authority, this time at the expense of postcolonial subjects, especially women.

What does this brilliant and influential argument (I have commented on it at length elsewhere)[12] tell us about au pair narratives, twentieth-century refunctionings of the *Bildungsroman* that have Third World women of color as their protagonists? Like *Jane Eyre*, both *Lucy* and "Jasmine" can be seen as allegories of upward mobility. In each, the nineteenth century's domestic move from the provinces to the capital is transposed into a transnational move from the periphery to the metropolitan core.[13] Structurally, or at least geographically, the genre seems therefore to flatter the metropolis as inevitable destination and saving source of freedom and happiness. In a sort of female Naipaulism, the personal trajectory from the Caribbean to the metropolis becomes paradigmatic of a Hegelian passage from primitive, unselfconscious barbarism to universal civilization, thus relegating those who remain behind to a familiar sort of colonial stasis and inferiority.[14]

Taken to the museum by her employer, Kincaid's Lucy finds an image of herself in

> some paintings by a man, a French man, who had gone halfway across the world to live and had painted pictures of the people he found living there. He had been a banker living a comfortable life with his wife and children, but that did not make him happy; eventually he left them and went to the opposite part of the world, where he was happier. I don't know if Mariah meant me to, but immediately I identified with the yearnings of this man; I understood finding the place you are born in an unbearable prison and wanting something completely different from what you are familiar with, knowing it represents a haven. (95)

Though Lucy does not seem to seek the material comforts that the painter has fled, her non-European inversion of European escapism looks much like the metaphysical and political error that is involved, Spivak says, in taking "Eurocentric economic migration as moment of origin." Metropolitan readers may not welcome a genre that literally advises the entire population of the Third World to emigrate, but they are seldom averse to hearing that the Third World is a prison and the First World a haven. The warm reception of the genre among metropolitan readers (if not among academic critics) must therefore be greeted with some misgiving. As Spivak warns, "The struggle of the marginal in metropolitan space cannot be made the unexamined referent for all postcoloniality."[15]

Lucy, immediately after identifying with the Gauguin-like painter, remembers her differences—that is to say, her additional disadvantages: "I was not a man; I was a young woman from the fringes of the world, and when I left my home I had wrapped around my shoulders the mantle of a servant" (95). Yet all this might also be said, without much distortion, about Jane Eyre, and at least in Spivak's reading, it does not sufficiently extenuate Jane's complicity with the imperial project. Is anything altered by Lucy's handicaps—a list from which race is notably missing—if the trajectory of her narrative nonetheless resembles so closely the "great expectations" formula of the nineteenth-century European bourgeoisie? For the metropolitan readership that gratefully climbs the rising curve of Lucy's story, does it offer anything more than a suitably displaced opportunity to reexperience that primal thrill? And for critics in particular, is Kincaid's moral significantly different from that which Spivak reprimands in *Jane Eyre*?

There are differences, I think, but they show only because of further similarities. *Lucy* and the two "Jasmines" share other narrative structures with *Jane Eyre*: notably, the narrative perspective of the servant or governess in the master's house and the motif of transgressive, transclass sexuality.[16] Again like *Jane Eyre*, these narratives stage their upward mobility around the servant's erotic energies. They associate those energies with the privilege of narrative perspective, on the one hand, and with a threat to disrupt the couple formed by master and legal wife, on the other. The short story "Jasmine" ends with the au pair willingly seduced by the paterfamilias (a professor of biology), while his wife, a performance artist, is away on tour. In *Lucy*, the opening chapter ends with the au pair telling the husband and wife a dream in which the husband chased her, naked, through the house, while the wife urged him on. And in the last chapter, the couple breaks up and, apparently neither as cause nor as effect, the protagonist departs, though the husband's adultery has not been with her and her own sexual explorations have not been with him.[17]

Here, then, is a large difference: marriage between master and servant, which has served to figure the reward of the servant's upward striving at least since Samuel Richardson's *Pamela* (1740), is apparently no longer on the agenda. By this means, Mukherjee apparently resists (though this is less true in the novel of the same name) the narrative of a migratory elite's upward mobility. The last line of the short story runs as follows: "His hand moved up her throat and forced her lips apart and it felt so good, so right, that she forgot all the dreariness of her new life and gave herself up to it." The ambiguity of "it"—lovemaking as figure for the new life—along with the forcing of the lips and the dreariness of the life seem to point a moral—perhaps that of the book's *Village Voice* reviewer, reprinted as a sentence fragment on the paperback: "Particularly chilling because the heroine has no idea she's being exploited." Unconscious exploitation would, of course, give a twist to the *Pamela/Jane Eyre* story of upwardly mobile eroticism. Here, one might say, a Third World sunk in ever deeper immiseration finds its figure in the cheery immigrant woman whose sexual transgression with the master can no longer be cashed in for any enduring social advantage.[18]

Yet Mukherjee clearly has trouble holding to the allegory of a Third World class or collectivity that is *not* rising. The idea of Jasmine's life as "dreariness" in the last line comes as something of a surprise. Up to this point, she has not seemed to mind her work at all. In short, Mukherjee seems to be making a last-minute effort to impose a moral on her story—a moral which the story defies. Many readers (not only those who have political doubts about her) will recognize that, like her heroine, Mukherjee is clearly more than half in love with the heady new Americanness of Jasmine's life. Jasmine likes it, for example, that in Ann Arbor men do the cooking, that her employers encourage her to take courses at the University of Michigan and to be "more selfish" (131), that a mother's helper isn't like a servant but "seemed to be as good as anyone" (128). Mukherjee and Kincaid both seem to buy into the American Dream of self-invention from nothing. "I was inventing myself" (135), Lucy says; and while making love at the end, Jasmine thinks of herself as "a bright, pretty girl with no visa, no papers, no birth certificate. Nothing other than what she wanted to invent and tell."

Are we left, after all, with an allegory not of seductive exploitation but of celebratory Americanization? Perhaps the options need not be so symmetrical. It would be provincial of American readers, recognizing here a disparity between American dreams and American realities, to see nothing *but* American reality— as if the reversals of the social order Jasmine knows are of no significance except as an affirmation of American values, as if nothing about Jasmine's new life could possibly be preferred over her old one by her own, non-American criteria. And it would be provincial not to see that adding race to Brontë's class and gender terms is bound to produce (as Brontë herself already produced) more complex relations between characters and collectivities than a zero-sum allegory.[19] It is clear that these texts prolong and appropriate the *Jane Eyre* allegory; it is not clear that, in so doing, they are obliged to accept the zero-sum linearity of the social ladder, with its implication that my rise is necessarily your fall.

In the novel *Jasmine*, published one year after Mukherjee's short story, the au pair protagonist—this time an immigrant from India rather than from the Caribbean—again falls in love with her employer, or rather with "what he represented to me, a professor who served biscuits to a servant" (148). Unlike her namesake, she is given narrative room to end up successfully (if not yet legally) displacing the first, white, legal wife. Yet it is unclear how much the displace-

UPWARD MOBILITY: KINCAID, MUKHERJEE, AND THE AU PAIR

ment really signifies. The wife has initiated all this by seeking her own happiness with someone else. And for Jasmine, bonding with her former employer seems to mean responding less to him than to "the promise of America." Like the heroes of such modernist *Bildungsromane* as D. H. Lawrence's *Sons and Lovers* and James Joyce's *A Portrait of the Artist as a Young Man*, she reaches a conclusion, "greedy with wants and reckless from hope" (213–14), that is less a union than a fresh departure.

Keeping closer than the short story to the *Jane Eyre* materials, the novel even includes, in the series of men it offers its au pair heroine, an older, prosperous, and allegorically crippled husband. But this Jasmine leaves behind her cripple, a banker shot and paralyzed by an angry client, along with his prosperity, which is shown to be complicit with the bankruptcies and suicides of surrounding farmers. Indeed, she makes this decision soon after his child (again, as in *Jane Eyre*, foreign and adopted, and like Jasmine, a refugee from the explicit but unexplained horrors of Third World violence) also decides to leave. "The world is divided," she says, "between those who stay and those who leave" (203). Is Mukherjee saying that the only way up is to leave, and the only way to stay is to be crippled? I cannot entirely disagree with those who read her this way, but to do so is to miss other, more interesting things that she is also saying. Crucially, she is displacing the *Jane Eyre* narrative's emphasis from an *upward* to a *lateral* move. Her biscuit-serving professor and his (also adopted) daughter belong, no less than the banker, to the class of those who can afford to pay for personal rather than institutional child care. In choosing them, the former au pair is not making any visible or significant sacrifice of economic privileges or life possibilities.[20] Allowing Jasmine to move within one social level rather than between levels, Mukherjee displaces the narrative interest onto a choice between modes of being: specifically, between a mode of staying that, like the banker's, slowly chokes those who are similarly forced to stay on their land and a mode of mobility, not profitable but pleasurable, that is committed to no positive or alternative values, only to not being or doing or submitting to *that*. Leaving, which occupies the space of terminal marriage, identifies the ending as a choice between being a victim and being a victimizer while it also evades that choice; Jasmine could as easily be the latter as the former, it suggests bravely, but it is better to be neither. If Mukherjee's answer is mobility, in other words, it is not necessarily upward mobility. If opting between different middle-class attitudes toward social injustice is not opting out of social injustice, neither is it the luxury of perpetual cosmopolitan tourism or the frivolity of free erotic choice without social consequences.

The same evasion or reinterpretation of upward mobility informs the ending of the short story "Jasmine." The story's concluding ambiguity is not technically subtle, but its very willedness—rough, unprepared for, tacked on abruptly at the end—might be said to foreground the question of will, especially Jasmine's own will and the value the reader will place on it. This Jasmine, even more than her counterpart in the novel, is presented as smart, active, ambitious, choosing her fate—and choosing to make love with her employer. Can consensual sex be interpreted as, like money, the object of a zero-sum calculation? Placed in a uniquely determining position, can sex function effectively as the stakes in a race, class, or gender allegory? The heavy weight that Mukherjee drops onto Jasmine's consenting consciousness in the moment of sexual relation makes that consciousness (or unconsciousness), like Pamela's, into a crucial space of interpretive ambiguity, a battleground where conflicting allegories collide. At this moment, is she an unconscious representative of her race or class? A conscious representative of her sex?[21] Neither of the above? By ending in an ambiguous instant of silencing and pleasure, stopping short before the social consequences of the lovemaking can appear—a decision reflected in the generic difference between short story and novel—Mukherjee opens up the possibility of an allegory that aims neither at marriage and displacement of the lawful wife (sex as gain) nor at exploitation (sex as loss) but at some other conclusion, including the pure provisionality of pleasure seized for its own sake in and despite hierarchical power. Given the booming transnational sex trade, this is a morally risky suggestion; but Mukherjee does not preclude the option that sex may not, in itself, mean anything—that it can be a possession or a gift; can belong to an economy of scarcity or an economy of abundance; can be an act of hostility toward the wife or irrelevant to her; can be an allegory of class or of gender or of neither.[22] She suggests that in striking off away from the *Jane Eyre* structure of marriage as social microcosm, this text may not be *failing* to achieve *Jane Eyre*'s social ambitions or its allegorical centrality but may rather be *succeeding* as one allegory of a society of multiple subject positions where there is no such center. It poses as a question, in other words, the zero-sum model according to which there can only be one (male) master and one master's wife.[23]

Here, it is instructive to compare the place of sex and marriage in *Lucy*. Lucy does not sleep with her employer, although much of the *Jane Eyre* structure is still intact—above all, the breakup of the master/wife couple, coinciding with the erotic and professional rise of "the young girl who watches over the children" (7). The parallel seems deliberate. "In my own mind," Lucy says, "I called myself other names: Emily, Charlotte, Jane. They were the names of the authoresses whose books I loved" (149). Like Jane Eyre, Lucy reacts strongly against people who are physically beautiful; she plays out some of the same opposition between birth and merit that makes *Jane Eyre*, among other things, a reading of the French Revolution. Sex, unlike beauty, can be aligned with merit, and Lucy takes a serious interest in it. It signifies various things for her: an achievement wrested from a bleak place, a rebuke to her mother's morals, a proof of her independence:—"life as a slut was quite enjoyable, thank you very much" (128). It is an object of competition: a girl who has had an experience that might be described as "sexual abuse" makes her jealous; she wishes it had happened to her (105). But for Lucy, sex is precisely *not* a way to rise to the social achievement marked by upwardly mobile marriage. Marriage, like sex between master and servant, does not interest her; wanting not to be married is one of her most conscious motives.[24] Though she records and presides over the breakup of her employers' marriage, and though she unloads much of her anger on the wife, Lucy shows no conscious desire to replace her in the arms of her too-handsome husband. One might say that for her, too, sex is lateral rather than vertical. In not needing or wanting sex from or in the married couple she serves, not bonding with them in a cross-class marriage plot, Lucy retains the negative, critical side of that plot while taking her own story off on a tangent.

Generalizing a bit recklessly, one might make this a sort of postmodern allegory of a decentered society in which one woman's rise is not necessarily another's woman's fall, and in which the multiplicity of subject positions suggests that significant movement may be neither rise nor fall. I add that it is possible, in comparison to *Jane Eyre*, to see the broken and incomplete marriages, the inconclusive and lateral sex of these texts, as very much a step up, or at least in the right direction. A reviewer of Kincaid in *The Nation* remarked that much of the unease she seemed to inspire in readers came from the "protagonist's failure to accede to white people—i.e. power—as a determining factor in her life" (208).[25] Such remarks remind us that the exhaustive closure of zero-sum allegory, even if that allegory captures in microcosm a struggle with white power, can serve as a sort of consolation prize to that power, a backhanded means of insisting on its illusory centrality.

In this sense, Kincaid's strongest revision of the *Jane Eyre* story is her commentary on the theme of the other woman versus the lawful wife. Brimming with anger, Lucy aims much of it at the First World middle-class feminist, who cannot understand her and drives her wild with rage when she brags of having "Indian blood." "How do you get to be the sort of victor," Lucy asks herself, "who can claim to be the vanquished also?" (41). It is this anger, I have suggested, that finds indirect expression in the smashing of the marriage, which Lucy catches, marks, and joins in an unforgettable moment with her camera. As if unaware of what is going on, she tells the miserable, quarreling couple on the couch, "Say cheese!" But for all this, the contrast with *Jane Eyre* is striking. The wary, hesitant friendship between the two women survives the breakup of the household, as it also survives the wife's sense of betrayal when Lucy breaks her contract and leaves. Some of the inconclusiveness of sex and marriage in *Lucy* perhaps is there because the real story has shifted to the women. The struggle is not over who will share the male's power but over their own vexed and difficult solidarity. The upward mobility of the Third World au pair may not require the displacement of or eternal antagonism to the First World upper-class feminist or professional woman. The wife may be something like a class enemy to Lucy but her gender ally at the same time. Because there is no central contradiction in society, no one linear path of historical development, the logic that links multiple actors must be complex.

If this seems an unnecessarily roundabout way of repeating the platitude that class is not the single, ultimately determining instance, it does not mean that class can be ignored. If sex has become lateral, it is in part because the class a writer such as Mukherjee represents has, indeed, made a lateral move. Her particular diaspora from the Indian subcontinent is largely middle and upper middle class, arriving in the United States with relatively well developed, salable skills or a certain capital.[26] In a sense, then, Mukherjee is doing nothing but projecting her particular class experience onto the au pair narrative.

It is a tricky and ambiguous projection. Domestic service remains one of the major sources of employment for women displaced by the international division of labor and traveling from country to city, whether or not across national borders. Yet as all of these texts take the trouble to note, the au pair, like the governess before her, cannot simply be labeled a domestic servant. The term comes from *pair*, meaning "equal," as in equality of exchange of currencies between countries. Strictly speaking, according to Larousse, to be "au pair dans une maison" (the noun form is a spin-off) means "être logé et nourri sans appointements, en échange de certains services" ("to be lodged and fed without wages, in exchange for certain services"). The experience of travel, with its implicit promise of trading on the cultural capital thus acquired, is bartered against nonwage domestic services. This not only keeps the care of children, and the women who provide it, protected from risks and opportunities of the wage economy; it also keeps them apart, at least potentially, from class difference.[27] The protagonist of Mukherjee's short story is the daughter of a doctor. Like Mukherjee herself, she can be seen as seeking to reproduce her class position, rather than as seeking to rise out of it, in the hostile territory where Third World middle class can all too easily become First World lower class.[28]

Moreover, it is understood that au pair work will be temporary, a brief stage in the life of a woman who may well go on to pay, or may already be paying, another woman to take care of her own children.[29] The class indeterminacy of the au pair, who can be an educated, relatively privileged figure or, on the contrary, a domestic servant forced to do the dirtiest, most isolating, and most poorly remunerated job, is in a sense no more than the multiple logic of a time when gender and racial identities cannot be reduced to class terms, when the so-called new social movements that do not define themselves in national terms have been globalized, when a certain social indeterminacy has therefore been generalized by the international division of labor.

In the ending of *The Country and the City*, which may be described, from one angle, as a meditation on the geography of the *Bildungsroman*, Raymond Williams tries to extend his previous argument into the larger world of the British Empire and the global neocolonialism that has followed it—to do, that is, what the au pair narrative does with *Jane Eyre*: the country, he says, is now the Third World, while both the city and the country that he has been discussing—British city and British country—suddenly become the imperial "city" to that country. The difficulty is the "suddenly." In fact, this "new" division goes back through much of the history Williams's book has traversed; the British country has been part of a global city, that is, for two or three centuries. To see the country/city opposition in the context of the international division of labor is thus to relativize it dramatically. The same is true for the categories of class, race, and gender that the *Bildungsroman* and the au pair narrative graft onto the geography of country and city. Relative to the superexploited Indian textile workers, whose industries were closed down before English textiles replaced them, the British working class is not simply a working class. And the reverse is also true: in the international division of labor, native elites are not simply elites.[30]

Freely adapting a well-known saying, Spivak has occasionally described the imperative behind her work as follows: "Promise them anything, but give them the international division of labor." It is a very artful line: the flippant allusion to perfume quietly undercuts the appeal to an ultimate foundation that the international division of labor otherwise seems to be making. This stylish undercutting is not frivolous, for the point of invoking the international division of labor is precisely and concisely to insist, without a laborious trotting out of additional social categories of the injured and excluded, that even the gravest social injustices are never completely reducible to a simple class allegory. As a transnational figure, the literary au pair stands in for global capitalism's systematic destabilization of local class divisions, which is by no means the effacing of those divisions. This is perhaps how to understand the au pair's distinctive class indeterminacy. The industrious artisans of the 1820s and 1830s could stand at once for those above and those below them in the social hierarchy, for the factory owner as well as the factory operative; thus they did the work of political representation, which is never reducible to the reflection of any constituency, while both running its risks and exercising its powers. The au pair of the 1980s

UPWARD MOBILITY: KINCAID, MUKHERJEE, AND THE AU PAIR

and 1990s runs no less visible risks, among them the risk of being read as a postcolonial fetish that magically obliterates the domestic injuries of class. But attention must also be paid to the potential powers.

It is, above all, those left behind on the periphery who oblige us to distrust the exemplary value of the au pair's tale. One cannot straightforwardly conclude that a story of the displacement of the white First World wife is actually aimed at displacing people of color who have not left home. To be sure, making a new life in the metropolis cannot be the story of the postcolonial subject as such, as Spivak points out. But once we agree that there is no such single, paradigmatic story, it may become easier to see that, through the mediations and displacements that all reading presumes, the au pair narrative in fact possesses allegorical, generalizing powers that need not be ruthlessly curbed or renounced. The trope of one-way travel need not mean, after all, that nation and race are merely skins to be shed in the interest of quicker acculturation. If race can stand for that which should not be left behind, it is also that which Lucy brings with her and makes her mission to communicate, especially to her feminist employer. As a genre, the au pair narrative seems devoted, on the one hand, to spurning uplift or worldly success in strictly economic terms and, on the other, to finding expression for explosive, even unconscious anger. Offering a story of resistance to assimilation as much as a story of assimilation, the genre simultaneously questions racial difference (as a metropolitan obstacle to be overcome), insists on racial difference (as a historically sedimented experience), and reinscribes and even reinvents racial difference within the new, shifting social landscape of the metropolis—a landscape populated by Irish nannies, Vietnamese refugees, and white middle-class feminists who have no pregiven place in premigratory binaries. These reinscriptions and reinventions, with their newly discovered hostilities and tentative internationalist solidarities, are enough to give the genre a real claim to represent an alternative upward mobility, an imagination of unrealized social progress.

In an essay called "Whose Nation?" historian Linda Colley argues that in the period from 1780 to 1830, the British state did not encourage nationalism, as one might have expected, but actually tended to resist it. It did so at a time when the word *patriot* meant a dangerous subversive, because nationalism was seen as a cover for dangerous self-assertion and upward mobility on the part of the lower classes. "For many social conservatives," Colley writes, "placing a premium on service to the nation was opening the door dangerously wide to a meritocracy" (106).[31] It follows from Colley's argument that, conversely, a more democratic state might well be more nationalist, and this is precisely what one finds in Prime Minister Benjamin Disraeli's Crystal Palace speech of 1872, which is often credited with first uncovering England's imperial mission. England would "have to decide," Disraeli said, "between national and cosmopolitan principles. The issue is not a mean one. It is whether you will be content to be a comfortable England . . . or whether you will be a great country—an Imperial country—a country where your sons, when they rise, rise to paramount positions, and obtain not merely the esteem of their countrymen, but command the respect of the world" (32). Through the rising sons, nationalism offers the working and middle classes a field for upward mobility. More surprising, the elitist cosmopolitanism that Disraeli sets against them is a source of resistance to imperialism itself.

These liberal mid-century cosmopolitans, not-so-distant ancestors of Hobsbawm's intergalactic historian, are far from an imitable ideal. The same evolutionary assumptions that qualified their support for nationalism—nations were, in Hobsbawm's paraphrase, "a second-best to world unity" (31)—also provided the prototypes of academic racism.[32] Yet Hobsbawm is right, I think, not to dismiss them out of hand, for one precedent they set is the resistance to "democratization and mass politics"—Disraeli's mobilizing of mass support, in the name of race and nation, for imperial rivalry—in the name of a larger and higher notion of democracy. Cosmopolitan intellectuals refused to be paralyzingly accountable to a national public opinion geared up for imperialism, yet they were no less accountable to the wider, though merely potential, public of imperialism's victims. If they refused Disraeli's appeal to upward mobility, they did so not by refusing upward mobility as such but rather by offering another version of the story of upward mobility, with another, more populous collective subject.

Hidden away within the laziness of democratic pieties are all the strenuous problems of minorities and majorities, of contradictory loyalties to multiple and overlapping social units and identities. It would clear the air somewhat if, instead of the usual breast-beating, there were a corresponding recognition that elitism is inevitably as various, fissured, and problematic as the versions of democracy to which it is contrasted. Most obvious, the intellectual who refuses the effort to become a national voice may thereby become a member of a smaller, "elite" collectivity—say, a professional one—and at the same time may be claiming or seeking democratic participation in a much larger collectivity that stretches beyond the nation. The modes of belonging and participation are unlikely to be identical at these different scales—but this is all the more reason not to bring to bear on them a single standard of political judgment.

The fate of the nineteenth-century story of upward mobility as it is reappropriated and refunctioned by Third World writers seems to demand the same sort of discrimination. If, like *cosmopolitanism*, terms such as *progress* and *modernity* lend themselves to metropolitan self-flattery, it is more such self-flattery to believe that this usage always and everywhere defines their political meaning. Those who urgently need to "change their lives" do not speak lightly of progress, even if they rightly distrust the universalized, inevitabilist gradualism that has been its frequent ideological form. While it presents itself as metropolitan self-critique, the unreflective scorn for modernity among Western intellectuals actually functions as metropolitan self-aggrandizement. Like a certain left-wing antiprofessionalism, aimed obliquely at the new place women and people of color have made for themselves in the academy, this apparent self-critique denigrates in the metropolis precisely that which is now being desired and demanded by intellectuals on the periphery. This is kicking away the ladder one has climbed oneself; it ensures that the necessarily higher ground from which the critique emanates remains in metropolitan hands and defines the metropolis's continuing superiority.[33]

Perhaps conferring the honorific of "cosmopolitan" on the au pair can be interpreted as the same kind of self-legitimizing move on the part of today's transnational intellectuals that Spivak diagnosed in establishment feminism's use of *Jane Eyre*—the professors serve the biscuits to the servants and eat them too, as it were. But if so, isn't it equally likely that metropolitan purposes are served by making Spivak's point, and my own? No reference to the purposes of the metropolis as a whole can resolve disputes within it. A wider political standard is needed—and that, I argue, is just what would-be cosmopolitan critics can legitimately take from the parallel that Mukherjee and Kincaid offer them. For critics, as for au pairs, the crossing of national boundaries is less a step up in the world than a destabilization of the world. One aspect of that destabilization is an imperfect yet peremptory match between new privileges and new responsibilities. Critics, like au pairs, bring the international division of labor into the intimacy of metropolitan space and thus become vehicles for anger and confrontation as well as possible participants in the fashioning of fragile new transnational solidarities. Both the anger and the solidarity are indispensable steps in the transnational stretching of criticism's public accountability, in its acknowledgment that the public sphere in which it must now participate extends beyond the circle of its past interlocutors—in short, in its cosmopolitanism in the most positive sense. From this perspective, the metropolitan anger that has greeted academic criticism's transnational extension of interests is perhaps a sign that some work of representation is being done. Among its other referents, then, upward mobility is perhaps a narrative figure for the surplus value added by this work—a value that has its own impersonal but ultimately progressive trajectory.

Edward Said's negotiation between the metropolis and Third World intellectuals in *Culture and Imperialism* offers a useful concluding paradigm. Said's metropolis is newly but now ineluctably self-divided. As a result of "adversarial internationalization in an age of continued imperial structures," opposition has arisen in the modern metropolis, emerging out of the precarious coalition of personal mobility and impersonal representativeness: "Anti-imperialist intellectual and scholarly work done by writers from the peripheries who have immigrated to or are visiting the metropolis is usually an extension into the metropolis of large-scale mass movements."[34] In one of his many provocations to the established protocols of scholarly disillusionment, Said allows what he calls "the voyage in," the story of how these visitors and immigrants have both integrated themselves into and transformed metropolitan culture, to supply an unexpectedly and incongruously cheerful undertone to the book. The collective *Bildungsroman* of Third World intellectuals who have come to live and work in the metropolis, repeating in transnational terms the country-to-city journey of the nineteenth-century novel, also works its way into Said's innovative treatment of the novel of disillusionment. In an indirect reply to Franco Moretti's darkly Lukácsian view of the genre, Said appreciatively displays Third World reversals of Conrad's *Heart of Darkness*, such as Tayeb Salih's *Season of Migration to the North*. Moretti sees the genre dying a modernist death when European men, losing faith in their own projects, have tired of it.[35] Said's insistence on its continuing vitality in the hands of Third World men and women appears, on the contrary, to express the intelligent optimism of a stratum or category that is still rising, energetic, confident of its powers. Or if optimism seems too strong, call it by the neologism coined by another great Palestinian writer: "pessoptimism."[36]

6

SECULARISM, ELITISM, PROGRESS AND OTHER TRANSGRESSIONS

ON EDWARD SAID'S "VOYAGE IN"

In what has come to be called "colonial and postcolonial studies," there seems to be a gathering consensus that the institutional rise of the field is somehow an anomaly and an embarrassment.[1] To judge from recent essays and conference presentations, the best thing to do with its success story, as perhaps with any success story, is to subject it to the most scathing critique possible. A certain sarcasm about the field's sociogeographical position—which seems irresistible even to observers who are otherwise quite opposed to one another, such as Aijaz Ahmad and his many critics—takes the characteristic form of a more or less personal belittling of the field's practitioners, identified as upwardly mobile both in terms of their place of origin (Third World) and their class of destination (bourgeois). According to Kwame Anthony Appiah, "Postcoloniality is the condition of what we might ungenerously call a comprador intelligentsia: of a relatively small, Western-style, Western-trained, group of writers and thinkers who mediate the trade in cultural commodities of Western capitalism at the periphery."[2] According to Arif Dirlik, "Postcoloniality is the condition of the intelligentsia of global capitalism," and "the popularity that the term *postcoloniality* has achieved in the last few years has less to do with its rigorousness as a concept or with the new vistas it has opened up for critical inquiry than it does with the increased visibility of academic intellectuals of Third World origin as pacesetters in cultural criticism."[3] For "Third World intellectuals who have arrived in First World academe," Dirlik argues, "postcolonial discourse is an expression not so much of agony over identity, as it often appears, but of newfound power" (339). It expresses their scandalous "complicity" in the "hegemony" (331) of global capitalism.

Such attacks on the field's metropolitan location and the power, privileges, and priorities that stem from that location raise one immediate tactical objection: they forget that the legitimacy and the institutional toehold enjoyed by such studies in the metropolis remain extremely fragile. It is often claimed that critical attention to the (post)colonial deviously serves the interests of neoimperialism. Unfortunately, nothing obliges neoimperialism to agree that its interests are so served, and there are no guarantees that it will think or act accordingly. Indeed, there are many signs that post–cold war nationalism in the United States does not wish to recognize its supposed interest in sustaining all those left-wing critics, many of them originally from Third World countries, who are teaching unpatriotic lessons to American youth. And if the tendency to delegitimate and defund continues, the ultraleft paranoid view of the rise of postcolonial criticism will appear, retrospectively, to have been as misguided (to paraphrase Régis Debray) as Communist attacks on progressive French universities on the eve of the Nazi invasion.[4]

Still, it should be possible to admit the partial truth of observations such as Dirlik's without also endorsing the crushing conclusions that Dirlik draws from them about the illegitimacy and misguidedness of postcolonial studies generally—conclusions that offer comfort and consolation to the field's political opponents. Yes, the existence of (post)colonial discourse does express "newfound power" as well as agonies of identity on the part of its practitioners. And so? Would this not be the case for any successful intellectual movement, any movement that wins provisional popular or institutional support for its terms and agendas, whatever the criteria of progressiveness it is judged by? Or have we actually come to believe that any success in winning support is in itself a fatal sign of co-optation or evidence that the movement was not progressive to begin with? If not, then the failure to answer the many critiques like this—indeed, the seemingly masochistic tendency to repeat and delight in them—seems to indicate an incoherence at the point where class and (inter)nationalism intersect that is rather mysterious. And this incoherence is also dangerous; for the lack of a vocabulary that would offer (post)colonial critics some other way of connecting between nationalism and class also means the inability to represent themselves and what they do in public. What (post)colonial studies needs, it seems to me, is not a political purge or purification (although like everyone else, I have points of disagreement with various routine assumptions). It needs a different and impious view of its own authority (such as it is), some narrative of how it arrived at that authority, and some explanation of what that authority has to do with the transnational circle or sphere to which it holds itself newly accountable.

This project is more than I am presently prepared to embark on. But it is with this task in mind that I make some remarks about the recent work of Edward Said, and in particular about the distinctive version of internationalism that clusters around his favored phrases "secular criticism" and the "secular intellectual."[5] Said is one of the few academic figures in the United States who have managed to give public voice both to serious criticism of American foreign policy and, with more difficulty, to solidarities that are not centered on or limited to the unquestioned priority of the American national interest.[6] Most remarkable, he has managed to defend the interests of the Palestinian national movement while maintaining an extremely skeptical view of nationalism as such. Indeed, perhaps the most crucial meaning of *secular*, in his usage, is as an opposing term not to *religion* but to *nationalism*. In the interview with Jennifer Wicke and Michael Sprinker published in the latter's *Edward W. Said: A Critical Reader*, Said sets the "ideal of secular interpretation and secular work" against "submerged feelings of identity, of tribal solidarity," of community that is "geographically and homogeneously defined."[7] "The dense fabric of secular life," Said says, is what "can't be herded under the rubric of national identity or can't be made entirely to respond to this phony idea of a paranoid frontier separating 'us' from 'them'—which is a repetition of the old sort of orientalist model." "The politics of secular interpretation proposes a way . . . of avoiding the pitfalls of nationalism" (233).

The word *secular* has usually served as a figure for the authority of a putatively universal reason or (narratively speaking) as the ideal end point of progress in the intellectual domain. In appropriating the word as a sort of insignia, then, Said clearly runs the risk of (in Tim Brennan's words) "assuming the nineteenth century mantle of progress and enlightenment."[8] Naturally enough, this usage has not gone uncontested among critics of Eurocentrism. R. Radhakrishnan, for example, objects to how "'the secular' as a western norm is made to operate naturally and therefore namelessly."[9] "What we have to realize," Peter van der Veer writes in *Orientalism and the Postcolonial Predicament*, "is that the very distinction between religious and secular is a product of the Enlightenment that was used in orientalism to draw a sharp opposition between irrational, religious behavior of the Oriental and rational secularism, which enabled the westerner to rule the Oriental."[10] Meanwhile, the Subaltern Studies group have stressed the further connection between secularism and indigenous elites. Extending the argument from Western Orientalists to the secularism of Indian nationalist elites, Ranajit Guha argues, for instance, that the latter, "unable to grasp religiosity as the central modality of peasant consciousness in colonial India," necessarily fail "to conceptualize insurgent mentality except in terms of an unadulterated secularism."[11] Or as Dipesh Chakrabarty puts it, secular nationalism in India has meant "an act of appropriation by elite (and elitist) Indians, on behalf of their project of building an Indian state, of diverse historical struggles of the subaltern classes."[12] The case against elites and the case against secularism seem to be one and the same.[13]

Having seen a certain *ressentiment* directed at his professional renown and his privileged position in an elite metropolitan university, Said shows some bravery in standing together with so authoritative a term as *secularism*. At the same time, his descriptions of the intellectual try to *evade* this authority. As he says in the Wicke-Sprinker interview, his version of secularism is an attempt to avoid nationalism's "us and them" without espousing what he calls "'universal values'" (235). If he speaks positively of "globalism" and "worldliness" (242), he says a distinct no to "cosmopolitanism and intellectual tourism" (242), to any internationalism that would express a "superior detachment . . . a general all-encompassing love for all of humanity" (235).[14] In other words, the word *secular* seems to aim at a version of internationalism that would do without the direct authoritative backing either of a putatively universal class, as in the Marxist version, or of disinterested rationality. Is it, then, a sort of postmodern secularism that attempts to do without any authority?[15]

Here, another implication of *secular* is pertinent: the suggestion that the so-called clerisy must learn to work without the quasi-theological guarantees and quasi-theological self-conceptions that have served it in the past. At the end of his final Reith lecture in the summer of 1993, published in *Raritan* and in *Representations of the Intellectual*, Said declared that "the true intellectual is a secular being. However much intellectuals pretend that their representations are of higher things or ultimate values, morality begins with their activity in this secular world of ours—where it takes place, whose interests it serves."[16] Rather than some sort of exemplary otherworldliness, being a secular intellectual here means resigning oneself to an inevitable profane untidiness, an impurity, a political incorrectness. Yet it also draws energy and authority from that refusal of virtue. This is perhaps because, implicitly, it entails biting the not entirely bitter bullet of institutional privilege. According to the Oxford English Dictionary, secularism is "the doctrine that morality should be based solely in regard to the well-being of mankind in the present life to the exclusion of all considerations drawn from belief in God or in a future state." If intellectuals should be "worldly" or even "profane," at least partially subdued to the untidiness of an unjust and hierarchical world, then perhaps they must do some strategic acquiescing in institutional or professional hierarchies.

The last lines of the final Reith lecture, "Gods That Always Fail," go as follows: "As an intellectual you are the one who can choose between actively representing the truth to the best of your ability, or passively allowing a patron or an authority to direct you. For the secular intellectual, *those* gods always fail." Add to this the refusal of all orthodoxy and dogma, of any "kind of absolute certainty" or any "total, seamless view of reality," and you get a secular intellectual who submits to *no* authority, even that of his or her own beliefs or findings.[17] Given this somewhat deconstructive thrust of the term *secular*—not just antinationalist but against any grounding of intellectual mission and activity—one would imagine that Said would be quite harsh with Julien Benda's *La Trahison des clercs*, a text that grounds its attractive antinationalism in a shamelessly sacred view of the intellectual. Surprisingly, he is not.[18] On the key issue of the clercs' betrayal, he comes down on Benda's side; that is, he implicitly endorses, here and throughout the Reith lectures, the sense of high vocation without which there could be no betrayal. This stubborn fidelity to an ideal of vocation is clearly one reason Said's work is so moving to so many people. But it is all the more reason to ask on what grounds, on what secular authority, this sense of mission might be based. The question is absolutely crucial, for it seems to promise a *different difference* between intellectuals and nonintellectuals, an articulation between the two that does not demand that the first simply dissolve into the second, and at the same time an authority that is specifically and uncompromisingly internationalist.

The secular ideal of the intellectual who "speaks truth to power," which Said celebrates in Benda and elsewhere, pays no explicit attention to the decisive question of why power would listen, what might *make* it listen, what makes *anyone* listen. That is, it has nothing explicit to say about the source of *counterauthority* that intellectuals must be assumed to counterpose to "power." This absence of critical or countervailing authority is all the more evident given that the term *secular* functions elsewhere in Said to frustrate the usual answers to the authority question: the dogmatic authority of disinterested truth and the authority of an ethnically purified local or national community, as we have already seen, and also the borrowed sanctity of the professional community. In the introduction to *The World, the Text, and the Critic*, titled "Secular Criticism," Said mobilizes the term *secular* in an attack on what he calls—again from the theological lexicon—the "*cult* of professional expertise" (2), with its sense of "vocation" and its "quasi-religious quietism" (25).[19]

What sorts of authority might there be, then? One hint comes from Said's most sympathetic words about Julien Benda, which suggest a sort of *economy* of authority. Intellectuals, Said says, "have to be in a state of almost permanent opposition to the status quo." And this is why "Benda's intellectuals are perforce a small, highly visible group." Here, intellectual authority would seem to come from the presumed rarity or scarcity of those willing to confront nonintellectual authority. It would come, that is, from a *rarefaction* of intellectuals—I borrow the term from Said's influential appreciation of Foucault—that formally resembles the dread concept of elitism but that offers the restrictiveness of the group an ethico-political legitimacy (the unusual courage needed for opposition to the status quo), rather than a meritocratic one. Or perhaps it would be fairer to say that, rather than the profession deciding who is a competent scholar, it is power that decides who is a real intellectual, whose dissent is painful or threatening enough to be worthy of public expressions of dislike. The authority of the intellectual is a faithful inversion of the authority of power itself and is thus dependent on it. Here, the amoral connotations of secularism lie not far beneath the surface. Practically speaking, an *ethical* scarcity defined by opposition will be indistinguishable from a *social* scarcity that is a potential source of profit and prestige. An undesired visibility, resulting from the political hostility of the powers that be, can and perhaps must be exchanged for celebrity—the prized, often apolitical currency of honors and economic rewards.

This line of thought seems interestingly continuous with another answer to the question of where intellectuals get such authority as they possess—Anna Boschetti's analysis of the success of Sartre. For Boschetti, Sartre's trick was to manage a transfer of cultural capital accumulated in one domain to another domain; thus Sartre brings the prestige of the École Normale Superieure and the discipline of philosophy to literature, and he then brings that newly accumulated sum to his political activities, the government's dramatic reactions to which feed back into his literary and philosophical esteem.[20] For all its problems, the concept of "cultural capital" makes a valuable stab at quantifying and mapping such transfers, translating an otherwise vague "guardianship of the archives" into a diversified and dynamic economy of cultural resources. And this import/export model brings out some distinctive features of—indeed, enables us to recognize as such—the authorizing story of the intellectual that Said calls, in *Culture and Imperialism*, "the voyage in"—the movement of Third World writers, intellectuals, and texts into the metropolis and their successful integration there.

From one point of view, this movement can be described as a form of upward mobility, and to these as to other such narratives, critics have reacted with various degrees of alarm. Can Third World fictions and careers that aim at and are embraced by the metropolis ultimately signify anything other than an opportunistic affirmation of the metropolis? The grounds of Said's qualified optimism are clearly not that the story of an upwardly mobile elite can literally be everyone's story. It is hard to imagine that American readers would react so favorably to Jamaica Kincaid or Bharati Mukherjee, for instance, if they thought the entire Third World was being advised to emulate their upwardly mobile au pair heroines and head for the nearest international airport.[21] Said's point, rather, is that the center can be and has been changed. There has been what he calls "adversarial internationalization in an age of continued imperial structures" (244).[22] Opposition has arisen in the modern metropolis—an opposition there was little sense of in his *Orientalism*. In the universities, the "impingement" of Third World intellectuals on metropolitan space has resulted in "the transformation of the very terrain of the disciplines." This implies that the story of Third World intellectual migration has conferred a certain authority on oppositional intellectuals in and from the First World, including many for whom the work of representing colonial and postcolonial experience must unequivocally be work, that is, for whom the work cannot be misperceived as a matter of effortless identity. And all this has been possible—this is the key point—because of the risky and unstable fusion of personal mobility and impersonal representativeness: "Anti-imperialist intellectual and scholarly work done by writers from the peripheries who have immigrated to or are visiting the metropolis is usually an extension into the metropolis of large-scale mass movements."

Let me offer a brief and schematic national contrast. In what I might call the French model of intellectual authority, as in Anna Boschetti and Pierre Bourdieu, the sole source of cultural capital is existing institutions. Bourdieu's model of the "oblate," for example, describes the rewards given to a poor child without social capital, whose upward mobility has depended entirely on the educational institution that elevated him and to which he responds with unconditional loyalty. Conservative reaction against disciplinary change often comes, Bourdieu writes in *Homo Academicus,* from "those I call 'oblates,' and who, consigned from childhood to the school institution (they are often children of the lower or middle classes or sons of teachers) are totally dedicated to it" (xxiv).[23] "The 'oblates' are always inclined to think that without the church there is no salvation—especially when they become the high priests of an institution of cultural reproduction which, in consecrating them, consecrates their active and above all passive ignorance of any other cultural world. Victims of their elite status, these deserving, but miraculously lucky, 'survivors' present a curious mixture of arrogance and inadequacy which immediately strikes the foreign observer. . . . They offer to the academic institution which they have chosen because it chose them, and vice versa, a support which, being so totally conditioned, has something total, absolute, and unconditional about it" (100–101). In this model, no authority is ascribed to the place from which the mobile oblate sets out; all authority is imagined to flow from the institutional destination. There is no possibility that the protagonist's initial poverty might serve in any way the (legitimating) purposes of the institution or—more important— that the protagonist's rise from that origin might help change that destination in any way, or change the composition of the cultural capital subsequently transmitted to others.

Said's "voyage in" narrative redistributes the emphasis radically. While it does not underestimate the continuing authority of metropolitan institutions, neither does it treat the composition of cultural capital as fixed once and for all or assume that to accept it is necessarily to offer the donor unconditional loyalty in return. National origin matters; transfers from the periphery to the center do not leave the center as it was. The transnational story of upward mobility is not just a claiming of authority; it is also a redefinition of authority, and a redefinition that can have many beneficiaries, for it means a recomposition as well as a redistribution of cultural capital. In short, progress is by no means inevitable, but it is possible.

Ironically, critiques of postcolonial studies that declare their fidelity to Marxist orthodoxy also turn out to be those that, unlike Marx, seem to preclude the untidily dialectical existence of progress. Arif Dirlik, for example, agrees that success stories such as those of Third World writers and intellectuals must offer some answer to the crucial question of where the newfound authority comes from: "Merely pointing to the ascendant role that intellectuals of Third World origin have played in propagating *postcolonial* as a critical orientation within First World academia begs the question as to why they and their intellectual concerns and orientations have been accorded the respectability that they have." In Dirlik's view, the metropolitan success of Third World intellectuals that has given the term *postcolonial* its currency has been "dependent on the conceptual needs of the social, political, and cultural problems thrown up by [a] new world situation," that is, by changes in world capitalism (330). "In their very globalism, the cultural requirements of transnational corporations can no longer afford the cultural parochialism of an earlier day"; they have "a need to internationalize academic institutions (which often takes the form not of promoting scholarship in a conventional sense but of 'importing' and 'exporting' students and faculty.")[24]

The messiness of the word *secular* seems a necessary antidote to this invocation of world capitalism, which might be described as overtidy or even theological. Dirlik assumes global capitalism is not only "organized" (a matter of dispute among Marxist economists) but ubiquitous and omnipotent; whatever happens expresses its will, which is undialectically unified and, in terms of its effects on Third World peoples, invariably malignant. There is no room here for a cunning of reason that, to cite Marx's famous discussion of the British in India, could bring forth unintended political progress even from the worst horrors of colonialism. It is hard to see how, within this worldview, any progress is conceivable that would not, on its emergence, immediately demand to be reinterpreted as the result of capitalism's disguised but malevolent intentions.

The common assumption for all of us who begin, in the study of colonial and postcolonial culture, with the intolerable facts of global suffering and injustice ought to be, on the contrary, that progress is an absolute necessity. Of course, as Anne McClintock points out, the word itself is entangled with a history of racism and Eurocentric self-congratulation, as, too, is *postcolonial*.[25] Any historical instance of progress will obligatorily be compromised in any number of ways, just as the rise of (post)colonial studies is compromised by its metropolitan and class location. But this does not mean the word *progress* is so contaminated as to be unsayable; we are not so rich in instances that we can afford to throw any out in the name of an ideal purity. Progress must be believed to be possible before it can be fought for, and narratives of progress, including narratives of upward mobility, do just this work. Thus such narratives cannot be disposed of by the simple thought that for most of the world's people, there has been no upward mobility. The incongruities between narratives of upward mobility and the static or declining state of the world cannot be corrected by some voluntary gesture of self-discipline, whereby narrative would henceforth allow no image of fulfilled desire not statistically guaranteed by actual improvement on the part of *x* thousands or millions of people; for narratives, including metanarratives, are obliged to make use of desire, and there is no politics without them. As literary critic Alan Sinfield has noted, the rise of British "left culturism," including the careers of Raymond Williams, E. P. Thompson, and Richard Hoggart, was by no means an easy or inevitable fact of postwar cultural life, and their legitimation was secured in part by narratives of "upward mobility through education," which was "a story that society, or parts of it, wanted to tell itself, not a record of experience."[26] Anyone who sees (post)colonial studies as a ruse of world capitalism should be prepared to say that the cultural scene would have been better off without these figures or that the current scene would be better off without the equally contingent presence of figures such as Said, Gayatri Spivak, and Stuart Hall.

In describing what he calls "the global cultural economy," Arjun Appadurai has distinguished between "finanscapes," or flows of capital, and "ideoscapes," or flows of ideologies and images. His point is that a "disjuncture" exists between these flows; no one of them (he provisionally distinguishes five levels) is a mere effect of any other.[27] No account of global capitalism can afford to forget this disjuncture, which makes a space for redistributions of cultural capital that are neither simply metaphorical nor simply epiphenomena of the real thing. I am suggesting, a bit obliquely, that the new internationalism or multiculturalism of the academic left can be seen as one effect of a recomposition of cultural capital—an effect that Said's "voyage in" narrative risks the charge of elitism to authorize and legitimate. The power of *anti*elitism, whether in Richard Rorty's denunciation of rootless cosmopolitans or elsewhere, does not, of course, depend on refusing narratives of upward mobility but only on controlling them. Said's "voyage in" can, I think, be seen as a courageous and well-timed effort to take back these narratives, to use them in a different sharing out of intellectual authority. It is more than incidental that, in so doing, it also offers an implicit answer to the enigma of where the postcolonial critic's secular authority comes from. The authority of internationalism, according to this narrative, comes from the national itself, or even from nationalism—though not everyone's nationalism, and not a nationalism that can itself be unchanged by taking part in the operation.

In the vocabulary of Abdul JanMohamed, we may say that the precarious but necessary authority that Said gives to secular internationalism is founded on an ambiguous border crossing: neither simply an exile (which privileges the place of origin) nor simply an immigration (which privileges the destination), but both an exile and an immigration at once.[28] It is tempting to stress the Americanness of the optimistic narrative that Said thus counterposes to the French "oblation," and even to allow for some legitimate pride one might feel in belonging, in this somewhat modified version of John F. Kennedy's words, to "a nation of immigrants."[29] With all due gratitude, however, for the support that the United States thus offers to the multicultural project of changing the center, I prefer to express my affiliation internationally, with the many otherwise situated groups and individuals, in the United States and elsewhere, who take this secular, progressive project as their own.

7

SAD STORIES IN THE INTERNATIONAL PUBLIC SPHERE

RICHARD RORTY ON CULTURE AND HUMAN RIGHTS

In 1994 the *New York Times* published an op-ed piece by the philosopher Richard Rorty under the title "The Unpatriotic Academy."[1] The trouble with the academic left in the United States, Rorty argued, is that "it is unpatriotic. In the name of 'the politics of difference,' it refuses to rejoice in the country it inhabits. It repudiates the idea of a national identity, and the emotion of national pride." Rorty concludes, "If in the interests of ideological purity, or out of the need to stay as angry as possible, the academic left insists on a 'politics of difference,' it will become increasingly isolated and ineffective. An unpatriotic left has never achieved anything. A left that refuses to take pride in its country will have no impact on that country's politics, and will eventually become an object of contempt."[2]

This is ugly stuff. I cannot imagine that the friends outside the university it may have won for Rorty—the sort of people who, in other times and places, snarled at "rootless cosmopolitans"—will make up for the academic friends it has lost him. Still, I think it is worth speculating that this attack was intended in a good cause: that of negotiating an alliance between liberals like himself and the "academic" or "cultural" left, one that would invite the latter into a joint defense of the ever more endangered social welfare state.[3] As I suggested in the Introduction, this is an invitation that, in my opinion, those of us who identify with the academic left have excellent reasons to entertain, among them our immediate institutional self-interest and, however paradoxical it may seem, our residual interest in the prospects for socialism. It is as the source of this invitation—a somewhat impolite but nonetheless reasonable and even peremptory invitation—that Rorty and his version of liberal common sense merit the most respectful and open-minded scrutiny.

What would be the terms of such a left-liberal alliance? Everything depends on what each side is asked to give up. Rorty's op-ed piece suggests that the academic left should give up two positions that currently discourage any collaboration: its rejection of "patriotism" and its embrace of a "politics of difference." I argue that, rather than simply standing between us and the alliance Rorty proposes, these two sets of investments—in cosmopolitanism or internationalism, on the one hand, and in culture or culture-as-difference, on the other—ought to have a large hand in defining that alliance, though not an entirely free hand. Thus my point of reference throughout this chapter is what I call *human rights internationalism*. Though I do not discuss human rights or the controversies surrounding them in any detail, I consider human rights internationalism as an imperfect but actually existing project that might well be shared by U.S. liberals and academic leftists both inside and outside the national territory of the United States—as a transnational common ground, in other words, that is uncomfortable both for Rorty's liberal ethnocentrism and for the academy's cosmopolitan multiculturalism, and that both can therefore learn from.

GLOBAL PRIVACY

As Nancy Fraser points out, Rorty himself has always displayed an unusually strong commitment to culture, and this commitment forces its way into some of the most troubling and contradictory aspects of his writing.[4] According to Fraser, Rorty's recent thought is structured around a series of collisions between "Romanticism and pragmatism, poetry and politics" (94). Fraser distinguishes three ways in which he tries to reconcile these contradictory impulses toward transgressive aesthetics and toward liberal or reformist politics. The first is the "invisible hand" conception, which asserts that the two are "natural partners," that the "strong poet" and the "reform politician" are "variants of the same species." The second is the "sublimity or decency?" conception, which suggests that "one has to choose between the sublime 'cruelty' of the strong poet and the beautiful 'kindness' of the political reformer" (94–95). The third, and most recent, is the "partition" position, which declares a truce by allotting to each a separate sphere of influence. "The Romantic impulse will have free rein in what will henceforth be 'the private sector.' But it will not be permitted any political pretensions. Pragmatism, on the other hand, will have exclusive rights to 'the public sector.' But it will be barred from entertaining any notions of radical change that could challenge the 'private' cultural hegemony of Romanticism" (95).

In the light of Fraser's analysis, it seems clear that for Rorty, the unforgivable sin of the contemporary academic left is its claim to be *political* by virtue of its attention to *culture*, for this claim ignores any need for Rorty's emphatic demarcation of private and public. It asserts or assumes that the private (culture) is already sufficiently public (political). Thus it might seem to return to Rorty's first position, where the aesthetic stood in for pragmatism's own distance from the ideal of objectivity. Fraser describes it (not very sympathetically, it should be said) as a "Sorelian temptation": admiration for the visionary artist-leader who transgresses social norms, whose actions are revolutionary creations both in aesthetics and in politics. Unfortunately, as Fraser and Rorty seem to agree, this cultural model of politics is both undemocratic and impractical; for "to say goodbye to objectivity is not necessarily to say hello to a single, unitary solidarity and . . . what's good for poets is not necessarily good for workers, peasants, and the hard-core unemployed" (102). The question of whether cultural politics is necessarily reducible to these formulations can be left for later.

Rorty's turn against cultural politics is expressed unambiguously in a debate with Andrew Ross in the pages of *Dissent*. There he sets up an opposition between the real politics of the old left, which is electoral politics (drafting and passing bills), and the merely academic politics of the new left, which is cultural politics (the demand for total social transformation, for change at the deep level of language, and so on). Cultural politics can be negatively defined, for Rorty, as politics that doesn't have to do with legislation, with passing bills into laws. "It is true that the Old Left ignored a lot of injustices and inequalities," he writes, "but it is also true that it struggled, with good effect, against a lot of other injustices and inequalities. The utility of this left is illustrated by its role in drafting and passing Lyndon Johnson's Great Society bills. The inutility of Ross's left is suggested by its disdainful refusal to think in terms of drafting and passing bills" (265).[5]

It is worth noting that there is no mention of patriotism or nationalism in this argument. If Rorty has no need of the patriotism theme here, it is because the substance of his reproaches against the "unpatriotic" academy is already contained in his reproaches against those who make claims for cultural politics. In other words, too little attachment to the nation produces the same undesirable effects, for Rorty, as too great an attachment to culture. The two sins are mysteriously and suspiciously interchangeable. But something must be wrong if two such unlike adjectives as *cultural* and *unpatriotic* can function as equivalents for each other.

And something is indeed wrong. If we extract the national/international problematic from the argumentative choler of "The Unpatriotic Academy," dust it off, and carefully insert it back into Rorty's argument against cultural politics, it turns out to lead somewhere very different.

Let us translate Rorty's opposition between law and culture—the first real and public, the second unreal and private—from the national to the international scale. In the absence of a world government, human rights instruments are not international law in the strict national sense; they are usually referred to as "soft" law. But they are certainly *public* in the ordinary meaning of that term, that is, objects that invite widespread discussion and demand universal application. Hence we seem to get a parallel opposition to the law/culture dichotomy between human rights internationalism, on the one hand, based on the universality of the law, and a sort of cultural cosmopolitanism, on the other hand, based on respect for the unique particularity of different cultures. On the cultural particularity side we would find only those privileged academic elites whom Rorty describes, in a killing association with aestheticism, as "connoisseurs of diversity."[6] On the legal universality side we would find a solid majority of popular opinion.

Given the opposition between real politics and cultural politics on which he so fiercely insists, one would expect Rorty to rejoice that human rights, like domestic legislation, are backed by an extensive democratic sense of fairness and decency. One would expect him to prefer human rights to culture's vanguardist appreciation of diversity and aesthetic skepticism about norms. And one would thus expect him to argue that human rights represent just the right style of politics on an international scale—a style of persuasive rather than forceful intervention that remains faithful, as he says is "inevitable and unobjectionable" for a Westerner, to "distinctively Western social democratic aspirations."[7] For culture, he has argued, should not matter to politics on an international scale any more than it matters on the national scale. "We can suggest that UNESCO think about cultural diversity on a world scale in the way our ancestors in the seventeenth and eighteenth century thought about religious diversity on an Atlantic scale: as something to be simply *ignored* for purposes of designing political institutions."[8]

Rorty does indeed speak in the name of human rights. He does so, at least, on occasions when he can thereby chide the academic left for a selective or nonexistent concern for human rights—the inevitable counterpart, he suggests, of its respect for cultural diversity.[9] He refers, for example, to

> what Lévi-Strauss once disdainfully called "UNESCO cosmopolitanism," the sort of cosmopolitanism which is content with the status quo, and defends it in the name of cultural diversity. Such cosmopolitanism was, when UNESCO [United Nations Educational, Scientific, and Cultural Organization] was founded in the 1940's, prudently and respectfully silent about Stalinism; nowadays it remains prudently and respectfully silent about religious fundamentalism and about the blood-stained autocrats who still rule much of the world. The most contemptible form of such cosmopolitanism is the sort which explains that 'human rights' are all very well for Eurocentric cultures, but that an efficient secret police, with subservient judges, professors and journalists, at its disposal, in addition to prison guards and torturers, is better suited to the needs of other cultures. The alternative to this spurious and self-deceptive kind of cosmopolitanism is one with a clear image of a specific kind of cosmopolitan future: the image of a planet-wide democracy.[10]

The ponderous sarcasm in this passage is perhaps a sign, however, that Rorty is not speaking from a position with which he is entirely comfortable. And there is no secret about why he should experience some discomfort. He has famously and controversially criticized the very universalism that he seems here to espouse. He has argued, specifically, that "humanity" and "planetwide justice" are vaporous and unproductive abstractions and that people act, and should act, by appealing instead to local solidarities of a smaller but more concrete sort. Hence he has received such equally sarcastic responses, in the name of the humanity he repudiates, as Terry Eagleton's: "One could demonstrate compassion towards those in the next apartment, for example, while withholding it from those a mile down the street. Personally, I only ever manifest compassion to fellow graduates of the University of Cambridge. . . . Once one begins extending one's compassionate reach to graduates of Oxford too, there seems no reason not to go on to London, Warwick and even Wolverhampton Polytechnic, and before one knows it one is on the slippery slope to Habermas, universalism, foundationalism and the rest."[11]

Of course, Marxists cannot feel totally secure with regard to universal compassion or human rights, either—which is why Eagleton's sarcasm, too, should be read as somewhat evasive or symptomatic. But Eagleton's counterclaim to the universal suggests a point that I second and would argue at greater length: namely, that Rorty's case against the cultural left is seriously qualified by his own continuing but unacknowledged commitment to culture, especially and crucially asserted on the international scale. The planetwide democracy Rorty says he wants—and that the elitists of the cultural left are supposedly willing to do without—becomes impossible because democracy requires a public, and the domain of the international, as Rorty sees it, is the domain of the private: the domain of the cultural. On the international level, Rorty himself seems to acknowledge the existence of nothing *but* culture.

The sort of attention Rorty feels should be paid to cultural diversity on a world scale is spelled out in an essay called "Private Irony and Liberal Hope." To transcend one's given ethnocentrism, he argues there, is an excellent ambition—as long as the ambition remains private. "Ironists," he writes, "are afraid that they will get stuck in the vocabulary in which they were brought up if they only know the people in their own neighborhood, so they try to get acquainted with strange people (Alcibiades, Julien Sorel), strange families (the Karamazovs, the Casaubons), and strange communities (the Teutonic Knights, the Nuer, the mandarins of the Sung)." "Ironists read literary critics, and take them as moral advisors," he goes on, "simply because such critics have an exceptionally large range of acquaintance" (80).[12] Such a range of acquaintance may well have a deprovincializing, antiethnocentric effect on one's sense of self, and this is all to the good. What is not good, for Rorty, is to believe that such an effect can or should be *public*, in the double sense that (1) it can have a broad popular appeal and (2) it can be transmuted, therefore, into actual political institutions. The privacy of culture permits us to put ourselves in other people's places, without feeling we have to *do* anything about it. The refusal of ethnocentrism is not, strictly speaking, an action, so it can never be more than private. To be public is necessarily to be ethnocentric.[13]

"The rise of literary criticism to preeminence," Rorty writes, and with it the rise of ironists, has "widened the gap between intellectuals and the public" (82). That is, the same gap that he accuses the cultural left of culpably enjoying, in the *New York Times* article, is here described as the inevitable and proper result of the cultural left's concern with culture—a concern that he himself declares should not be more public, should not be allowed to escape from the domain of the private, for we must uphold "a firm distinction between the private and the public" (83). Culture is a matter of private fantasy; no public use should be made of it. It is and should remain, he says, "largely irrelevant to public life and to political questions" (83). Literature and its ironies constitute a sort of synthesis: privacy *with* and even perhaps *for* others, but privacy all the same. In other words, despite the "range of acquaintance" metaphor, these others are not necessary or even possible conversational partners. That key meaning of the term *public* does not include them. Therefore, they need not be dragged into practical discussions about reality, whether political or otherwise. They constitute not a new international *public* sphere but what can only be called the international *private* sphere.

It is this logic, rather than his momentary and inconsistent sarcasm at the expense of the cultural left, that expresses itself in Rorty's account of human rights for Amnesty International. Decisively and disturbingly, Rorty also places human rights in the private sphere.

Asked by Amnesty to speak in 1993, in the midst of horrifying reports of Serbian "ethnic cleansing," Rorty did not describe human rights in the public vocabulary of justice or law, which would presumably hold domestically. He described them as a private matter of imagination, of "sympathy," of literature. Progress in human rights will not be made by winning support for universals, by getting more and more people to overcome the parochialism of "kinship and custom," by inducing them to accept the universal "obligations imposed by recognition of membership in the same species" (133). It will be made by "manipulating their sentiments" (127); for progress in human rights thus far "seems to owe nothing to increased moral knowledge, and everything to hearing sad and sentimental stories" (118–19). Human rights talk, Rorty argues, should aim at inducing "the sort of reaction that the Athenians had more of after seeing Aeschylus' *The Persians* than before, the sort that white Americans had more of after reading *Uncle Tom's Cabin* than before" (128). You can and should talk about justice and then go on to legislate accordingly—the problem with the cultural left, remember, is that it did not. But you can talk about justice only, it appears, within your own nation. Extended across national borders, matters of justice become not legislation but literature. Or (in a phrase Rorty borrows from the Argentinian jurist Eduardo Rabossi), they become "human rights *culture*" (115, my emphasis).[14]

Rorty is right in a sense. As employed by human rights advocates, the expression "human rights culture" refers to the goal of creating social conditions in which human rights are likely to be respected. But the phrase also acknowledges that human rights are a culturally specific product. As the advocates also acknowledge, if more intermittently, this culture of human rights—which can be described from without, as well and as badly as other cultures are described—is a culture whose particularity sometimes interferes with its laudable political aims, for example, when it unconsciously assumes its own universality and does not pay enough attention to its particular interlocutors. But Rorty's use of the phrase makes a different point. In describing human rights as cultural rather than juridical, and thereby denying them any foundational status, he is not merely taking up the (to my mind, inescapable) challenge of supporting human rights without positing any universal human nature, a definition of humanity, known in advance, on which those rights can be based. What it means not to have a foundation, he implies, is to exist on the level of culture, on the level of "sad and sentimental stories." But this is true only beyond the nation; for there is such a thing as law, and law is what politics is properly about. And law has a better foundation. But law exists, for Rorty, only *within* the nation.

One reason is, as I noted above, that no supranational executive power exists at present, or is likely to exist in the near future. But if even the prospect of such a world state would excite at least as much worry as relief, especially in liberals concerned with individual freedom, then it seems doubtful that its absence is truly the decisive factor. Rorty's identification of the international with the private would seem to rely less on conventional liberal usage (for which the "public" is, strictly speaking, the state as opposed to the market) than on a strange swerve in his own, more original equation of the public with democratic dialogue. Strangely, it is only within the nation that Rorty is willing to recognize that other foundation on which law is properly based, the alternative to culture or aesthetics that he calls "conversation" or "solidarity" or "consensus."[15] There is no law outside the nation not because there is not yet an international executive power but because outside the nation, Rorty refuses to recognize the legitimating base that such a power would require. For him, there is no public outside the nation, no collectivity "viewed as possible [or necessary] conversational partners," no set of people whose opinions need to be consulted.[16] Hence there is no need for discussion beyond the nation. The international is the private. Beyond the nation, all the rest is literature.

DEMOCRACY AND REDISTRIBUTION

If those affected by decisions are to have influence over those decisions, they must be consulted. Where there is no public, there is no democracy. It should thus come as no surprise that, talk of planetwide democracy notwithstanding, Rorty's most recent writing chooses not the democratic and reform-minded William James but the aristocratic and aesthetic Nietzsche as the figure who should preside over international realities.[17] Yet the idea that democracy should be championed within our borders but might have to be abandoned outside them is precisely the double-standard relativism for which Rorty had earlier ridiculed the left and its supposed "UNESCO cosmopolitanism."

This inconsistency is not something to which the left can have a single or simple reaction. Yes, Rorty's willingness to let the line between national and international settle his divided loyalties to democracy and to culture tends to confirm some of the left's fears about the meaning of a left-liberal alliance. It implies that alliance with liberalism would mean giving up, in the name of a proper effort to reduce domestic inequalities, any effort to correct the even greater inequalities that separate rich nations from poor nations. In this case, of course, joint defense of the social welfare state would become an explicit defense of fortress America, a decision to protect, by withdrawal from the world, a prosperity gained in large part through exploitation of the world. That program might be a fantasy—it would not result in any withdrawal from the process by which the world's resources continue to be converted into our commodities—but it could have real consequences as a stick to beat the left on such issues as immigration and foreign policy.

But these fears, however reasonable, should not be the end of the story, for we cannot be content with the real international consequences that our commitment to culture already produces. When Rorty identifies the cultural and the international, in order to lessen the importance of both, he also challenges the cultural left to formulate that connection differently. And he challenges us, if only indirectly, to formulate it in such a way as to invite the effective participation of the liberals. He also suggests, again indirectly, that the liberals are closer to us than they may think.

The essay in which Rorty steps away from the goal of expanding democracy to an international scale, titled "Who Are We? Moral Universalism and Economic Triage," is equally interesting for another of its shifts. If Rorty has earlier appealed to democracy as a higher value than culture, here he trumps democracy itself with the still higher value of economic redistribution: "[William] James took for granted the universalistic assumption, common to Christianity and the Enlightenment, that our moral community should be identical with our biological species. . . . This amounts to the project of distributing the planet's resources in such a way that no human child lacks the opportunities for individual development, the life chances, available to any other human child." However, he adds, "nobody has written a scenario which shows how the people in the lucky industrialized democracies might redistribute their wealth in ways that create bright prospects for the children of the undeveloped countries without destroying the prospects of their own children and of their own societies. The institutions of the rich democracies are now so intertwined with advanced methods of transportation and communication, and more generally with expensive technology, that it is hardly possible to imagine their survival if the rich countries had to reduce their share of the world's resources to a fraction of what they now consume." In effect, Rorty here offers a more limited, more conditional version of his earlier critique of humanist universals. It is only *if such a redistribution cannot happen*, he now argues, that talk of planetwide democracy is cruel and delusive; for there is no genuine sense of common membership without a readiness to come to the assistance of other members, coupled with some capacity to do so. It is "self-deceptive or hypocritical for those who do not believe that the industrialized democracies can bring either hope or human rights to the billions who lack both to use the term 'We, the people of the United Nations.' . . . Moral identification is empty when it is no longer tied to habits of action."

This argument offers a somewhat different solution to the split allegiances that Rorty elsewhere deals with by separating the public from the private, the national from the international. It is a clear improvement, I think, in the sense that it no longer takes for granted the centrality of U.S. national interests. On the contrary, it recognizes the weight of potentially intrusive ethical claims from outside our borders. And it is an improvement in that action to rectify injustice in the global distribution of resources also draws public and private, liberal reform and aesthetic empathy, back together again. Unlike "sad stories," such action produces an effective solidarity that is not merely private. But unlike "legislation"—and there may be less improvement than continuity here—this rectifying action does not seem to require the existence of a democratic public. Rather, it is presented as a precondition for constituting such a public.

How can an international public sphere be constituted? And how can such a sphere contribute to the redistribution of the world's resources? These are the right questions, and Rorty is right to link them. The question I am left with is whether he has set himself up so as to be unable to answer them. To describe effective action as the precondition for an international public sphere may be seen as a way of continuing not to recognize the extent to which such a sphere already exists. And to stake all bets on action may be seen as a way of continuing to suggest that culture makes nothing happen, that cultural politics is a waste of time.

If so, human rights would also seem to be a waste of time. Rorty's notion that effective action against global economic injustice must happen before any genuine transnational dialogue can occur offers a bizarre echo of the argument, often put forward by certain Third World governments, that development must precede any talk of human rights. Like ethnocentrism, action makes strange bedfellows. Here, Rorty finds himself side by side with just those "blood-stained autocrats" with whom he earlier tried to force the cultural left into guilty association. But then, there never was much room for human rights in Rorty's account of decency. According to Norman Geras, Rorty's references to human rights before the Amnesty lecture are "invariably . . . negative and dismissive."[18]

This lack of respect for the human rights vocabulary emerges still more emphatically in a recent speech called "The Intellectuals and the Poor."[19] Here "the cultural politicians of the academic left" (17) are accused not of ignoring rights but, on the contrary, of relying on them excessively. "The difference between an appeal to end suffering and an appeal to rights," Rorty argues, "is the difference between an appeal to fraternity, to fellow-feeling, to sympathetic concern, and an appeal that exists quite independently from anybody's feelings about anything—something that issues unconditional commands" (15). Thus demands for gay rights, to take Rorty's example, are a mere "distraction" from the real political task, which is "an attempt by the straight to put themselves in the shoes of the gays . . . rights talk is the wrong approach to issues where appeals to human sympathy are needed" (16–17). Note that in this (primarily domestic?) example, rights figure as a denial of fellow feeling, a position to which we fall back, perhaps, when we no longer have faith in our ability to put ourselves in other people's shoes. Here, instead of valuing rights as essential to liberal decency, Rorty locates them still further away from the one true politics, which is again defined as action to remedy economic inequality.

What is action? And how far does the position based on it differ from the earlier argument that there is no alternative to ethnocentrism? This new position can be taken in at least two different ways. It can be interpreted as a desperate, provocative challenge to the international community to make good on its rhetoric in tangible economic terms. Or it can be seen as a way of regretfully resigning oneself to the impossibility of the needed redistribution, given the highly exacting conditions that such action would have to satisfy at home; for if action seems so simple and basic that one has every right to demand it, it also seems, as Rorty describes it, almost inconceivably difficult.

"A politically feasible project of egalitarian redistribution of wealth," Rorty writes, "requires that there be enough money around to insure that, after the redistribution, the rich will still be able to recognize themselves—will still think their lives worth living. The only way in which the rich can still think of themselves as part of the same moral community with the poor is by reference to some scenario which gives hope to the children of the poor without depriving their own children of hope."[20] The rich must still be able to recognize themselves. What is strange is not the demand that the children of the rich keep their hope alive—there can be no two opinions about that—but the sudden appeal to recognition, to *identity*. What decides the limits and feasibility of this *economic* calculation is an appeal to *culture*. In effect, what Rorty proposes is a rich man's identity politics. Appearances to the contrary, the criterion of action proves ultimately reducible to culture—the very concept it was introduced to dominate. Cultural identity is the decisive excuse for avoiding economic redistribution—for avoiding, in other words, both economic justice and the democracy that depends on it.

This means Rorty shares in the culturalism that he attacks. But it does not mean that culture itself is the problem. On the contrary, Rorty makes the point for his antagonists. He is exactly right: culture is indeed inextricable from democratic politics and economic redistribution. Though Rorty first makes redistribution seem too easy—a simple act of top-down social engineering—before he goes on to make it seem too difficult, he is certainly correct that it is difficult and that the difficulty is inextricably economic and cultural. Large-scale redistribution between the rich and poor countries would indeed require major changes in identity in the rich countries, and it could happen only by addressing the existing cultures of those countries. But such self-transformations are what cultural politics is about. When Rorty insists, whether sympathetically or merely pragmatically, that the rich must be able to recognize themselves afterward, he assumes that people overwhelmingly desire to remain fixed in the identities they already firmly possess. In other words, he takes for his own just that supposed multicultural dogma that he so forcefully rejects in his op-ed piece. And in embracing this caricature of multiculturalism and turning it into the major obstacle to global change, he wilfully evades the emergent common sense that he could have learned from his antagonists on the cultural left. For that common sense, culture signifies both membership and identity, on the one hand, and a loose, relativized, self-problematizing relation to membership and identity, on the other—one that assumes the persistence of injustice and inequality within identities as well as between them, and thus also assumes the need for a politics that is not mere reaffirmation of a prior identity. It is in this framework that one might imagine, for example, an ascetic ecopolitics in the industrial West that would take advantage of widespread disgust with consumerist waste—certainly a visceral part of Western culture—in order to maneuver toward global economic redistribution. Indeed, one might also argue, with James Livingston, that a strongly imaginative approach to redistribution is necessary if the United States is even going to sustain such democracy as it has, let alone work to extend it.[21]

I have argued elsewhere that the category of culture has functioned as a sort of Trojan horse by which the need to take the experience of distant others into account, along with a need for solidarity with or at least accountability to those others, could be smuggled into U.S. notions of political "reality" and the "public sphere"—notions which, to repeat the crucial point, Rorty and others seem rather too willing to confine within the nation and our patriotic duties to it.[22] As the price of alliance with beleaguered liberals, the (equally beleaguered) cultural left has been invited to shift our working vocabulary away from culture while restricting the working definition of the public to the scale of the nation-state. It seems clear that this is a price that should not, indeed cannot, be paid. As Rorty himself reminds us, culture will have to be at the heart of any feasible scenario that works toward global democracy and economic redistribution—

just as culture is also and already part of the action on behalf of both that is carried on in the liberal vocabulary of human rights.

HUMAN RIGHTS AT THE UNITED NATIONS

According to Rorty, "cultural diversity" should be "simply ignored" in the task of "designing political institutions." As one political institution where human rights internationalism assumes some real, if limited, agency, the United Nations is also a site where oppositions between culture, human rights, and economic redistribution have been fought out many times and continue to be debated. There is no room for me to rehearse these debates here. All I will do, continuing the line of argument begun above, is say a few words about the actually existing internationalism centered at the United Nations and about how opposed terms such as *sad stories* and *legislation, private* and *public, cultural leftists* and *reformist liberals* are already meeting on this less-than-ideal terrain.[23]

In the ten years between the fortieth anniversary of the founding of the United Nations and its fiftieth anniversary in June 1995, there has been at least one change in the somewhat feeble rhetoric by which the United Nations is defended. Today, as in 1985, one hears that its mere survival is a triumph;[24] that despite its inability to prevent wars, it is "better than nothing" (President Clinton's phrase);[25] that it's better for enemies to talk than not to talk.[26] One also hears, very properly, that the United Nations is only as good as its constituents. As Richard Falk wrote in 1985, for example, "The United Nations is neither better nor worse than the states that control its purse strings, and hence its operations" (234).[27] Eqbal Ahmad, in the same issue of *The Nation*, titled his contribution "Only as Good as Its Members" (242): "The failures of the United Nations are not its own. An organization of states can be only as good as its members" (244).

This remains common sense. And yet there is new evidence, since 1985, to suggest that the United Nations can no longer be described (if it ever could) as a transparent representation of the global balance of power, a sort of nonentity whose underlying and definitive reality is the unequal power of existing nation-states. That evidence comes from the dramatically increased impact, especially since the end of the cold war, of the so-called NGOs, or nongovernmental organizations—units that are precisely other than nations. Before 1970, NGOs had no voice at the United Nations. But we can see that something has changed when, for example, the French Communist Party petitions the United Nations for status as a sanctioned NGO and wins, thus winning the right to speak officially at the UN Social Summit. At the World Conference on Human Rights in Vienna in 1993, attended by some five thousand representatives of nine hundred organizations, these nongovernmental groups were arguably the decisive force that broke the sterile, state-induced impasse between First World universalists and Third World relativists—especially, it should be noted, NGOs from the so-called Third World. "Perhaps the most significant lesson to be learned from the experience," wrote Fateh Azzam, a Palestinian organizer, "was the new-found strength of the human rights movement, based in large part on the development and participation of Southern and national NGOs" (99).[28] The sense of paradox in the outcome was widespread. "In a curious kind of way," Upandra Baxi reported, "the global human rights movement triumphed at Vienna. Curious, because the measuring rod of illegitimacy and illegality of practices of power was provided by sovereign states themselves. . . . In an ironic gesture, the perpetrators of inhuman wrongs—the member-states of the United Nations—sat together with the representatives of people's human rights organizations to fashion a new charter of human rights" (1–2).[29]

How had it come about that member states could support the "vision and vitality" of a declaration derived, in Baxi's words, "from the solidarity in struggle of the world's peoples against perishable state sovereignties" (2)? How had it happened, in other words, that something like an international public sphere had come into being? As Azzam notes, one crucial factor was the impact of regional and national NGOs. Such NGOs often won international backing from their own and neighboring nation-states, even though these same states opposed them violently at home. The states agreed, however, that they and their regions required greater representation at the international level, to balance the weight of Western states and better-funded, Western-oriented international NGOs. In other words, the level of "international civil society" where NGOs are key actors had won for itself enough legitimacy, had sufficiently demonstrated its autonomous political importance, that states had an investment in compromising with those who could represent them there. Azzam mentions the expansion of NGO participation beyond those few NGOs with so-called consultative status, their strong joint statements to their governments stressing the universality and indivisibility of human rights, and new modes of organization "on the streets and in the local papers" (90). "It was evident that Asian governments had not anticipated so many NGOs beating on their doors with their demands" (94). When it was over, the *Human Rights Monitor* reported: "Too often in the past, Asian governments at the UN Commission have dismissed NGO criticisms as concerns of foreigners who do not know their cultures. With Asian NGOs speaking out so clearly, they will now find that a more difficult defence to adopt" (94).[30]

Yet this was not a simple embrace of universal public reason at the expense of the local, the private, and the cultural. On the contrary.[31] The single clearest triumph of the Vienna conference was a direct result of disputing the public/

private line that had previously governed the very definition of human rights. The feminist critique of human rights has always insisted, correctly, that "public" has been a gendered category; it has condemned male violence against women when it expressed itself through the state, but by the same token, it has ignored the abuse of women in its far more pervasive "private," or nonstate, forms.[32] In Vienna, the extraordinary success of NGOs in getting women's rights described as human rights involved forcing the so-called private into the so-called public—a doubling, one might say, of the shift in agency by which ostensibly private agents (NGOs) asserted their power against more public ones (states). And a doubling as well of a shift in formal means: in Vienna, much of the political work was accomplished by means of "sad and sentimental stories" of the sort Rorty mentions, including horrifying stories of violence and atrocity.[33]

Yet as I have already noted, Laura Flanders suggests that perhaps such stories had too large a place in Vienna; perhaps the urge to focus on first-person narratives of violence proved too hard to resist. "In a global women's movement rent by class, race, age, and national divisions," Flanders notes, "the experience of violence provides a powerful common ground. It's also sexy; sexier than labor rights, illiteracy, self-determination or poverty. The Vienna conference certainly demanded a clear, preferably dramatic profile. If the story's gruesome enough, the mainstream media may come along. What bleeds, as the familiar press maxim has it, leads" (175).[34] As a result, she concludes, "of the recommendations from the Women's Caucus, those that addressed violence mostly got accepted. Those that dealt with poverty and development did not" (177).

Here is a commentary on Rorty's "sad and sentimental story" account of human rights discourse. Another crucial result of the new power of NGOs in the 1990s has been an insistence on economic development (not always the preferred term) as part and parcel of the human rights agenda.[35] But in this domain, it is arguable that universal principles have had more purchase than local anecdotes. Fleeing the false universality of philosophy, which permits the illusion of building on a solid foundation, Rorty attributes just this missing progressiveness to fictions, perhaps because they make no claim to be foundational. But critics have reason to know, by our training, the inconclusiveness of sad and sentimental stories. We know how evasive they are, how susceptible to multiple and contradictory interpretations. We also know how often stories have functioned to "make strange" rather than to produce recognitions of sameness, and sometimes—one thinks of those unverified but highly functional anecdotes that set off rampages—to produce horrors rather than fend them off. The apparent universality of suffering and the apparent universality of the sentiments in the face of suffering are no less open to possible abuse than any other universality.

SAD STORIES: RICHARD RORTY

As Rorty himself admits in his lecture for Amnesty, many—perhaps most—of the human rights stories we have been hearing lately tend to make us feel about the perpetrators of atrocity just what the perpetrators, apparently, feel about their victims: that they are inhuman. If this is not the conclusion we want (and the stories themselves cannot be depended on to make this point), then philosophical reason cannot solve its problems in this domain by abdicating in favor of culture. It is not in the stories themselves but rather in the conversation about these stories—just the sort of discourse in which Rorty himself is engaging in his lecture—that such supplementary discriminations are properly made. And to go back to Flanders's discontent with feminist storytelling in Vienna, this is a discourse in which universality, if not necessarily philosophy's version of universality, has an essential place; for it is only more universality, not less—for example, attention to what Étienne Balibar calls the "real universality" of capitalism—that can widen our view, returning us to such issues as "poverty and development" that the sad stories of violence left undiscussed.

From the perspective of the rising NGOs at Vienna in 1993, the international public sphere looks less like a wish and more like a reality. But to celebrate the NGO at the expense of the state—or for that matter, to celebrate (private) culture at the expense of (public) reason—is to forget the immense differences among the NGOs; how little progress was made at Vienna toward opening up to public scrutiny the entirely "private" functioning of the World Bank and the International Monetary Fund (IMF) (Baxi calls for "a direct imposition of human rights conditionalities" on both [6]); how much the progress of the NGOs themselves owes to a "privatization" campaign by the United States and its most powerful allies. After all, the undermining of the nation-state in the name of human rights serves a variety of purposes, not all of them desirable; while it leaves untouched that other, economic power, represented by the World Bank and the IMF, which is more indirectly but no less effectively responsible for many of the world's human rights abuses. If power and its abuses are at the heart of human rights, then the state as such, like universality as such, cannot be *the* enemy.[36]

Though both unequal power and cultural difference exist in friction with the universality of human rights, the two differ in at least one crucial respect. The assertion of cultural difference is often understood as an all-or-nothing proposition that offers no substance for further debate. The assertion of unequal power, in contrast, opens out into a continuing discussion with more than two sides, indeed, with a profusion of tactical and principled complications to attend to. It relativizes the universal on a common ground of assumptions—from within universality itself, as it were.

I take as an example the Singaporean controversy over the so-called Michael Fay caning case of 1994. In an issue of *Commentary*, the journal of the National University of Singapore Society (NUSS), one writer points out that caning is a holdover from British rule, and the caning of U.S. student Michael Fay shows that "the prerogatives of the 'law and order' structures of the old colonial state have been indigenised, and have now been applied to a white person. Thus history plays its little cruel jokes" (164).[37] The same writer, C. J. Wee Wan-ling, adds that "the charges of barbarism against a white body smack of an implicit demand for extraterritorial rights of the sort which existed in the imperial era" (164). A similar point is made by the next writer, Leon Perera: "*The New York Times* appeal for phone calls to the Singapore embassy in Washington and to U.S. firms doing business with Singapore in order to pressure the Singapore government into pardoning Fay were not directed at abolishing the caning sentence itself in Singapore. As such, this appeal had more in common with nineteenth century Western requests for extraterritorial rights in imperial China than it did with a concern for universally applicable human rights norms. The same can be said for the disappearance of the issue from the media agenda in the United States subsequent to the caning, even though mandatory caning is still on the statute books here" (124).[38] He goes on, "The whole Fay saga has to be seen in the context of the postwar history of American foreign policy; concerns about democracy and human rights have always been selective and subordinated to the political agendas of *realpolitik* as articulated by the state planners of the day" (124).

The discrimination that has to be made here is one that Perera makes himself: between cultural relativism and national sovereignty concerns, on the one hand—which he criticizes for their mutual support (130)—and the insistence, on the other hand, that Singaporeans participate in the conversation about rights in their country and that, in this way and others, human rights discourse become truly universalistic. The national sovereignty defense "only works," Perera comments, "if the U.S. was unambiguously trying to secure exemption from punishment for Fay because he was an American . . . the U.S. should not only oppose Singapore's caning of Americans but also Singapore's caning of *Singaporeans* from a consistent human rights–based standpoint." Most American criticism, he writes, was not universalistic: it expressed outrage "that Singapore should presume to cane an American rather than that it should cane *anyone at all* irrespective of nationality" (122).[39]

Perera quotes one opinion from the newspaper the *Straits Times*: "Human rights have become a convenient weapon for sections of American opinion to set upon systems they do not like for whatever reason . . . human rights is actually an effort by dominant nations to keep down emergent powers, by denying them access to prosperous markets unless they agree to abide by externally-mandated human rights standards" (130).[40] He then comments that even the author of this position makes a concession to "the idea that there *are* universally valid human rights standards which may occupy a legitimate place in the debate" (131). When Singaporeans criticize the United States for a criminal justice system that doesn't work, they are acknowledging universality of a sort. This is precisely Perera's own position: "If the values embodied in our domestic political arrangements can be defended without recourse to arguments about incommensurable cultural differences, but rather using purely political ideas, isn't this an admission that the choice of values can be made on the basis of transcultural criteria? If stiffer penalties will deter crime in America as well as Singapore, then can't we say some things about desireable and feasible socio-political arrangements which apply to *all* societies? . . . Perhaps the Michael Fay saga will be remembered as a milestone in the evolution of mainstream discourse in Singapore: that it is moving towards the use of arguments based on universally valid socio-political values" (132).[41]

TOWARD AN ALLIANCE

The backlash against the so-called politicizing of culture has not been the ideal means of revealing what such politicizing signifies, for it hides the extent to which "politics-talk" has served as a way in which those who deal with culture professionally can make a dramatic (some would say, desperate) claim for the public significance of their work, and hence for its public legitimacy. In other words, cultural politics has brought to the forefront an element of hidden normativity, or cryptonormativism, that was always already there in culture.[42] In an essay called "Given Culture: Rethinking Cosmopolitical Freedom in Transnationalism," Pheng Cheah suggests that cultural arguments against universality, especially transnational universality, are often inconsistent: "The critique of the false universalism of cosmopolitical culture already harbors a desire for access to a true universal. The argument for the autonomy of the local presupposes the universal value of autonomy and proposes to apply it to every particular group or collective unit . . . the truth of cultural relativism is multicultural universalism" (179–80).[43] If the ostensibly cultural always involves cryptonormativism, then perhaps the cultural version of the universal/particular conflict is actually a conflict not for or against normativity itself but rather between two units or scales of normativity, or even between units or scales that can be shown (like nationalism and internationalism) to overlap and thus are susceptible of resolution.

This is not to suggest that cultural innovation and social justice go naturally together, that the first must invariably work toward the second, or, still less, that culture unerringly supplies all the actions that social justice might ever require. It is merely to suggest that the old equation of poetry with unacknowledged legislation does not preclude an effort to produce *acknowledged* legislation. The concept of culture need not be aligned against such normative concerns as human rights. Flawed and limited as both concepts undoubtedly are, they are tools with which good work is already being done.

In his essay "Two Cheers for the Cultural Left," Rorty objects to talk about the "transformation" of society, which he takes to be "more or less synonymous with 'revolution.' . . . I am not sure I want to see our society revolutionized, to see our basic institutions replaced."[44] Whatever one's opinion of Rorty's unrepentantly liberal preference for reform over revolution, one has to agree that something strange is going on when, as he points out, the demand for total or revolutionary transformation migrates out of the world of politics (where, in the United States at least, no one seriously believes it is on the agenda) and takes up exclusive residence in the concept of culture. It is this displaced, desperate habit of mind on the cultural left that makes culture seem an all-or-nothing, take-it-or-leave-it proposition—in effect, beyond discussion or debate. But our political imperatives are too urgent, there is too much both at home and abroad that needs discussion if it is to be done, for us to take refuge in the all-or-nothing paradigm. When culture is invoked, it should, I think, be as one component of local circumstances—that is, in a sense that both insists on particular realities and remains open to further debate on common or universal grounds. It is only by remaining at least potentially open to criticism, by not hiding behind the absolute protection that Charles Taylor calls "incorrigibility," that it can help engage the international intricacies of power.

To Rorty, liberalism means the existence of "functioning mechanisms of social improvement which rely on persuasion rather than force."[45] This is, on one level, a false dichotomy. Persuasion *is* force, as the cultural left is fond of repeating, especially when the means of persuasion are controlled by powerful private-owned interests that are neither elected nor appointed. But there is as much diversity among forces as among cultures. And the differences are just as significant. Human rights internationalism today is the inheritor of liberal premises, and it does not promise satisfyingly revolutionary transformation. But it has become a force to be reckoned with—a force the cultural left would be mistaken not to reckon with, especially when our own persuasions are in quest of more forceful international modes, venues, and allies.

8

ROOT, ROOT, ROOT

MARTHA NUSSBAUM MEETS THE HOME TEAM

COSMOPOLITANISM AND BOREDOM

"In the course of my life," Joseph De Maistre famously observed, "I have seen Frenchmen, Italians, Russians; I even know, thanks to Montesquieu, that one can be a Persian; but *man* I have never met."[1] De Maistre's genteel snubbing of "man" is still remembered, and usually with satisfaction. But the propriety of this snub has never seemed so open to doubt. Even if one could assume, with De Maistre, that the abstract universal "man" is vague and ungraspable, recent history has made it difficult to pretend that it can be neatly opposed to particular nationalities, assumed to be palpable and real. Those Frenchmen De Maistre saw with his own eyes—are we sure they weren't Alsatians or Occitanians of uncertain allegiance and identity? Could it be that his Russians were not really

Russians at all but Ukrainians or Georgians, Chechens or Abkhasians, whose day of national recognition had not yet arrived—and when it arrived would be contested in turn? Nationality, it would appear, is also an artifice, a fragile historical generalization, rather than a given fact of nature. And precisely because France and Russia must be acknowledged to be abstractions, it is increasingly difficult to avoid at least a nodding acquaintance with "man," who is nothing but a heftier and more footloose abstraction.

This devious line of argument expresses some of my ambivalence about Martha Nussbaum's essay "Patriotism and Cosmopolitanism" and the other essays, gathered around it, in *For Love of Country: Debating the Limits of Patriotism*.[2] In part because of my discomfort with the universal "man," I did not set out with overwhelming sympathy for Nussbaum's version of the cosmopolitan project, that of educating people into a primary allegiance to what she calls "the worldwide community of human beings" (4). According to this Stoic and Kantian ideal, there can be only one cosmopolitanism, one "world citizenship," for there is only one "worldwide community of human beings." Paradoxically, then, Nussbaum can defend the rest against the West only by means of an unrepentant reassertion of Western philosophical universalism.[3]

I warmed somewhat to Nussbaum's argument, however, for two reasons. The first was a sense of sneaky incoherence in positions that, like De Maistre's, base their counterappeal on the unquestionable self-evidence of the particular. After all, it is not just an abstract, universal "man" but very particular groups of noncitizens who can be treated as if they were not there, and *are* treated as if they were not there, because of a code of intellectual courtesy that prides itself on recognizing only particulars. The unrecognized include, among the victims of the war in Vietnam, the Vietnamese war dead, estimated at twenty times the number of U.S. casualties yet uncommemorated even on Maya Lin's admirable monument. They include apparel workers in the Honduran *maquiladoras*, where TV entertainer Kathie Lee Gifford's Wal-Mart clothing line is produced.[4] These workers have now emerged from their convenient invisibility, but that does not mean anyone is factoring them into calculations of global well-being. And the unrecognized include the undocumented immigrants who were both central to California disputes about Proposition 187, which denied their rights, and utterly rejected from these disputes, even by critics of the proposition. Linda Bosniak reports "the near-complete omission from the public debate of one particular opposing argument which might have seemed, in theory, an obvious one to make; this is the argument that Prop. 187 should be rejected on the grounds that its treatment of undocumented aliens is unjust" to the aliens themselves (567).[5] What were argued instead were the ill effects of Proposition 187 for U.S. citizens; even progressives could find little or no room for the interests of noncitizens.

Yes, terms such as *man* and *humanity* fail to attract and, indeed, are often repellent. Who wants them at the party? Yet the social bonds they work to cement—the bonds of recognition between, say, U.S. citizens and particular groups of noncitizens—are not more abstract than domestic social bonds, among national citizens. And it is work that clearly has to be done, even if some might prefer it be done in another vocabulary.

A second reason for putting my doubts about Nussbaum's argument on hold was seeing what massive hostility that argument provoked and how alien I felt among Nussbaum's attackers—even though, or perhaps because, the arguments of her attackers disquietingly echo the epistemological modesty of the American cultural left—its insistence on the limits of rationality. Most of the essays in *For Love of Country* are less interesting as critiques of Nussbaum than as instances of an emergent form of American nationalism, suddenly visible against the stark background of her cosmopolitanism, that clearly has a certain charm for the left as well as the right.

To the rest of the world, American nationalism may still seem, first and foremost, a hypocritical version of idealist universalism. Its primary associations are with the borderless-world globalism, at once capitalist and electronic, that hypes McDonald's and MTV along with free markets and carefully selected human rights. But recently there has been a retrenchment, a circling of the wagons, a scale-down of American nationalism in the direction of *Realpolitik*. These days, many American policy makers and media pundits no longer bother to pretend that what is good for us is good for the world. With a menacing modesty, they are now content to champion one national interest against all others. The mood, as James Der Derian puts it, is neo-medieval.[6] And the flower of the national intelligentsia, at least as far as it is represented in this book, seems intent on declaring itself unwilling or incompetent to pass judgment on this melee from anywhere outside or above it. With a silent bow in the direction of postmodern commonplace, they seem to say that if there is indeed no metalanguage, no metadiscourse, then so much the better for us. This limitation on thought turns out to have unexpected benefits for the world's most powerful nation, which can present itself as just another tiny particular locked in battle with a tyrannical, totalizing universalism. Faced with criticism of their country from the outside, liberal and rightist intellectuals can claim the protection that the cultural left has been according to smaller and more vulnerable collectivities.

Unlike, for example, Alain Finkielkraut in *The Defeat of the Mind* or David Hollinger in *Postethnic America*, Martha Nussbaum does not set her cosmopolitan ideal against the perceived excesses of atavistic nationalists abroad or academic multiculturalists at home. *For Love of Country* began as an essay, in the *Boston Review* in late 1994, that protested against recent statements by Sheldon

Hackney, chairman of the National Endowment for the Humanities (NEH), and by the philosopher Richard Rorty. Hackney, speaking for the Clinton administration, had recently called for shared values and national unity to counter the threats of excessive pluralism. In the "Unpatriotic Academy" piece mentioned above (see especially chapter 7), Rorty had sternly cautioned the cultural left to show more deference to "the emotion of national pride."

Nussbaum, a distinguished classical scholar, can hardly be mistaken for one of those mythical multiculturalists who supposedly refuse to teach the Greeks. Indeed, her counterattack has nothing either multi- or cultural about it. No multiculturalist could have written, as she does, that "the accident of where one was born is just that, an accident" (7). For the cultural left, the culture one is born and raised in can hardly be deemed accidental. Whatever controversy may exist over *when* cultural diversity should matter, or *how* and *how much*, there is widespread agreement that, in one way or other, it *does* matter. But for Nussbaum, culture has nothing to do with moral worth; hence it is "morally irrelevant" (5). Her demand is not that greater reverence be paid to the diversity of cultures. What she wants is respect for a universal ethical standard.

Nussbaum thus resembles the cultural left only in that she, too, insists on obligations and commitments that do not stop at the borders of the nation.[7] But those obligations and commitments may provide a more significant marker of current political alignments than the usual clashes of philosophical position, including that between Kantian and communitarian political philosophies. At any rate, the refusal to recognize foreign obligations and commitments certainly gathers up her critics into a sudden and coherent collectivity. It is quite a spectacle. With few exceptions, liberals and conservatives join in a smooth, bipartisan consensus against Nussbaum's or, it seems, any challenge to the American nation. Michael Walzer, forgetting what Stalin did to those he called cosmopolitans, tries to tar cosmopolitanism with the brush of Stalinism. Foreigners cannot be granted the moral rights of fellow citizens, says Nathan Glazer; otherwise, we would be forced to allow an unlimited number of Third World refugees into the United States. (This is a neat bit of illogic, on a par with believing that socialism means having to share your toothbrush.) Our boat is full. But cosmopolitanism itself is empty: according to Robert Pinsky, who, not coincidentally, has been named poet laureate, cosmopolitanism is as empty of affect and constituency as Esperanto. Cosmopolitanism is "a view of the world that would be true only if people were not driven by emotions" (87).

Emotions are among the many local particulars that the respondents, following De Maistre's lead, throw in the face of Nussbaum's fidelity to "man." Benjamin Barber argues that to "bypass" the local is to end up "nowhere," in mere "abstraction and disembodiment" (34). For Gertrude Himmelfarb, cosmopolitanism "obscures and even denies . . . the givens of life: parents, ancestors, family, race, religion, heritage, history, culture, tradition, community—and nationality" (77). Many of the arguments in the book follow the curve of this last sentence. The local, intimate "givens" lined up before the dash—"parents, ancestors, family, race, religion," and so on—are identified with the term after the dash—*nationality*—so as to lend to the nation their warmth, inevitability, inviolability. Only the dash itself hints at an unbridgeable difference in scale and kind. Religion and nation-state, it is implied, are both local. Since religion deserves protection from state interference, it becomes an apparent argument for sheltering the U.S. state itself, suddenly radiant with borrowed divinity, from any critique of its behavior toward noncitizens.

It is customary to see the American academy as a sanctuary of secular intellectuals, sheltered from the often eccentric religiosity of the American majority. To judge from these responses, however, it would seem that academic opinion on U.S. nationalism—or the absence of acknowledgment that such nationalism exists—reflects with uncanny exactness the petulant sensitivity of the sectarian believer. There is more than one irony in this. Multiculturalism is often charged with an uncritical celebration of cultural givenness. But one finds a much cruder celebration of cultural givenness here, among writers who are mainly vehement opponents of multiculturalism, than in multiculturalism itself, where a shared interest in diversity tends to force at least some relativizing of everyone's given culture.

Nussbaum's own favored image for how local givens relate to concern for humanity is "concentric circles." Borrowed from the Stoics, this image minimizes conflict between humanity and the local, urging us merely to make the outermost circle (humanity as a whole) more like the innermost circle (self and family). Yet it does suggest, however gently, the need for an educative progress from narrower to broader loyalties. This is already too much of an either-or for most of the respondents. They insist, rightly enough, that larger loyalties need not preclude or replace smaller loyalties: "We will not love those distant from us more," Michael McConnell writes, "by loving those close to us less" (82). (Of course, as Charles Taylor observes, Americans have not thus far displayed abundant love toward those closest to them: "The widespread opposition to extremely modest national health care proposals in the United States doesn't seem to indicate that contemporary Americans suffer from too great a mutual commitment" [126].) It is absurd to think that most of us can or should spend our time trying to fight free of our national or local entanglements. Nussbaum herself notes that the local deserves priority in at least one ethical sense: it is in your power to affect it more directly, for example, as a parent. Mrs. Jellyby, the character in *Bleak House* who neglects her children in favor of what Charles

Dickens calls "telescopic philanthropy," remains an object lesson. Her eyes "had a curious habit of seeming to look a long way off," as Michael Sandel reminds us in his case against cosmopolitanism, "as if . . . they could see nothing nearer than Africa."[8] But in his frequently less familial moods, Dickens himself owed much of his success as a social analyst and reformer to distanced ways of thinking and speaking that could certainly be described as telescopic philanthropy.[9] And his Mr. Vholes in the same novel, the Chancery lawyer who endlessly reminds everyone that he both has and is a father, offers an opposite but equally instructive lesson in how tender solicitude for one's family can stand in the way of reform. Dickens sums up Vholes's position thus: "Make man-eating unlawful, and you starve the Vholeses!"

Like Mr. Vholes, Nussbaum's respondents in *For Love of Country* treat local attachments as peremptory and absolute. Neither cannibalism nor the Court of Chancery shall be outlawed, they imply, if such measures mean that their loved ones will eat one morsel less. Walzer writes, "My allegiances, like my relationships, start at the center" (126). Starting at the center, Walzer gives us no reason to believe that his allegiances will go any distance away from that center. Michael McConnell quotes Edmund Burke: "To love the little platoon we belong to in society is . . . the first link in the series by which we proceed toward a love to our country and to mankind" (79). McConnell does not address the question of whether we do, in fact, proceed in that direction, or proceed far enough. The actual platoons, companies, and battalions that America has sent out into the world give some cause to wonder.

Amy Gutmann argues, in a similar vein, that "asking us to choose between being, above all, citizens of our own society or, above all, citizens of the world" is "morally misguided and politically dangerous" (71). But if choosing is not always called for, can one not at least acknowledge that sometimes it may be? Along with the necessity of choice, Gutmann and most of the others throw out even its hypothetical possibility. Thus they refuse to confront the core of Nussbaum's case, which is simply that loyalty to one's nation can and sometimes does contradict the manifest demands of justice as seen from any extranational perspective, even a subuniversalistic one. They acknowledge no moral or political leverage against the profound rootedness of caring first and always for our own.

Many of the respondents balk at being asked to treat strangers as lovingly as they would treat their own family or friends. One can see their point. As Elaine Scarry argues, it is quite possible that the confusion of strangers with friends is both unnecessary and a mistake. You don't have to pull off the neat trick of relating to the world's distant peoples with full imaginative and emotional intensity in order to lobby for better policies with respect to their well-being. And feeling obliged to try may lead you to neglect the legal machinery of the state, with which cosmopolitans must be glad to cooperate when they can, as well as NGOs operating in the politically ambiguous but increasingly material domain of international civil society. A third alternative would involve thinking of distant strangers neither as objects of loving concern nor as objects of policy but as interlocutors with whom one must enter into dialogue, common participants in a transnational public sphere whose goal would be some sort of coordinated action. This path might seem a mild, unthreatening extension of existing belief in participatory democracy. But the theorists of American democracy represented in *For Love of Country* decline to venture down it. "American patriotism," Benjamin Barber asserts defiantly, is "itself the counter to the very evils Nussbaum associates with American patriotism" (31).

Barber's patriotism, like the constitutional patriotism of Habermas, resembles the antidote to ethnic nationalism that Michael Ignatieff and others have called "civic nationalism": "The only guarantee that ethnic groups will live side by side in peace is shared loyalty to a state." This remains the crucial concept allowing Americans (and a few deluded others, such as Elie Kedourie) to deny that there is nationalism in the United States at all. But respect for the Constitution unfortunately guarantees very little. Quiet and constitutional rather than ethnic or tribal, American nationalism arguably has been and remains one of the world's most dangerous.

Whatever may be said on behalf of constitutional patriotism, it is of little use to noncitizens and nonresidents, especially those who are touched by U.S. power without living on U.S. soil. Even the most judicious interpretation of the Constitution will not make it protect those who stand outside it. Internally, constitutional patriotism may calm things down, shielding the status quo against bloody outbreaks of ethnic violence. But it cannot speak to the desperate need to *change* the status quo that is Nussbaum's point of departure. To get the haves mobilized behind a significant transfer of resources to the have-nots, you need more than even a cosmopolitan extension of decorous constitutionalism. You need something like religious fervor.

The true opposite of such fervor is not constitutionalism, however, but boredom. On the defensive from the outset, Nussbaum repeatedly rejects the charge that cosmopolitanism is as "boringly flat" (17) as it may seem. But this is a point that can be made more aggressively. Nussbaum could have said that boredom and indifference name the truth not about cosmopolitanism but about nationalism; for in countries such as the United States, at least, nationalism may do the most damage today not by its racist and xenophobic enthusiasms, real as these are, but rather because it encourages inertia, compassion fatigue, a normalizing of our all-too-human satedness with the demands of the distant, even when distant events are nothing but the sensational result of everyday domestic policy.

Strangely enough, many of Nussbaum's respondents seem to agree that the single largest cause of the world's curable unhappiness today is global capitalism. (More concerned with ethics than with politics, Nussbaum herself implies this but does not state it explicitly.) Indeed, they engage her in a spirited game of "more anticapitalist than thou." They accuse her of naively ignoring the complicities between her cosmopolitan ethics and "the market-driven globalism currently being promoted by transnational corporations and banks" (57). More damningly still, they treat her cosmopolitanism as if it were simply global capital's official line.

This pervasive style of romantic anticapitalism is worth pausing over. It looks very much like the dominant, academically respectable form that American nationalism is coming to assume. One distinctive feature is that capitalism is attacked only or primarily when it can be identified with the global. Capitalism is treated as if it came from somewhere else, as if Americans derived no benefit from it—as if, rather than being penetrated and, to a large extent, defined by many decades of capitalist development, American society and American nationalism were among its pitiable victims. Again and again, the case against cosmopolitanism is framed as a call to renew "our various intact moral communities" (84), to defend vestigial enclaves against an outside seen as chill and inhospitable. By refusing to acknowledge that these warm insides are heated and provisioned by that cold outside, these avowedly anticapitalist critics allow the consequences of capitalism to disappear from the national sense of responsibility. McDonald's and the IMF could not ask for better protection from ethical scrutiny.

The second distinctive feature of this supposed anticapitalism is that economic suffering registers only or primarily when it can be blamed on the globalists. One example among many is the demagogic description of cosmopolitanism as "the village of the liberal managerial class" (87). Class is indeed an issue worth raising here. But if they are so interested, why do her respondents want nothing to do with Nussbaum's numbers, the relative and absolute indicators of one population's wealth and another's desperate, almost unfathomable misery? If life expectancy is age 78.2 in Sweden and age 39 in Sierra Leone— with recent events in Sierra Leone, I'm sure the figures are now even worse— then "we are all going to have to do some tough thinking," as Nussbaum says, "about the luck of birth and the morality of transfers of wealth from richer to poorer nations" (135). Who among her respondents talks about transfers of wealth? Who offers to explain why such ideas are aborted in the richer nations before they can even be proposed, victims of an ethical ennui or paralysis that is, perhaps, the truest face of nationalism in the so-called developed world?

Almost none of Nussbaum's respondents concedes any connection between the unbearably unequal distribution of the world's resources and the future shape of American society. Only a few (Richard Falk, Amartya Sen, Immanuel Wallerstein) enter critically and constructively into Nussbaum's project by extending it beyond the domain of the ethical. No one at all, including Nussbaum herself, invokes or even questions the hypothesis that the riches of the West were and are produced by the active underdeveloping of those areas of the world that are now the poorest, and that the demand for redistribution is thus not a plea for benevolent humanitarianism but merely for restitution.

Pinning hopes for change on moral reasoning directed to the free individual conscience, as Nussbaum does, is not a self evident mistake. For a rich country such as the United States, despite our glaring and increasing inequalities, more equitable redistribution on a global scale would certainly entail some sacrifice in living standards, some willingness to postpone or dilute self-interest, even for ordinary or (as we say) "middle-class" people. In the United States, then, Nussbaum's high-minded universalism may prove a paradoxically necessary way of getting down to the grassroots, where "fairness" and the moral autonomy of the individual are influential notions. One might also flesh out Nussbaum's cosmopolitanism in another way. In her book *The Limits of Citizenship*, the sociologist Yasemin Soysal offers a kind of empirical translation of Nussbaum's case. Describing the transnational mechanisms that are already in place for the protection of guest workers in Europe who do not become citizens—for their contested but statistically impressive assimilation, without benefit of citizenship, into the apparatus of the various welfare states and the European Union—Soysal speaks of "a reconfiguration of citizenship from a more particularistic one based on nationhood to a more universalistic one based on personhood" (137), that is, based on human rights. In effect, Soysal complements Nussbaum's argument by suggesting that, at least in Europe, "man" is taking some hesitant steps toward acquiring just that institutional concreteness or grounding that, until now, has seemed reserved for particular nations.[10]

Perhaps Nussbaum's high moral line can be seen, rhetorically, as an oblique but practical means of addressing unnamed social collectivities. Still, one would like to know more about the collectivities—domestic or transnational, given or elective—that might be capable of translating her moral universalism into a historical force. Nussbaum is uninterested in this question, even when such collectivities are transnational rather than domestic and thus potential vehicles for or embodiments of cosmopolitan ideas like her own. And she is uninterested in negotiating the messy, soiling compromises between the normative and the descriptive that would inevitably follow from engagement with these collectivities. The only agent that can sustain the unblemished purity of the normative is, of course, "man." Nussbaum's love for this bulky figure is understandable. But as I suggested throughout this book, this is perhaps a moment for transnational politics to turn from Kant to Hegel, that is, from the purity of the normative to the impurity of the already existing, to cosmopolitanisms in the plural that include non-European, nonelitist, and ineligible versions. These lesser abstractions—ethnic minorities, diasporas, religions, worker solidarity movements, feminist and ecological organizations, and even (why not?) sovereign states—may attract passionate feelings toward cosmopolitan aims without the pretension to absolute universality. No less transnational than humanity, these actually existing cosmopolitanisms offer some reason to hope they will be more politically effectual.

ROOTING AND REALISM

Are we so sure that cosmopolitanism, as the poet laureate affirms, is "a view of the world that would be true only if people were not driven by emotions"? Consider the equal and opposite cliché that has emerged from the new globalism. In a personal experience of the so-called CNN effect, U.S. diplomat George F. Kennan awoke in December 1992 to watch American soldiers landing in Somalia, on a beach where reporters were already waiting to interview them. "If American policy from here on out, particularly policy involving the use of our armed forces abroad, is to be controlled by popular emotional impulses, and particularly ones provoked by the commercial television industry," Kennan wrote, "then there is no place not only for myself, but for what have traditionally been regarded as the responsible deliberative organs of our government."[11] Thanks to a new complicity between the media and foreign policy, the latter has passed out of the control of "responsible deliberative organs of our government," Kennan laments, and under the irresponsible sway of "popular emotional impulses." This is also Paul Virilio's reading of democracy in the era of the global village: "The space of politics in ancient societies was the public space (square, forum, agora . . .). Today the public image has taken over public space. Television has become the forum for all emotions and all options. . . . There is no politics possible at the speed of light . . . what is proper to democracy is the sharing of power. When there is no longer time to share, what do we share? Emotions."[12]

Outside the nation, say Virilio and Kennan, there is no time for deliberation—there is only emotion. On the contrary, say Nussbaum's respondents, outside the nation there is only a bloodless, abstract reason, utterly empty of emotion. Both groups cannot be right, though both might well be wrong. If emotion can be tied with equal facility to the national and the extranational, there are grounds to suspect that the real issue lies elsewhere. Kennan is worried that emotions relevant to foreign policy can suddenly bypass the customary restraints and authorities that politics as usual has slowly accreted, and that continue to dictate domestic policy. Nussbaum's respondents seem to assume that it is emotion itself that has built up these customary restraints and authorities, and that it is reason which, roving too freely abroad, threatens to give them the slip. But whether it is reason that needs to restrain flighty emotion or emotion that needs to grip and ground a dangerously nomadic reason, the site where the gripping, grounding, and restraining is called for is the same: the nation. These opposite invocations of reason and emotion hide a common anxiety: that extranational outflowings of reason and emotion might turn out to be "proper to democracy," in Virilio's phrase, and thus hard for a democratic polity to disavow, while they also stretch democracy uncomfortably, cracking the joints of the "national interest"—at least, as it has been commonly understood.

Though Virilio speaks in its name, democracy for him seems less an unfulfilled promise than an existing achievement. In speeding politics up, the media have allowed politics to overextend itself in space. Outside its proper, designated spaces—the agora and the nation—politics ceases to function. Until it was threatened by the new transnational emotionality, while it remained within its older, national limits, democratic tradition had apparently functioned well enough. This is certainly Kennan's assumption. Used to a certain leadership within the government's "responsible deliberative organs," Kennan takes for granted that responsible deliberation was once the rule. Were he a representative of some other, smaller nation instead of the grand old man of American diplomacy, his frank admission of media-induced redundancy ("there is no place . . . for myself") might invite a parallel between his "realism" and Mary Kaldor's analysis of the new nationalism in Eastern Europe as "a reaction to the growing impotence and declining legitimacy of the established political classes. From this perspective, it is a nationalism fostered from above" (49).[13]

Looking down from above, Kennan seems to fear excessive or uncontrolled democracy: enormous new quantities of opinion demanding to be taken into consideration, uninformed by expert, specialized knowledge but shaped, on the contrary, by the superficial and sensational reporting of the "commercial television industry." Television seems an unlikely source of this threat to proper decision making, given the notorious degree to which the media are under not only corporate control but the control of just four gigantic corporations: General Electric, Time Warner, Disney/Cap Cities, and Westinghouse.[14] Television matters, of course, but it also makes an easy target for anxieties that extend far beyond it. Kennan uses much the same language in relation to current media impact as was heard in the pretelevision past against proposals to extend the suffrage to blacks, women, the poor: the weak and uninstructed are vulnerable to sensational appeals. If democracy is enlarged, the nation will be at risk.

After the blind furies of the cold war, there is something to be said for Kennan's quietly elitist nationalism. Though it was he who authored the "containment" doctrine, the "great wall" of anticommunism that defined the cold war, he was opposed to any anticommunist intervention in China, as he was later to the U.S. misadventure in Vietnam. So it makes some sense that his brand of realism has recently been proposed (for example, in John Judis's book *Grand Illusion*)[15] as the proper antithesis of cold war evangelicalism, with its bipolar simplifications and the out-of-control emotionality they encouraged. Still, it helps to be reminded that Kennan "dismissed China and the rest of the Third World as unsuitable objects of policy," as Anders Stephanson says, because "so far as he was concerned, these regions were of no particular importance in the greater scheme of things and were basically unknowable anyway" (115). "The continuous disintegration of the Chinese regime, however lamentable, was thus a matter of indifference."[16] Presumably, realism would also produce indifference to Somalia and Rwanda, though not to Bosnia, the Caribbean, or Latin America.

The tradition of high moralistic pronouncements and free-market missionary zeal for which the United States is known around the world, all so weirdly disconnected from actual American foreign policy, can make a turn toward indifference look healthy. Acknowledging its own limited self-interest, the United States could acknowledge the limited self-interest of other states and, conceivably, let up a bit in its habit of preaching to them. Ethically, this sounds like a step in the right direction. However, aside from how consistent *Realpolitik* has always been with America's aggressive interference in its self-declared areas of interest, there is also the inconvenient fact that in taking the nation and nationalism for granted, realism would commit itself to some rather alarming ethical postulates. It would encourage people to identify themselves exclusively or primarily with their nation-states, as if no other primary identification were possible. It would mark off some large zones of indifference. And, to quote Thomas Pogge, it would fortify Americans in "the moral conviction that there is nothing seriously wrong, morally speaking, with the lives we lead" (273). The least one can say is that this will do nothing about what Pogge calls "the abundantly documented facts of widespread extreme deprivations and disadvantages" (273) elsewhere in the world.[17]

Consider the "warlord," a term that has been much in the news since the end of the Cold War. Both lexically and conceptually, the term "warlord" seems to fit the anti-visionary vision of fragmented, bitterly pragmatic international relations that Der Derian refers to as "neo-medievalism."[18] In this context, it seems to consecrate a necessary, realistic indifference, a tight scarcity economy both of acting and of caring. If it's a jungle out there, an amoral battleground where force is everything, then all we can do is look out for ourselves and our near and dear ones without asking universalistic questions about right, wrong, or the general welfare and without otherwise extending our engagements to anything too far away. Some might object that the quiet, elitist game of *Realpolitik* does not adapt well to Orwellian mass mobilizations of the "two minute hate" variety, and realism cannot win mass popularity.[19] But it is hard to believe there is an inherent complicity between mass media and evangelical foreign policy. For better or worse, the media seem perfectly capable of popularizing a shift from cold war moralism to a scaled-back, amoral brand of nationalism. Among the media vehicles of this new nationalism, for example, is the popular genre of violent, neomedievalist science fiction, such as the *Alien* movies and *Predator*, where postmodern knights and cyborg creatures struggle on a darkling plain, neither exhibiting emblems of good nor expecting to encounter emblems of evil, where victory often means only self-preservation. (This is also the burden of Tom Nairn's refreshingly minimalist case for nationalism as survival—a case on behalf of those who simply "fear disappearance.")[20] The numerically massive model of sports fandom also qualifies as such a vehicle. Here, identifications of self and other are presumed to be as natural and unideological as rooting for your team for no reason other than that it is yours.[21] I will say more about rooting and roots in a moment.

In Somalia, as it happens, "one team among others" is not what the term *warlord* has come to suggest. We were told that the Somali people were starving in a land of feuding warlords, without a government, because they had warlords *instead* of a government.[22] Like the drug lord, the warlord is a useful post–cold war scapegoat because it does not stand for the sovereign nation-state; it is the Other of the nation-state. According to the Oxford English Dictionary (OED), "warlord" may be a translation of *Kriegsherr*, one title of the German emperor. What is sure is that, though it sounds feudal, the term *warlord* was invented in the nineteenth century. It was invented in this period of nationalism and progress, one might conclude, to sanctify the nation *as* progress. The first citation in the OED is from Emerson in 1856: "Piracy and war gave place to trade, politics, and letters; the war-lord to the law-lord." Whether supranational emperor or subnational potentate, in other words, the warlord is supposed to belong to a Hobbesian past of brute force and disorder that has now been rendered obsolete by the nation-state.[23] Whether larger or smaller than the nation-state, the concept implies that violence is illegitimate when it falls into the hands of what is not the state, while legitimacy means the state's effective monopoly of violence—this monopoly being even less effective today than it was in the past.[24]

Neo-medievalism is such a suggestive term for postmodern or late capitalist international relations, according to Der Derian, because it recognizes, as realism does not, that nation-states can no longer be presumed to be the natural or rightful actors. But this is just the lesson post–cold war discourse has been trying to avoid, especially when it speaks of warlords. As the anomaly of brute force in the midst of a civilization guaranteed by nation-states, the warlord backs up the increasingly fragile equation of civilization with the state, thus permitting the state to back up its charity with its own brute force, *rather than by any other means.* The identification of Somalia with warlords, and of warlords with barbaric violence, avoids any obligation to negotiate with the socioeconomic organization of the "clan," let alone any larger social organization with a potential claim to social legitimacy on the national (or even more than national) level. Who has spoken to or even about peace-loving elements in Somalia that might have been supported without the intervention of U.S. or UN troops? Did anyone even look for them?

Such an inquiry would not be unprecedented. China in the 1930s, when Edgar Snow sought out the distant and almost unknown Mao Zedong, was the very paradigm of the nonnation: disintegrated empire on the one hand, warlords, bandits, and starvation on the other. For Snow, it is true, warlords figured as power centers that Chiang Kai-shek could not control, and who thus proved Chiang was less than a national leader. But they were also strategic allies in the struggle against the Japanese, and even allies of the Communist Party against Chiang. In short, they were not simple figures of barbarism and disorder. With them, as with Mao himself, Snow could make the same imaginative leap that Eric Hobsbawm makes in his *Bandits*; for Hobsbawm notes that Mao, "powerfully influenced by the native tradition of popular resistance," was quite self-conscious in aligning himself with Chinese bandit-guerrillas of the past.[25] Snow's was an exemplary act of cosmopolitan vision. It arrived at a prophecy about the future of the Chinese nation by paying attention to local matters that did not seem to fit a national model and would take many years to show up on the grid of America's "national interest."

TWO LOVE STORIES:
THE HOME AND THE WORLD AND *THE ENGLISH PATIENT*

At the beginning of "Patriotism and Cosmopolitanism," Nussbaum sums up the position she is arguing against by retelling the plot of Rabindranath Tagore's novel *The Home and the World*. As Nussbaum retells it, "the young wife Bimala, entranced by the patriotic rhetoric of her husband's friend Sandip," is seduced away from the cosmopolitan coolness of her husband, Nikhil, who reserves his worship, he says, "for Right which is far greater than my country" (3). Although an early supporter of the Swadeshi movement and its boycott of foreign goods, the husband was not sufficiently enthusiastic about the *Bande Mataram*, or "Hail Motherland," spirit that infused it. Such people are habitually, if wrongly, judged to be "boring, flat, [and] lacking in love" (17). His wife's passion flows instead toward nationalism and the nationalist.

Since Nussbaum says nothing about the gender politics of this text, it is perhaps not surprising that her respondents do not mention it either. Yet the assumption that emotion is born at home—which her respondents take to mean that, emotionally speaking, cosmopolitanism will always be a losing proposition—joins with the circumstance that the home has been the woman's sphere to imply that emotional investments in nationalism or cosmopolitanism will depend on what women are, or (in *The Home and the World*) on what Tagore thinks women really feel. It seems worth speculating that the superimposition of a gendered love triangle on the issue of nationalism and cosmopolitanism (wife/lover torn between cosmopolitan husband and nationalist seducer) probably predetermines the outcome in a way that says as much about gender as about nationalism. According to novelist E. M. Forster, Tagore "meant the wife to be seduced by the World, which is, with all its sins, a tremendous lover."[26] In fact, as Forster also notes, the world in this larger sense is never allowed into the novel.[27] What seduces Bimala is a smaller thing. Though Nikhil announces that he is trying to liberate Bimala from the woman's traditional position in the home, he also wants her to remain a woman—or rather, what he recognizes as a woman. In the sense that woman has been defined in and by the home, he wants her to stay close to home. And that is just what her passion for nationalism permits her to do.

"The home," Partha Chatterjee suggests, "was . . . the original site on which the hegemonic project of nationalism was launched."[28] Of course, some of the seduced wife's new emotions suggest a worldly liberation; nationalism offers Bimala a space in which she can both reanimate traditional female identifications and intuit unforeseen potential for herself. But more often, her new feelings merely extend and reinforce her subordination within the patriarchal home. Hearing Sandip's oratory, Bimala has "a feeling of worship"; her passion, acting the part of her seducer, "made as though it would tear me up by the roots, and drag me along by the hair" (68). To be dragged by the hair is not to be torn from her roots; it is to remain rooted in the posture of worship from which her husband aspires to release her. Bimala's dalliance with nationalism is a simple reflection of Nikhil's own desire for her to retain (but this time by freely choosing) the status of wife. Ironically, this recoding of the submission Bimala has already been taught involves submission to a power like her husband but still stronger than her husband. Just as Nikhil's political aspirations for the welfare of his tenants are couched in paternalist terms, so his and his creator's aspirations for change at home remain patriarchal, even if neither can be happy with the results.

This line of thinking suggests that cosmopolitanism is a loser only to the extent that the project of democracy itself fails, foundering over the mixed motives of its proponents. If the nationalism of the Swadeshi movement represented a kind of "home rule" in a double sense, as Chatterjee suggests, projecting into the political arena the values of the traditional home, then in sexual and class terms, it was not the democratic movement it seemed. Ranajit Guha's essay "Discipline and Mobilize" makes just this argument. Guha revalues the critique of the Swadeshi movement offered by Tagore, "who had done more than any other of its leaders to generate the enthusiasm of its initial phase" (122). The real issue that Tagore was addressing, Guha writes, was "the balance of force and consent in nationalist practice" (122). Tagore's Nikhil is a landlord, and he is wounded at the end by his tenants; the familiar identification of cosmopolitanism with class superiority seems firmly in place. But according to Guha, the real issue for Tagore was that Swadeshi was being promoted by "blackmail, deceit, assault, and plain robbery" (109). "It goes without saying that no mobilization based on such violence could have any claim to popular consent. . . . Social coercion was, for Tagore, at least as obnoxious as physical coercion" (110). Moreover, coercion often took the form of "caste sanction" (111). "The ancient and conservative ideology of caste came to be grafted on a developing nationalism supposed to be modern and progressive" (120). The necessity for coercion was inscribed in this choice of conservative means. It was the movement's "social conservatism" (111), its eagerness to protect the existing social hierarchy, that obliged it to use force in order to achieve a popular mobilization it could not achieve by consent, that is, by offering the Indian masses a radical change in Indian social structure.[29] What might look like antielitism in the nationalist response against Tagore and his character Nikhil is thus, in fact, a defense of elite privilege. In the specific situation dealt with in *The Home and the World*, Tagore's cosmopolitanism is superior to the nationalism of the Swadeshi movement, for Guha, because it is more, not less, democratic.

This is a point that can be generalized. "Not so long ago," Neil Lazarus writes, "to speak of Vietnam or Cuba or Algeria or Guinea-Bissau . . . was to conjure up the spectre of national liberation. . . . Today, things are very different. It is not so much that the setbacks and defeats that have had to be endured throughout Africa and Asia have been bitter and severe, though that is certainly true. Rather, contemporary theorists tend to argue that the national liberation movements never were what they were" (39).[30] Lazarus quotes Guha on "the failure of the Indian bourgeoisie to speak for the nation" (37). But what Guha means by this phrase is just what Lazarus is arguing against: "that the national liberation movements never were what they were." If I read Guha correctly, he is saying that in the Indian case, the national liberation movement indeed never was what it was, never was a proper or genuine movement of national liberation. There was, of course, a peasant nationalism, but the nationalist elites could only intermittently claim to speak for it. The successful nationalist movement that won India its independence in 1947 is also the movement that produced the unspeakable horrors of Partition. These horrors cannot be conveniently attributed either to British colonial tactics or to the more distant agency of global capital; they result from the failure of national elites to mobilize the mass of the Indian population, to rally the nation around a program of radical social change that would have jeopardized the elite's own place in the social hierarchy. This is the legacy of anticolonial nationalism that has stalled social change in India and Pakistan—that continues to define the present. In short, the interests of democracy do not demand eternal respect or affection for the brands of nationalism that have produced the system of states presently in force, including the former colonies.

"I have my desire to be fascinated," Bimala says, "and fascination must be supplied to me in bodily shape by my country" (38). Fascination, even democratic fascination, can come in very different bodily shapes. It does not necessarily take the shape of countries. It can come in the shape of lovers, but also in the shape of teams. Teams are offered as an example in Timothy Brennan's *At Home in the World*, which picks up both Tagore's title and the argument with Nussbaum. "To understand and appreciate the values of all humans," Brennan writes, "is to understand what Nussbaum does not: the rights of small nations—patriotism and all—including that embarrassing, but sizable, variant of socialist nationalism that is also an internationalism."[31] Small nations are underdogs and have the right to patriotism; large nations, apparently, do not. Brennan opposes cosmopolitanism on the grounds that it is "the way in which a kind of American patriotism is today being expressed" (26). Along with the difference between small and large nations, Brennan demands respect for "key distinctions" between, for instance, "the patriotic carnival of the 1984 Los Angeles Olympics" and "the 1995 South African Rugby World Cup in which mostly white players embraced the new South Africa of Nelson Mandela" (25).

But why should these distinctions be respected? To what exactly are they "key"? The fact that socialist nationalism is "sizable"—if this is, indeed, a fact—is surely no more of a guarantee that it is desirable than the size of the United States is a guarantee that its patriotism is undesirable. (India is not a

ROOT, ROOT, ROOT: MARTHA NUSSBAUM

"small" nation either.) The real markers of desirability here are terms such as *socialist* and *democracy*, not size. Presumably, what Brennan is trying to say is that the United States is a more powerful nation than others and has often used that power against socialism and democracy elsewhere—fair enough. But the historical record does not favor any other holders of power. To judge from the troubled decades since decolonization, dividing the world into good nations and bad nations has not been a very rewarding mode of political analysis, especially for those who take the fortunes of socialism and democracy to heart. It seems perverse to agree in advance that, as long as it retains its comparative strength, the United States will always play the bad nation, and that no political events within or outside its borders can pry it loose from that role. Can infallible political bearings really be taken anywhere in the world from this fixed point? Does it provide any useful guidance for political movements inside the United States?

If the symbolic uniting of different races behind a common purpose is worthy of celebration in South Africa—this does not go without saying—then perhaps it is also worthy of celebration in the United States. Moving displays of sports-related cross-racial solidarity are not hard to come by in the United States. Indeed, it is just such an example that Robert Pinsky offers in evidence against Martha Nussbaum. What Pinsky asks us to call patriotism is his feeling for the old Brooklyn Dodgers, "the team of Jackie Robinson and of Roy Campanella, the Italian-African-American catcher."[32] There are more accurate ways to describe fandom in Brooklyn, but for better or worse, the breaking of the color line in major-league baseball is probably just the sort of thing that Americans think of when they think affectionately of their nation. According to Benedict Anderson (following the lead of Leslie Fiedler on James Fenimore Cooper and Mark Twain), nothing could be more characteristic of North American nationalism than "imaginings of fraternity" across a racial divide. "Male-male bondings" of black and white do not so much represent a "national eroticism," Anderson suggests, as "an eroticized nationalism."[33]

Anderson himself is studiously neutral on the question of whether there is anything to celebrate in this eroticized nationalism, and both his neutrality and his analysis of nationalism's emotional power can be taken one step further. Given the argument thus far, one could predict the hesitant and equivocal emergence of an internationalist parallel: an eroticizing of bonds not just across different races within one nation but across different nations. And that is just what one finds in Michael Ondaatje's novel *The English Patient*.[34] Behind the glamorous heterosexual love story that occupies the film version is a homosocial love story of male bonding in the novel: a story of the fraternal solidarity of men in the desert, exploring together, though they come from nations soon to be at war, sharing and then losing a consciousness that is explicitly and passionately antinational: "Everywhere there was war. Suddenly there were 'teams.' The Bermanns, the Bagnolds, the Slatin Pashas—who had at various times saved each other's lives—had now split up into camps" (168). Nations are the novel's only villains. "We were German, English, Hungarian, African—all of us insignificant to them [the desert tribes]. Gradually we became nationless. I came to hate nations. We are deformed by nation-states. Madox died because of nations." (138) The death of Madox, Almásy's English friend and fellow explorer, is a moral touchstone to which the novel returns repeatedly. Madox, says the Hungarian Almásy, was a "man I loved more than any other man" (240). In 1939 he returned to England, "heard the sermon in honour of war, pulled out his desert revolver and shot himself."

Of course, this is also a heterosexual love story. But *The English Patient*, unlike *The Home and the World*, casts the cosmopolitan as the successful lover. This time, it is the cuckolded husband who represents the nation. Moreover, by means of the romanticized desert locale, Ondaatje's novel inscribes the lover's principled cosmopolitanism into his sexual appeal. While the husband turns out to be an agent of the British government, Almásy stands against nations and against domesticity: "The desert could not be claimed or owned" (138). "Erase the family name! Erase nations! I was taught such things by the desert" (139). Surprisingly and refreshingly, the values that link him to the other men are the same values that link him to Katharine Clifton. And they also separate him from her. "You slide past everything," she tells him, "with your fear and hate of ownership, of owning, of being owned, of being named. You think this is a virtue. I think you are inhuman" (238). But this inhumanity, this promise of a life outside both nation and home, is the real center of Almásy's sexiness. "All of us, even those with European homes and children in the distance, wished to remove the clothing of our countries" (139). This nakedness is what draws her, investing the removal of clothing, the descriptions of bodies and sexuality, with the desert's rich emptiness. Her lover's nakedness also eventually drives Katharine back, in muted private parallel with public preparations for war, to her husband and her nation. Still, it is important that, rather than another banal instance of the woman who breaks up an ideal male fraternity (and dies for it), this male-female romance resembles the male-male romance in being set against the stupidity of national belonging and national hatred—specifically and self-consciously, if also temporarily and ambivalently, cosmopolitan.

This transnational fraternity's hostility to the home implies that, as one would expect, it is ultimately ineligible as a moral cosmopolitanism in other ways. The passage about Madox's death follows immediately on another story,

ROOT, ROOT, ROOT: MARTHA NUSSBAUM

in which Almásy tells of visiting the tent of a fellow explorer and finding, tied up in his bed, "a small Arab girl" (138). This story is not treated as a moral touchstone, but it serves as a tangible reminder that alternatives to domesticity do not always improve on it. This version of transnational bonding also transparently depends on "a half-invented world of the desert" (150)—in other words, on the presumption that the desert is populated by fellow nomads, who have no interest in nations and no national hatred of the invasive Europeans. It depends on a massive denial of the anticolonial resistance that was a historical fact of the prewar period.

But in the ending of the novel, this denial is registered and undone. A national or anti-imperial feeling gets the last word. And this word can also be claimed for internationalism.

Kip, the Sikh defuser of bombs, is another of the novel's "international bastards" (176). Indeed, he offers a sustained parallel to Almásy. His Madox is a fellow sapper named Hardy, whom he, too, loses to the war. Kip lives in a style that can also be described as inhuman. Though he belongs to an army, it is not the army of his nation, and he, too, communicates as fully and readily with his enemies as with those for whom he is fighting: "His only human and personal contact was this enemy who had made the bomb and departed" (105). Burnt in the crash of his plane, Almásy becomes "a man with no face" (48); Kip is metaphorically faceless, "a result of being the anonymous member of another race" (196). Like Almásy, he is part of a fanatically loyal band, detached from ordinary humanity: "The sappers kept to themselves for the most part. They were an odd group as far as character went, somewhat like people who worked with jewels or stone, they had a hardness and clarity within them, their decisions frightening even to others in the same trade. Kip had witnessed that quality among gem-cutters but never in himself, though he knew others saw it there" (110). This is the same hardness and clarity that Kip appreciates in the statues and murals he seeks out in Italian churches, artworks that he examines through the tools of his trade: a rifle sight, a flare. Italian art is to him what the desert is to Almásy: compelling because of its cold, inhuman transcendence of national rivalries and their mortal consequences. And his love affair with Hana, like Almásy's with Katharine Clifton, builds on and expresses these cosmopolitan attractions. The film, for once finding an appropriate equivalent to the novel, treats us to a wonderful love scene: Hana is hoisted up by her lover to the ceiling of a church, a military flare burning in her hand, to inspect the paintings that are invisible from the ground. She rises to an unusual height in order to see up close, swinging like a child to make contact with something that transcends the rivalry between nations.

But the end of this affair is different. Almásy's great love ends with a reassertion of the rights of national proprietorship, both within Katharine and with the onset of World War II. Almásy assents to none of this. Kip leaves Hana when he hears that the atomic bomb has been dropped on Hiroshima and Nagasaki. The enemy of bombs, he realizes he has been helping the worst bombers of all. "They would never have dropped such a bomb on a white nation" (286). Kip goes back to being Kirpal Singh, who "does not know what he is doing here" (287). He assents to an alienness that he had earlier refused. And in so doing, he briefly becomes a voice for all the Arabs whose silencing made possible the cosmopolitan fantasy of a mapless desert. It's no wonder that all this is cut out of the film.

But this does not mean that the novel backs down from its cosmopolitanism. The identity of "Sikh" to which Kip returns is pointedly subnational, and, of course, an allusion to divisions within the nation that have made the world news. The self-identification as "Asian" that he acquires, thinking of the victims at Hiroshima and Nagasaki, is larger than national. In acting on both, he also acts out the cosmopolitan advice he has been receiving throughout the novel. Caravaggio, another cosmopolitan, asks, "What is he doing fighting English wars?" (122). One might say that in the ending, Kip merely politicizes the detachment from national conflict that has already defined him and that has aligned him with the apolitical Almásy.

It is tempting to think of Almásy, burned beyond national recognition and eager to die for his countrylessness, as a sort of cosmopolitan saint—an inhuman incarnation of the nationless "humanity" that De Maistre claims never to have met. He is actually a martyr to love, rather than to internationalism. And yet that is perhaps just the reason for considering him as an irreverent candidate for commemoration in whatever postnational monument may one day succeed the Tomb of the Unknown Soldier. Benedict Anderson's point about these national monuments is that they are reverenced because they are "either deliberately empty or no one knows who lies inside them." We do not want to know that, up close, love of one's country may look like a very different sort of love, or no love at all. Thus "one has only to imagine the general reaction to the busybody who 'discovered' the Unknown Soldier's name or insisted on filling the cenotaph with some real bones. Sacrilege of a strange, contemporary kind!" (9). Lately, Americans have been treated to the suggestion that Ronald Reagan's henchmen may have deliberately covered up the identity of Lieutenant Michael J. Blassie, shot down over Vietnam in 1972, in order to install his remains in the Tomb of the Unknowns.[35] There does not seem to have been a general sense of outrage, even against the behavior of the Reagan administration, which

ROOT, ROOT, ROOT: MARTHA NUSSBAUM

is known to have done worse. In *The English Patient*, it is discovered that the "English patient" is a Hungarian who has aided the enemy, and this, too, makes no difference, either to his fellow characters or to readers who vicariously share his passion. Small signs, perhaps, that cynicism about the nation and its representatives is lurching unsteadily toward some alternative moral code, in which love and internationalism will at last be coupled.

AFTERWORD

"If Kip had been asked whom he loved most he would have named his ayah before his mother" (226).[1] To judge from this detail in *The English Patient*, Ondaatje rests Kip's worldliness—which is affirmed, rather than discredited, when Kip renounces his part in the war—on much the same narrative of moral development as Martha Nussbaum offers in defense of hers. Her critics, Nussbaum says, rely on an account of how children grow that is familiar but flawed: "When a child is little, it recognizes and loves only its own particular parents; then, after a while, it comes to know and love its other relatives, then its region or local group, then its nation—and finally, if at all, we get to humanity on the outside."[2] Moving outward from its natural center in the family, love would inevitably decrease in power. In Nussbaum's alternative account, however, the infant begins with "universal needs" that will "form the basis for later recognition of the common" (142). In the beginning, the infant recognizes neither the particular people around it nor its own separate existence. Learning to tell these people apart happens "roughly at the time that [the infant] is learning to demarcate itself from them." It is only later that the child will be asked "to consider herself as one person among others, and not the entire world" (143).

The title of this book was meant to acknowledge from the outset the understandable skepticism with which it is likely to be received. The phrase "feeling global" suggests infantile pretensions to divine ubiquity, if not to omniscience or omnipotence. It also alludes to that "feeling as of something limitless, unbounded—as it were, 'oceanic'" that Freud discusses in *Civilization and Its Discontents*.[3] Freud declared himself a stranger to this feeling. (But then, he also developed his theory of the Oedipus complex from a dream about his nurse, not about his parents.) He is not persuaded that this "feeling of an indissoluble bond, of being one with the external world as a whole" (12), is at the origin of religious sentiments. Relating it, instead, to the experience of "an infant at the breast," which "does not as yet distinguish his ego from the external world" (13)—perhaps the account on which Nussbaum is drawing—he suggests that it is proper to infancy and must be grown out of. In the name of epistemological modesty, ethical parity, and political realism, the same might well be said about the varieties of global feeling or worldliness that have been discussed here.

Freud, however, also relates the oceanic feeling to the experience of "being in love," when "the boundary between ego and object threatens to melt away" (13). Freud's description of love fits well with Ondaatje's: "To fall in love," Almásy says, is to "be disassembled" (158). This sounds like an experience one would be more likely to run from than to seek out. Why would we crave to have our identities disassembled? And yet, neither the craving nor the experience is unusual. Nor is love exclusively private. The film *Titanic*, which deploys its ocean backdrop together with its first class/steerage divide to amplify and enrich its otherwise banal central romance, shows that one need not go far to find public uses for oceanic love. Kip's preference for his ayah is hardly the rule and certainly does not propel Kip toward abolishing the hierarchy that determines that some have and others are ayahs. Still, Ondaatje seems to suggest that love's psychological regressiveness, which is always capable of reactivating the primal inclusiveness of infantile feeling and blurring once more the boundaries between self and world, is a foundation that something can be built on. Others like Kip can hear on a portable radio the news of a distant bombing. They can be disassembled, like him, by bad news from a place they have never been. They can reconsider what they do every day, as Kip reconsiders the work of defusing bombs. They can find ways of acting on their conclusions, if probably less dramatic ways. One might argue that this is, in fact, the foundation that democracy requires.

According to Eric Lott, the problem with Walter Benn Michaels's "new cosmopolitanism" is its antagonism toward group self-interest: "The defense of your own because it is your own is, as Michaels puts it, 'the essence of nativism'" (121–22).[4] Michaels is unconcerned by the transnational dimension of the subject, but he is right about this: radical democratic politics rarely permits a direct or simple expression of group interest. It demands that, facing an antagonist or issue they share, a given group will articulate its interests together with the interests of other groups, negotiating strategic commonalities. Neither the interests nor the group identities themselves emerge from this process unchanged.[5] In other words, democracy is like love. This principle holds equally for democracy on the national and on the transnational scale. Worldly or cosmopolitan politics is not intrinsically altruistic or magnanimous; it does not automatically confer the high moral ground. It cannot claim that—unlike nationalism, which requires external enemies or internal scapegoats—its only antagonist is antagonism itself. Any solidarity that helps someone will also hurt or ignore someone, if not in equal proportions. But if worldliness is not disinterestedness, it does require a certain disassembling of the self that is self-interested. As Gopal Balakrishnan observes in regard to Benedict Anderson, both nations and world religions have long demanded of their members a disassembling and reassembling of identity. Each has been "open, even cosmopolitan in its horizons . . . both [nation and religion] are premised on conceptions of membership which *cancel* the raw fatalities of birth, kinship, and race" (63).[6] The same is true, I suggest, for international feminism, human rights, and environmentalism.

Anderson's difference of opinion here would probably hinge on "raw fatality" in a literal rather than a metaphorical sense. In his argument, the advantage nations have is that, like religions in the past, they acknowledge the fact of mortality and help people deal with it. They connect the generations; they redeem the dead. And this newer transnational solidarities cannot do. For Anderson, as for Tom Nairn, it is death that draws the decisive line between the nation and the world.[7] After all, what are you ready to die for?

The question is dramatic. But perhaps it is the wrong question. Perhaps only radical simplifications like this—some would describe them as philosophical simplifications, or masculine ones—allow international feeling to seem bloodless, abstract, and unlikely. "The greatest gift one human being can offer another," Zygmunt Bauman writes, "is the gift of one's life" (200). Building on Emmanuel Levinas, Bauman goes so far as to suggest that dying for another is "the only truly individual" human act, "the constitutive act of human individuality and uniqueness" (200). He can say so because the background or contrasting vision is society as "monotony" and "indifference" (201). Only an ultimate sacrifice of the self can possibly annul "the absurdity of my being-in-the-world. . . . Existential significance rests, and can only be found, away from the realm of quotidianity" (203). "The care for the Other, . . . and that care only, makes life worth living" (208).[8]

The other side of Bauman's sacralization of dying for the Other is an ostentatious contempt for ordinary life, a blank incomprehension of what else might possibly make it worth living. Bauman is no nationalist, but his argument crystallizes the sort of nationalist common sense to which I offer an alternative. Perhaps the nationalism/internationalism argument would look different if the examples had more to do with ordinary forms of life, such as love and child care, that are repeated everywhere every day than with extraordinary, one-shot choices of life or death. Perhaps the more pertinent questions are not what you would die for but what you live for, how you live, what you eat, whose children you take care of, who takes care of yours—all the ways in which the personal, as Cynthia Enloe has put it, is international.

I have been arguing that the knittedness of culture—the thick, dense embodiedness that is so easily accepted as a domestic fact—cannot be refused to claims and relationships that cross national boundaries. There is no coherent world culture any more than there is a world government, but the odds and ends of transnational experience produced by global commodities and global tourism, mass migrations and mass media, add up to something; and that evolving something is not absolutely different in kind from the incoherent and unfinished national cultures that preceded it. Moreover, it is something on whose evolution the future success of global movements such as human rights and environmentalism depends. I do not mean to imply that culture is the one missing ingredient or key term, as if we had failed to attain blissful achievements in such domains only because we put too much emphasis on rationality. On the contrary, I would point out the existence of a right-wing culturalism that, though it comes in more palatable forms, is epitomized by Samuel Huntington's famous "clash of civilizations" thesis: "In the post–Cold War world, the most important distinctions among peoples are not ideological, political, or economic. They are cultural" (21). Huntington is critical of universalism: "The West's universalist pretensions increasingly bring it into conflict with other civilizations, most seriously with Islam and China," he argues. But what conclusions follow from this familiar point? "The survival of the West depends on Americans reaffirming their Western identity and Westerners accepting their civilization as unique not universal and uniting to renew and preserve it against challengers from non-Western societies" (20–21).[9] Refreshing in its antiuniversalistic honesty, Huntington's culturalism is nonetheless a call to arms in defense of "our" culture—a call that sounds more like the preparation for another offensive. And this call to arms needs to assume only, in Immanuel Wallerstein's words, that culture is "by definition particularistic. Culture is the set of values or practices of some part smaller than some whole" (184). World culture is a logical impossibility, Wallerstein concludes, because "culture is a collective expression that is combative, that requires another" (198).[10]

But *culture* seems inherently particularistic and combative only if *reason*, the contrasting term, is assumed to be inherently universal and pacific. There are real conflicts between national and international loyalties, but they are not reducible to conflicts between cultures or to conflicts between the concepts of culture and reason. Indeed, these conflicts might be easier to resolve if they were merely definitional. National loyalties clash with international loyalties over the welfare state, for example. It is not for nothing that defenders of nationalism such as Richard Rorty and David Miller do their defending in the name of the welfare state. In claiming "that a proper account of ethics should give weight to national boundaries," Miller is also arguing "that in particular there is no objection to ethical schemes—such as welfare states—that are designed to deliver benefits exclusively to those who fall within the same boundaries as ourselves."[11] There is common ground here, as I suggested earlier, but it has yet to be exploited with much success. In October 1996 a much-publicized conference at Columbia University brought together representatives of the academy and representatives of the U.S. labor movement, now under new and more energetic leadership. To many of us who attended the conference, it seemed that the single largest obstacle to any meaningful reconciliation between unions and academics was the issue of nationalism and internationalism. As evidenced by historical references to the war in Vietnam, on the one hand, and to current issues such as immigration, on the other, the line between the organized working class and the institutionalized intellectuals seemed to repeat itself in an ideological divide between nationalism and internationalism. On the whole, the unions were more nationalist; the academic leftists were more internationalist.

Still, as with other conflicts, that between academics and the labor movement is not beyond the reach of political creativity. Support for feminism, human rights, and the environment comes in both national and international scales or emphases, but ways exist in which such support could be channeled into struggles that recognize some, though not all, of what each party wants, and which could thus avoid a debilitating choice between them. This is a goal for the political imagination in the new millennium. What would it take to win support in the rich countries for a tax on all international financial transactions? What would it take to win support in the poor countries for child labor laws such as those the International Labor Office has applied to textile workers in Bangladesh? What would it take to get the different national populations or blocs to agree about land rights for indigenous peoples, worker rights to organize, public scrutiny for the IMF and the World Bank? How can unions and ecologists get themselves onto the same side? How can humanitarian groups be held accountable for their unelected power over foreign policy? These are practical questions without being local questions. They are distressingly difficult questions, and they require an education in global or internationalist feeling.

NOTES

NOTES TO THE INTRODUCTION

1. Timothy Brennan, *At Home in the World: Cosmopolitanism Now* (Cambridge, MA: Harvard University Press, 1997), 27.
2. Judith Butler, "Contingent Foundations: Feminism and the Question of 'Postmodernism,'" in Judith Butler and Joan W. Scott, eds., *Feminists Theorize the Political* (New York and London: Routledge, 1992), 3–21.
3. I discuss Said's use of *worldly* in "The East Is a Career: Edward Said," in *Secular Vocations: Intellectuals, Professionalism, Culture* (London: Verso, 1993), 152–79.
4. Jonathan Arac, *Commissioned Spirits: The Shaping of Social Motion in Dickens, Carlyle, Melville, and Hawthorne* (New Brunswick, NJ: Rutgers University Press, 1979), 190.

5. Eric Lott, "The New Cosmopolitanism," *Transition* 72, 6, 4 (Winter 1996), 108–35. "It may be hard to remember today," Craig Calhoun writes, "but from the 1780s to the 1870s [nationalism] flourished as a liberal, cosmopolitan discourse emphasizing the freedom of all peoples." See Craig Calhoun, *Nationalism* (Minneapolis: University of Minnesota Press, 1997), 86.

6. Peter Waterman, "Internationalism Is Dead! Long Live Global Solidarity!" in Jeremy Brecher, John Brown Childs, and Jill Cutler, eds., *Global Visions: Beyond the New World Order* (Boston: South End Press, 1993), 257–61.

7. See my introduction to Pheng Cheah and Bruce Robbins, eds., *Cosmopolitics: Thinking and Feeling beyond the Nation* (Minneapolis and London: University of Minnesota Press, 1998).

8. Columbus Coalition for Democratic Foreign Policy, "Questions You Won't Get to Ask at the Town Meeting," Columbus, Ohio.

NOTES TO CHAPTER 1

1. Susan Sontag, "A Lament for Bosnia: 'There' and 'Here,' " *The Nation* (December 25, 1995), 818–20.

2. Susan Sontag offers more testimony from Bosnians, along with useful reflections on the limits to what foreign intellectuals can do, in her "Godot Comes to Sarajevo," *New York Review of Books*, October 21, 1993, 52–59.

3. Liam Kennedy, *Susan Sontag: Mind as Passion* (Manchester and New York: Manchester University Press, 1995), 103–6.

4. Of course, Orwell went to Spain as a soldier.

5. David Rieff describes some of those who called for humanitarian intervention as follows: "They wanted an outcome that required a war to obtain, but they did not want to face the fact that even a just war causes the most terrible suffering" (13). Sontag says nothing that would enable us to distinguish her from them. See David Rieff, *Slaughterhouse: Bosnia and the Failure of the West* (New York: Simon & Schuster, 1995). For a brilliantly nuanced treatment of the opposition between "real politics" and "the politics of conscience" in Sontag, see Sohnya Sayres, *Susan Sontag: The Elegaic Modernist* (New York and London: Routledge, 1990), 130–39.

6. Émile Durkheim, *Professional Ethics and Civic Morals*, trans. Cornelia Brookfield, preface by Bryan S. Turner (1957; reprint, London and New York: Routledge, 1992), xxxv.

7. World War I was not technically a genocide, but even if it had been, it seems clear that the simplicity of fellow feeling would not have been a sufficient guide in addressing the question of intervention in it.

8. "Sentiment was a poor guide during the Croatian war," Rieff writes, in what might be a commentary on Sontag's declaration, "and it has been a poor guide during the slaughter in Bosnia" (*Slaughterhouse*, 41). Rieff suggests that the humanitarian approach was worse than (as it was called) a mere Band-Aid; it was a positive hindrance to other, more effectual options.

9. Kjell Goldmann, *The Logic of Internationalism: Coercion and Accommodation* (London and New York: Routledge, 1994), 1. A few examples of this cheery, official, policy-level discourse about transcending the nation-state include Jean-Marie Guéhenno, *The End of the Nation-State*, trans. Victoria Elliot (Minneapolis: University of Minnesota Press, 1995); David Held, *Democracy and the Global Order: From the Modern State to Cosmopolitan Governance* (Stanford: Stanford University Press, 1995); and Suheil Bushrui, Iraj Ayman, and Ervin Laszlo, eds., *Transition to a Global Society* (Oxford: Oneworld, 1993).

10. An example, among many, is Eugene R. Wittkopf, *Faces of Internationalism: Public Opinion and American Foreign Policy* (Durham and London: Duke University Press, 1990). It is in this sense that John Sweeney, president of the American Federation of Labor and Congress of Industrial Organizations (AFL-CIO), says, "The question is not whether America must lead, but where we must lead. . . . It is not whether we are internationalists, but what values our internationalism serves" (quoted in Robert L. Borosage, "Fast Track to Nowhere," *The Nation* [September 29, 1997], 20–22, esp. 21).

11. A parallel point is made about morality by Robert McKim and Jeff McMahan in *The Morality of Nationalism* (Oxford: Oxford University Press, 1997): "At least some moral questions cannot be evaded even by the most resolutely pragmatic person. When they are not explicitly acknowledged, moral and evaluative assumptions lie beneath the surface of every program of action" (4).

12. Richard Falk, "Intervention Revisited: Hard Choices and Tragic Dilemmas," *The Nation* (December 20, 1993), 755–64. Falk argued against intervention in Bosnia, even supervised and supported by the United Nations, on the grounds that it would mean the use of military power with the aim of political restructuring, yet without the consent of those concerned. He concluded, "Nonintervention is intolerable, but intervention remains impossible" (757).

13. Susan Sontag, *On Photography* (New York: Dell, 1977), 11–12.

14. See Marcie Frank, "The Critic as Performance Artist: Susan Sontag's Writing and Gay Cultures," David Bergman, ed., in *Camp Grounds* (Amherst: University of Massachusetts Press, 1993), 173–84.

15. David Miller, *On Nationality* (Oxford: Clarendon Press, 1995).

16. Patchen Markell makes a useful distinction of these terms in his "Making Affect Safe for Democracy? On 'Constitutional Patriotism'" (paper delivered at American Political Science Association, Washington, DC, August 1997).

17. Not for the first time, America is thus set up as the paradoxical exception to all rules: a culture without culture, the national source of a nation-corroding cosmopolitanism.

18. Yael Tamir, *Liberal Nationalism* (Princeton: Princeton University Press, 1993), 166–67.

19. A widely publicized use of McDonald's in just this way is Benjamin R. Barber, *Jihad vs. McWorld: How Globalism and Tribalism Are Reshaping the World* (New York: Ballantine, 1996).

20. Thomas L. Haskell, "Capitalism and the Origins of the Humanitarian Sensibility, Part 1," in Thomas Bender, ed., *The Antislavery Debate: Capitalism and Abolitionism as a Problem in Historical Interpretation* (Berkeley: University of California Press, 1992), 107–35. My thanks to Jim Livingston for the reference.

21. See my introduction to Pheng Cheah and Bruce Robbins, eds., *Cosmopolitics: Thinking and Feeling beyond the Nation* (Minneapolis and London: University of Minnesota Press, 1998).

22. Can McDonald's rightly signify the emptiness of global homogenization? For a reality check, see John Heilemann, "All Europeans Are Not Alike," *New Yorker* (April 28 and May 5, 1997), 174–81, on how advertising for global firms such as McDonald's necessarily adapts to particular national cultures. The article quotes Thom Kettle, McDonald's' vice president for marketing: "We've never commissioned a pan-European ad, and we probably never will" (179). David Miller expresses the habitual sneer when he mentions a Body Shop lapel pin that displays a quotation from H. G. Wells: "Our true nationality is mankind" (*On Nationality*, 13n.).

23. Julia Kristeva, *Strangers to Ourselves*, trans. Leon S. Roudiez (New York: Columbia University Press, 1991).

24. Reviewing Peter Unger's *Living High and Letting Die: Our Illusion of Innocence* (Oxford: Oxford University Press, 1996), Martha Nussbaum makes a very similar point. Unger, who proposes that people give away most of their property to organizations such as Oxfam and UNICEF in order to end world hunger, "seems not to have asked himself any questions about what would actually happen if people took his advice. This would appear to be because he has assumed that people will not take his advice and that he will remain one of a small band of moral heroes, in a world of moral sloth and corruption" (18). See Martha Nussbaum, "If Oxfam Ran the World," *London Review of Books*, September 4, 1997, 18–19.

25. For contrast, consider Timothy Brennan's turn to a strong religious vocabulary; Brennan suggests that a proper appreciation of cross-cultural difference would entail "the sort of mental shift one traditionally has called 'conversion'" (*At Home in the World: Cosmopolitanism Now* [Cambridge, MA: Harvard University Press, 1997], 27).

26. This talk was eventually published as "Comparative Cosmopolitanism," *Social Text*, no. 31/32 (1992), 169–86; reprinted, with revisions, in Bruce Robbins, ed., *Secular Vocations* (London: Verso, 1993), and in Cheah and Robbins, eds., *Cosmopolitics*. A more elaborate discussion of Greek cosmopolitanism can be found in Martha Nussbaum, *Cultivating Humanity: A Classical Defense of Reform in Liberal Education* (Cambridge, MA, and London: Harvard University Press, 1997), chap. 2.

27. Robert Pinsky, "Eros against Esperanto," in Martha Nussbaum et al., *For Love of Country: Debating the Limits of Patriotism*, ed. Josh Cohen (Boston: Beacon Press, 1996), 85–90.

28. John Patrick Diggins, "Let Every Faction Bloom," *London Review of Books*, March 6, 1997, 22–23.

29. Richard Rorty, "Intellectuals in Politics," *Dissent* 38 (Fall 1991), 483–90. A response by Andrew Ross, "On Intellectuals in Politics," and "Richard Rorty Replies" are in *Dissent* 39 (Spring 1992), 263–67.

30. Michael Lind, *The Next American Nation: The New Nationalism and the Fourth American Revolution* (New York: Free Press, 1995), 149n. Lind's source is James Fallows, "Low-Class Conclusions," *Atlantic Monthly* (April 1993), 43–44.

31. Milton J. Bates, *The Wars We Took to Vietnam: Cultural Conflict and Story-telling* (Berkeley: University of California Press, 1996), 88. Bates tellingly concedes, however, that "the workers themselves were not always conscious of their liberalism and would not have worn it as a badge of honor. . . . Americans tend to support the president on issues that are remote from their personal experience, such as foreign policy" (89).

32. Robert B. Reich, *The Work of Nations: Preparing Ourselves for Twenty-first-Century Capitalism* (New York: Vintage, 1992), 3.

33. David Miller, too, defends nationalism as if it were likely to produce a live-and-let-live world "in which different peoples can pursue their own national projects in a spirit of friendly rivalry, but in which none attempts to control, exploit, or undermine any of the others" (*On Nationality*, 189–90).

34. Juliet Schor, *A Sustainable Economy for the Twenty-first Century*, Open Magazine Pamphlet Series, no. 31 (Westfield, NJ: Open Media/New Party, 1995), 21.

35. Economics is an area in which we are already causally connected to each other, for better and for worse, and not merely by our acts of omission. This is another reason Sontag on genocide is not representative: there is much more of a direct link between, say, American consumption and Third World poverty than between American TV watchers and ethnic cleansing, and a link of such a nature as to produce different possibilities for action. For an account of the relevant moral responsibilities, see, for example, Henry Shue, *Basic Rights: Subsistence, Affluence, and U.S. Foreign Policy*, 2d ed. (Princeton: Princeton University Press, 1996). Anyone curious about the recent figures on global inequality can find them in the United Nations Development Programme's *Human Development Report 1997* (New York and Oxford: Oxford University Press, 1997).

36. One lesson to be learned from the culture wars is that the disciplinary commitment to culture (as aesthetic defamiliarization, uncertainty, and mystery) has obscured an underlying commitment to universalizing rational critique, without which the internationalism of the cultural critics would be inconceivable. See Amanda Anderson, "Cryptonormativism and Double Gestures: The Politics of Post-Structuralism," *Cultural Critique*, 21 (Spring 1992), 63–95.

37. Goldmann, *Logic of Internationalism*, 1.
38. Michael Ignatieff, *Blood and Belonging: Journeys into the New Nationalism* (New York: Farrar, Straus & Giroux, 1993), 13.
39. Nussbaum, "If Oxfam Ran the World," 18.
40. David Rieff, "Multiculturalism's Silent Partner," *Harper's* (August 1993), 62–72, quoted in Gregory S. Jay, *American Literature and the Culture Wars* (Ithaca and London: Cornell University Press, 1997), 33–34. In Jay's paraphrase: multiculturalism is "the shadow cast by global capitalism" (34).
41. Michael Mann, "As the Twentieth Century Ages," *New Left Review*, no. 214 (November/December 1995), 104–24. Mann further states, "Indeed, it is doubtful whether, in many respects, capitalism is more transnational than it was before 1914, except for the special case of the increasing integration of the European Union. This is hardly an economic base on which to ground any grand generalizing theories of the end of the nation-state" (117–18).
42. David A. Hollinger, *Postethnic America: Beyond Multiculturalism* (New York: Basic Books, 1995), 148.
43. Fredric Jameson, "Five Theses on Actually Existing Marxism," *Monthly Review* 47, 11 (April 1996), 1–10; for a parallel argument contrasting the epoch of Richard Hoggart and Raymond Williams positively with the "anarcho-reformism" (36) of the present day, see Francis Mulhern, "A Welfare Culture? Hoggart and Williams in the Fifties," *Radical Philosophy*, no. 77 (May/June 1996), 26–37.
44. Étienne Balibar, "Le citoyen aujourd'hui?" *Raison présente*, no. 103 (1992), 27–44, esp. 35.

NOTES TO CHAPTER 2

I am grateful to Geoffrey White and the East/West Center, Honolulu, Hawaii, where I first tried out these ideas; to Rob Wilson and Wimal Dissanayeke; to the fellows of the Cornell University Society for the Humanities, 1994–1995, and in particular its director, Dominick LaCapra; and to Andrew Ross and the members of the *Social Text* collective, all of whom provided helpful commentaries and criticisms.

1. Edward W. Said, *Culture and Imperialism* (New York: Knopf, 1993), 244. I have not entered here into the argument over whether or when an internationalist impatience with nationalism is desirable. For a useful corrective, see David Lloyd, "Nationalisms against the State: Towards a Critique of the Anti-Nationalist Prejudice," in John Gershman and Walden Bello, eds., *Reexamining and Renewing the Philippine Progressive Vision* (Diliman, Quezon City: FOPA, 1993), 215–33.
2. I take as a premise here that journals define themselves in dialogue with their readers and contributors, as well as in competition for readers and contributors against other journals in a common field of intellectual interest, and that they thus acquire identities that never simply reflect their original or

180

NOTES TO CHAPTER TWO

self-conscious intentions. I also assume that since, unlike individual authors, journals are collectively edited and institutionally funded, they are more broadly representative than individual authors.

3. Carmen Wickramagamage, "Relocation as Positive Act: The Immigrant Experience in Bharati Mukherjee's Novels," *Diaspora* 2, 2 (Fall 1992), 171–200.

4. Yossi Shain, "Marketing the Democratic Creed Abroad: U.S. Diasporic Politics in the Era of Multiculturalism," *Diaspora* 3, 1 (Spring 1994), 85–111. Shain's argument raises the question of whether some logic connects identification with diaspora to identification with the state.

5. Consider, as a problematic example, the model of German solidarity with the Germans of the Sudetenland before the Nazi annexation.

6. Christopher L. Connery, "Pacific Rim Discourse: The U.S. Global Imaginary in the Late Cold War Years," *boundary 2* 21, 1 (Spring 1994), 34.

7. Note, in this issue, the potentially significant difference between the interests of *global* capital (Arif Dirlik) and the interests of *national* capital (Connery). Can we not even imagine the interests of global capital interfering with the national interests of the United States—for example, in the Gulf War, when it seemed clear that neither German nor Japanese capital was much worried by the threat of greater Iraqi control over Middle Eastern oil? In contrast, the United States was manifestly doing what it said Saddam Hussein was doing: namely, in an era of national economic decline, trying to convert one remaining national asset—a large military—back into economic advantage. Perhaps the lukewarm interest of much global capital, if it did not stop the war from happening, can be linked to the fact that the war did not go any farther.

8. For example, the editors note, one discussion of "the rise of the Pacific Rim" proceeds "without once factoring in even one Pacific Basin country or island culture as a political-economic player or, for that matter, without even mentioning the state of Hawaii as a space caught between the Pacific Rim geo-imaginary hallucinations of Los Angeles and Tokyo" (Arif Dirlik and Rob Wilson, introduction, *boundary 2* 21, 1 [Spring 1994], 5). "Cultures and politics of difference within the Asia/Pacific region are all but . . . ignored as sources of innovation and production" (6).

9. It is not that the editors ignore the positive potential of larger-than-local groupings, whether of people or of conceptual space (the slash between Asia and Pacific, they write, indicates "linkage" as well as difference [ibid., 6]), but rather that their critique of the global (capital) is articulated solely in the name of the local, as if that potential had no practical effect. This should, of course, be said without claiming that fluidity means identifying "flow" with resistance, as certain "diasporist" metaphors seem to do.

10. J. K. Gibson-Graham, "Waiting for the Revolution, or How to Smash Capitalism while Working at Home in Your Spare Time," *Rethinking Marxism* 6,

2 (Summer 1993), 10–24. "Through its architectural or organismic representation as an edifice or body, Capitalism becomes not an uncentered aggregate of practices but a structural and systemic unity, potentially coextensive with the (national or global) economy as a whole. . . . Capitalism cannot be chipped away at, gradually replaced, or removed piecemeal. It must be transformed in its entirety or not at all" (14). Such a way of thinking about capitalism "makes unimaginable a current and present socialism in places like the United States" (18). "When capitalism is presented as a unified system coextensive with the nation-state or with the world, when it is portrayed as an economic form that marginalizes and demotes all other economic forms, when it is allowed to define our entire societies and not merely an aspect of our economic lives, it becomes . . . too ultimate and millenial, too embracing and total" (21).

11. See the introduction by Dirlik and Wilson in the issue "Asia/Pacific as Space of Cultural Production." Articulating what is implied by *boundary 2*, Nicholas Garnham deduces the necessity of universalism from the ubiquity of capitalism: "If we accept that the economic system is indeed global in scope and at the same time crucially determining over large areas of social action, the Enlightenment project of democracy requires us to make the Pascalian bet on universal rationality. For without it the emancipatory project of the Enlightenment is unrealizable and we will in large part remain enslaved by a system outside our control" ("The Mass Media, Cultural Identity, and the Public Sphere in the Modern World," *Public Culture*, 10 [1993], 263).

12. Fredric Jameson, "Third-World Literature in the Era of Multinational Capitalism," *Social Text*, 15 (Fall 1986), 65–88.

13. Thus, in a sense, the journal's present global Marxism is more continuous with its past Heideggerian attachments than might at first appear to be the case.

14. Here the Spring 1994 issue of *Diaspora* offers a useful contrast. An article by Liisa Maalki, "Citizens of Humanity: Internationalism and the Imagined Community of Nations," demonstrates the importance of the international, the image of "the community of nations," to Hutu refugees living in Tanzania in the mid-1980s. Part of the self-definition of a local group (though also a displaced group) is to see itself attached, in one way or another, to transnational groupings.

15. George Yúdice, "We Are *Not* the World," *Social Text*, no. 31/32 (1992), 202–16. "Outside of the university and the unemployment line, the U.S. army, that global defender—or, more accurately, mercenary—of free trade in the interests of transnational capital, was projected as the epitome of multiculturalism by the televisual charade that promoted the Gulf War to markets around the world" (213).

16. Aijaz Ahmad, "Jameson's Rhetoric of Otherness and the 'National Allegory,'" *Social Text*, no. 17 (Fall 1987), 3–25.

17. Alejandro Colás, in "Putting Cosmopolitanism into Practice: The Case of Socialist Internationalism," *Millenium* 23, 3 (1994), 513–34, argues that any future socialist internationalism must take both class and the state more seriously. For a summary of early positions, see Michael Löwy, "Marxists and the National Question," in *On Changing the World: Essays in Political Philosophy, from Karl Marx to Walter Benjamin* (Atlantic Highlands, NJ, and London: Humanities Press, 1993).

18. Reflecting on those controversies that have made news and won readers for particular journals, as well as those significant silences that are no less a part of the historical record for this slice of civil society, it is interesting to note how the debate between Jameson and Ahmad passed from *Social Text* to *Public Culture*, which devoted a special issue (6, 1 [Fall 1993]) to Ahmad's arguments.

19. Katherine Verdery, "Beyond the Nation in Eastern Europe," *Social Text*, no. 38 (Spring 1994), 1–19. Note that by this argument, Verdery also saves a theoretical site for the sort of voice in which she herself speaks.

20. Faye Ginsburg, "Aboriginal Media and the Australian Imaginary," *Public Culture*, no. 11 (1993), 557–78. For another essay that usefully exemplifies this popular internationalism, see Michael Peter Smith, "Can You Imagine? Transnational Migration and the Globalization of Grassroots Politics," *Social Text*, no. 39 (Fall 1994), 15–33.

21. María Milagros López, "Post-Work Selves and Entitlement 'Attitudes' in Peripheral Postindustrial Puerto Rico," *Social Text*, no. 38 (Spring 1994), 111–33.

22. As López does *not* say, this also means that the metropolitan culture rejoined thereby can be both parallel to and continuous with emergent cultural forms elsewhere—a distinct, if not an absolute, privilege.

23. *Social Text* has also made space for discussion of *intellectuals*, a term that exceeds the cultural in the direction of the state, even if a characteristic theme has been the difficulty intellectuals face in defining themselves *other* than in some relation to the state. See Arturo Torrecilla's "Watermelon Intelligentsia," *Social Text*, no. 38 (Spring 1994), 135–47; and Verdery, "Beyond the Nation," 1–19.

24. I'm grateful to Samira Kawash for her remarks on this point.

25. Michael Shapiro, "Moral Geographies and the Ethics of Post-Sovereignty," *Public Culture*, no. 14 (Spring 1994), 479–502; Charles Taylor, "Modes of Civil Society," and Partha Chatterjee, "A Response to Taylor's 'Modes of Civil Society,'" *Public Culture* 3, 1 (Fall 1990), 95–132. For further worry over the concept, see Benjamin Lee, "Critical Internationalism," *Public Culture* 7, 3 (Spring 1995), 559–92.

26. Jean L. Cohen and Andrew Arato, *Civil Society and Political Theory* (Cambridge, MA, and London: MIT Press, 1992), ix.

27. In this regard, there is an interesting dialogue over "policy," titled "Against Power," in the journal *Transition*, no. 64 (1994), 113–69. See also Michael

Bérubé, *Public Access: Literary Theory and American Cultural Politics* (London: Verso, 1994), 225 and passim.

28. On civil society at the international scale, see the special issue of *Millenium: Journal of International Studies* 23, 3 (1994).

29. See, for example, Joseph Buttigieg, who writes in "Gramsci on Civil Society" that "there has been a tendency to stress the non-violent, non-coercive character of the hegemonic relations that obtain in civil society and thus to under-emphasize the extent to which these are *uneven relations of power* that strengthen and help perpetuate the grip of the dominant classes over the state as a whole" (23). Manuscript available from Buttigieg, Department of English, University of Notre Dame, Notre Dame, Indiana. A German version of the essay, "Ethik und Staat: Zivilgesellschaft," appears in a special issue of *Das Argument* devoted to civil society, no. 206 (July–October 1994).

30. Gayatri Chakravorty Spivak, "Who Claims Sexuality in the New World Order?" (paper based on her speeches at the United Nations ICPD Conference, Cairo, in September 1994, delivered at the Conference on Culture/Sex/Economics, LaTrobe University, Melbourne, Australia, December 1994).

31. See, for example, Ernest Gellner, "From the Ruins of the Great Contest: Civil Society, Nationalism, and Islam," *Times Literary Supplement*, March 13, 1992, 9–10.

32. John Keane, ed., *Civil Society and the State: New European Perspectives* (London and New York: Verso, 1988).

33. Chatterjee, "A Response to Taylor's 'Modes of Civil Society,'" 120. In a similar vein, Neil Lazarus remarks that the implicit price of championing "the achievements of European liberalism" at home, as proposed by the social theory of Chantal Mouffe, is Mouffe's "apparent unawareness of the social costs that have been borne outside of Europe, and by non-Europeans, in order that European 'democracy' could register the 'achievements' that she so cherishes" ("Doubting the New World Order: Marxism, Realism, and the Claims of Postmodernist Social Theory," *differences* 3, 3 [1991], 94–138, esp. 100). Both points are complicated, of course, by the genuine question of what value to put on concepts and institutions of civil society that, for all their putatively European roots and associations, may be of real service to people outside Europe struggling against despotic forces both local and distant.

34. Jeffrey C. Alexander, "Modern, Anti, Post, Neo," *New Left Review*, no. 210 (March/April 1995), 63–101. See also Jeffrey C. Alexander, "Citizen and Enemy as Symbolic Classification: On the Polarizing Discourse of Civil Society," in Michele Lamont and Marcel Fournier, eds., *Cultivating Differences* (Chicago: University of Chicago Press, 1992), 289–308.

35. Arjun Appadurai, "Patriotism and Its Futures," *Public Culture* 5, 3 (Spring 1993), 411–29. Appadurai continues: "These basic motives can either be far darker than anything having to do with national sovereignty, as when they

seem driven by the motives of 'ethnic purification' and genocide. . . . Or they can be simply idioms and symbols around which many groups come to articulate their desire to escape the specific state regime that is seen as threatening their own survival. Palestinians are more worried about getting Israel off their backs than about the special geographical magic of the West Bank" (418).

36. Arjun Appadurai, "Disjuncture and Difference in the Global Cultural Economy," *Theory, Culture and Society* 7 (1990), 295–310.

37. Masao Miyoshi, "A Borderless World? From Colonialism to Transnationalism and the Decline of the Nation-State," *Critical Inquiry* 19 (Summer 1993), 726–51. The version or sector of international civil society (or perhaps one should say, of international popular culture) that these journals intervene in is relevant here. Miyoshi concludes that the TNCs have succeeded in "converting academics—us—into frequent fliers and globetrotters" (750). How much capitalist complicity does this mobile hybridity bring with it? Perhaps not so much after all. On the one hand, the journals we work for operate on an academic market that is no longer as protected from the "trade" market as it once was. This may explain the weakened ideological resistance to capitalism reflected in some of their pages. But perhaps it also explains their shared impulse to be more public and more political than was once the rule for journals in the humanities. Both are judgments of their publicness—as is their distance from the unconscious nationalism of the mass media, print as well as electronic, which pretty well guarantees that they will not cross over from an academic to a genuine mass public. On the other hand, as interdisciplinary journals they all participate, more or less consciously, in an alternative system for the distribution and creation of cultural capital that clearly cuts athwart (and is often resented by) individual disciplines and departments. America's reputation for excellence in higher education surely does not suffer from this. Yet within the university system, these journals also count as strenuously and subversively cosmopolitan.

38. John Judis, "Looking Left and Right: The Evolution of Political Direction," *In These Times* (June 12–25, 1991), 12–13.

39. Meaghan Morris, "Lunching for the Republic: Feminism, the Media, and Identity Politics in the Australian Republicanism Debate," in David Bennett, ed., *Multicultural States: Difference and Identity* (New York and London: Routledge, forthcoming).

40. Lee, *Critical Internationalism*, 559–92.

41. There is an interesting comparison to be drawn here between Rorty's patriotic anticulturalism and Jürgen Habermas's notion of "constitutional patriotism." Habermas, too, downplays the importance of culture, which he sees as divisive, in favor of something like civil society, which he sees as conciliatory and inclusive. But he does so in order to argue that immigrants to Germany are best defended by reminding German citizens that a common cultural identity is not, after all, essential to the stability of German society. See

Jürgen Habermas, "Struggles for Recognition in the Constitutional Democratic State," in Amy Guttmann, ed., *Multiculturalism: Examining the Politics of Recognition* (Princeton: Princeton University Press, 1994), 107–48.

42. A parallel case, inspired by Thatcherism's success in dismantling the more extensive British welfare state, is offered by the so-called New Times proposals in the United Kingdom. The ensuing argument can be seen, in retrospect, to have pitted supporters, who largely took for granted the overriding priority of domestic politics, against critics, who insisted on maintaining an internationalist perspective. See the special issue of *Marxism Today* titled "New Times" (October 1988); and A. Sivanandan, "All That Melts into Air Is Solid: The Hokum of New Times," in *Communities of Resistance: Writings on Black Struggles for Socialism* (London: Verso, 1990), 19–59.

43. Craig Calhoun, "Civil Society and the Public Sphere," *Public Culture* 5, 2 (Winter 1993), 267–81.

44. Arjun Appadurai, Lauren Berlant, Carol A. Breckenridge, and Manthia Diawara, "Editorial Comment: On Thinking the Black Public Sphere," *Public Culture* 7, 1 (Fall 1994), xii. See also, in the same issue, Regina Austen, " 'A Nation of Thieves': Consumption, Commerce, and the Black Public Sphere"; Rosemary J. Coombe and Paul Stoler, "X Marks the Spot: The Ambiguities of African Trading in the Commerce of the Black Public Sphere"; and Reebee Garofalo, "Culture versus Commerce: The Marketing of Black Popular Music," 225–87.

45. Hortense J. Spillers, "*The Crisis of the Negro Intellectual:* A Post-Date," *boundary 2* 21, 3 (Fall 1994), 65–116. According to Spillers, West's view of black intellectuals is too dependent on "the kinetic orality and emotional physicality" that is modeled on the black preacher and musical performer. To preaching and performance she contrasts the more autonomous models of "writing" and "theoretical practice" (99).

46. Miriam Hansen, "Unstable Mixtures, Dilated Spheres: Negt and Kluge's *The Public Sphere and Experience*, Twenty Years Later," *Public Culture* 5, 2 (Winter 1993), 201.

47. For a move in the direction of international policy relevance, see, however, George DeMartino and Stephen Cullenberg, "Beyond the Competitiveness Debate: An Internationalist Agenda," *Social Text*, no. 41 (Winter 1994), 11–39, which tries to remedy the lack of any internationalist economic policy for the U.S. left. The usual competition-enhancing strategies, the authors argue, "might be expected *at best* to displace social dislocations such as declining living standards onto others, rather than eliminate them" (12). Their proposal, a "Social Index Tariff Structure," tries to explore "new international linkages and mobilizations to overcome some of the most debilitating instances of political fragmentation today (not least among nationally segregated labor movements)" (33). The universalizing pressure of policy making can perhaps be felt, however, in the injunction that such a solution "must

not carry a bias either in favor of or against developing countries" (32). Affirmative action in favor of the Third World continues to set a sort of limit.

48. Eric Lott, "Cornel West in the Hour of Chaos: Culture and Politics in *Race Matters*," *Social Text*, no. 40 (Fall 1994), 39–50. On the international dimension of rap, see, for example, Nina Cornyetz, "Fetishized Blackness: Hip Hop and Racial Desire in Contemporary Japan," *Social Text*, no. 41 (Winter 1994), 113–39.

49. Hans Magnus Enzensberger, *Civil War* (London: Granta Books [in association with Penguin], 1990, 1992, 1993).

50. Andrew Ross, *Strange Weather: Culture, Science, and Technology in the Age of Limits* (London and New York: Verso, 1991), 195.

51. Andrew Ross, *The Chicago Gangster Theory of Life: Nature's Debt to Society* (London and New York: Verso, 1994).

52. James Livingston, *Pragmatism and the Political Economy of Cultural Revolution, 1850–1940* (Chapel Hill and London: University of North Carolina Press, 1994).

53. Ibid., 71.

54. See, for example, Roger Rouse, "Thinking through Transnationalism: Notes on the Cultural Politics of Class Relations in the Contemporary United States," *Public Culture* 7, 2 (1995), 353–402.

NOTES TO CHAPTER 3

I am grateful to Pheng Cheah, Marjorie Howes, Gayatri Chakravorty Spivak, and Linda Zerilli for generously taking the time to discuss these issues with me.

1. Karl Marx, "Economic and Philosophical Manuscripts," in *Early Writings*, introduced by Lucio Colletti, trans. Rodney Livingstone and Gregor Benton (Harmondsworth and London: Penguin and New Left Books, 1975), 342.

2. Mary Louise Pratt, *Imperial Eyes: Travel Writing and Transculturation* (London and New York: Routledge, 1992).

3. Nancy Hartsock, "Foucault on Power: A Theory for Women?" in Linda J. Nicholson, ed., *Feminism/Postmodernism* (New York: Routledge, 1990), 171.

4. Amanda Anderson, "Cryptonormativism and Double Gestures: The Politics of Post-Structuralism," *Cultural Critique*, no. 21 (Spring 1992), 63–95.

5. Vivek Dhareshwar, "Marxism, Location Politics, and the Possibility of Critique," *Public Culture*, no. 12 (1993), 41.

6. Gertrude Himmelfarb, "Not What We Meant at All," *Times Literary Supplement*, June 10, 1994, 8–9. Himmelfarb is reviewing Joyce Appleby, Lynn Hunt, and Margaret Jacob, *Telling the Truth about History* (New York: Norton, 1994), who see their "new history" as opposing an " 'imperialist' history that sought to establish 'universal' ('synonymous with Western') laws of progress" (8).

7. Common sense regarding the work that needs to be done these days would seem, rather, to share the mixed motives that Joan Landes expresses in

Women and the Public Sphere in the Age of the French Revolution (Ithaca: Cornell University Press, 1988). Her book, Landes says, "had to challenge the Revolution's claim to universality at its *political* core, to display the posturings of the particular behind the veil of the universal." But this could not be its sole or even primary purpose. "Although the Revolution's *universal* political significance is contested, its *general* importance for feminist modernity has been underscored" (201). Or, as David Simpson concludes, generalizing this distinction between the universal and the general, "Universals, of course, were never the issue: between the local and the universal (and within the local), the question is one of workable theories and productive generalities, not transcendental norms" (*The Academic Postmodern and the Rule of Literature: A Report on Half-Knowledge* [Chicago: University of Chicago Press, 1995], 128).

8. For a deconstructive critique of Kant's cosmopolitanism, see, for example, Geoffrey Bennington, "Mosaique: Politiques et frontières de la déconstruction," in *L'Ethique du don: Jacques Derrida et la pensée du don*, comp. Jean-Michel Rabaté and Michael Wetzel (Paris: Métailié-Transition, 1992), 178–93.

9. Yossi Shain, "Marketing the Democratic Creed Abroad: U.S. Diasporic Politics in the Era of Multiculturalism," *Diaspora* 3, 1 (Spring 1994), 85–111.

10. George Yúdice, "We Are *Not* the World," *Social Text*, no. 31/32 (1992), 202–16.

11. Slavoj Žižek, *The Sublime Object of Ideology* (London: Verso, 1989), 25–26.

12. Among the ways in which universalism remains inscribed, problematically, in a discourse that otherwise declares itself antiuniversalist, consider the universalizing of the aesthetic ("everything is discourse," or textuality, or what have you), as well as the unconscious universalizing that underlies any critique in the name of inclusion (*x* may seem like an attractive democratic position, but it excludes *y*). The assumption that any exclusion invalidates the excluder is an assumption that only universal inclusiveness is acceptable, which is to presume, in turn, that universal inclusiveness is possible.

13. Ernesto Laclau and Chantal Mouffe, *Hegemony and Socialist Strategy: Towards a Radical Democratic Politics*, trans. Winston Moore and Paul Cammack (London: Verso, 1985), 103.

14. Naoki Sakai, "Modernity and Its Critique: The Problem of Universalism and Particularism," in Masao Miyoshi and H. D. Harootunian, eds., *Postmodernism and Japan* (Durham: Duke University Press, 1989), 93–122, esp. 105. Sakai writes: "Contrary to what has been advertised by both sides, universalism and particularism reinforce and supplement each other; they are never in real conflict; they need each other and have to seek to form a symmetrical, mutually supporting relationship by every means in order to avoid a dialogic encounter which would necessarily jeopardize their reputedly secure and harmonized monologic worlds. Universalism and particularism en-

dorse each other's defect in order to conceal their own; they are intimately tied to each other in their accomplice. In this respect, a particularism such as nationalism can never be a serious critique of universalism, for it is an accomplice thereof" (105).

15. Nicholas Garnham, "The Mass Media, Cultural Identity, and the Public Sphere in the Modern World," *Public Culture*, no. 10 (1993), 263.

16. Étienne Balibar, "Ambiguous Universality" (talk presented at the Bohen Foundation, New York City, February 1994).

17. Étienne Balibar, "The Nation Form," in Étienne Balibar and Immanuel Wallerstein, *Race, Nation, Class: Ambiguous Identities* (London: Verso, 1991), 89.

18. Neil Lazarus, "Disavowing Decolonization: Fanon, Nationalism, and the Problematic of Representation in Current Theories of Colonial Discourse," *Research in African Literatures* 24, 4 (Winter 1993), 70. Lazarus also argues, with Garnham, that there is no need "to concede the terrain of universality to . . . Eurocentric projections" (93).

19. Ibid., 78.

20. Amitav Ghosh, *In an Antique Land* (New York: Knopf, 1993). On cosmopolitanism in this sense, see Paul Rabinow, "Representations Are Social Facts," in James Clifford and George E. Marcus, eds., *Writing Culture: The Poetics and Politics of Ethnography* (Berkeley: University of California Press, 1986), 234–61; and James Clifford, "Traveling Cultures," in Lawrence Grossberg, Cary Nelson, and Paula A. Treichler, eds., *Cultural Studies* (New York: Routledge, 1992), 96–116; as well as Louisa Schein, "Itinerant Ethnography of the Postnational: China, the U.S. and a Globalizing Minority" (manuscript available from Schein, Department of Anthropology, Rutgers University, New Brunswick, New Jersey 08903).

21. Note that Pratt refuses the cliché of a desiring spectatorship, turning the spectator instead into a version of the passionless, disembodied citizen.

22. Richard Rorty, "The Unpatriotic Academy," *New York Times*, Sunday, February 13, 1994, E15.

23. Benedict Anderson, *Imagined Communities: Reflections on the Origin and Spread of Nationalism* (London: Verso, 1983).

24. Ibid., 15. Anderson opens *Imagined Communities* by describing the nation as "*imagined* because the members of even the smallest nation will never know most of their fellow members, meet them, or even hear of them, yet in the minds of each lives the images of their communion. . . . In fact, all communities larger than primordial villages of face-to-face contact (and perhaps even those) are imagined."

25. Martha Nussbaum, "Patriotism and Cosmopolitanism," *Boston Review* 19, 5 (October/November 1994), 6. Nussbaum's defense of "universal reason" does not seem necessary to her defense of cosmopolitanism or her critique of Rorty's op-ed piece.

26. Étienne Balibar, "Fichte and the Internal Border," in *Masses, Classes, Ideas: Studies on Politics and Philosophy before and after Marx*, trans. James Swenson (London and New York: Routledge, 1994), 74.

27. In an appeal for "A Liberalism of Heart and Spine" (*New York Times*, March 27, 1994, Op-Ed page), Henry Louis Gates Jr. has also denounced the lack of affect that accompanies a "moral relativism" among intellectual leaders, which is really "moral indifference."

28. Étienne Balibar, "Racism as Universalism," in *Masses, Classes, Ideas*, 203.

29. See chapter 5.

30. Charles Taylor, *Philosophy and the Human Sciences* (Cambridge: Cambridge University Press, 1985). The incorrigibility thesis is not the only safeguard against one's own ethnocentricity, Taylor argues; "the error in this view is to hold that the language of a cross-cultural theory has to be either theirs or ours. If this were so, then any attempt at understanding across cultures would be faced with an impossible dilemma: either accept incorrigibility, or be arrogantly ethnocentric. . . . But as a matter of fact, while challenging their language of self-understanding, we may also be challenging ours . . . the adequate language in which we can understand another society is not our language, or theirs, but rather what one could call a language of perspicuous contrast. This would be a language in which we could formulate both their way of life and ours as alternative possibilities in relation to some human constants at work in both" (125).

31. Françoise Lionnet, "Feminisms and Universalisms: 'Universal Rights' and the Legal Debate around the Practice of Female Excision in France," *Inscriptions* 6 (1992), 109.

32. Naomi Schor, "Feminism and George Sand: *Lettres à Marcie*," in Judith Butler and Joan Scott, eds., *Feminists Theorize the Political* (New York and London: Routledge, 1992), 41–53.

33. Rey Chow, "Violence in the Other Country: China as Crisis, Spectacle, and Woman," in Chandra Mohanty, Ann Russo, and Lourdes Torres, eds., *Third World Women and the Politics of Feminism* (Bloomington: Indiana University Press, 1991), 85.

34. C. Douglas Lummis, "Globocop? Time to Watch the Watchers," *The Nation* (September 26, 1994), 302–6.

35. David J. Depew, "Narrativism, Cosmopolitanism, and Historical Epistemology," *Clio* 14, 4 (1985). Depew's argument continues: "Positive cosmopolitanism must oscillate uncertainly between these poles. Cosmopolitanism, then, *considered as a positive ideal* . . . generates antinomies that undermine its internal coherence. . . . Considered, however, as a critical ideal, these difficulties largely disappear" (375). That is, cosmopolitanism should serve only negatively, to block false totalization.

36. Tom Athanasiou, "After the Summit," *Socialist Review* 22, 4 (October/December 1992), 57–92, esp. 82.

37. Christopher Hitchens, introduction to Adam Bartos and Christopher Hitchens, *International Territory: The United Nations 1945–95* (London and New York: Verso, 1994), 33.
38. Laura Flanders, "C. MacKinnon in the City of Freud: Hard Cases and Human Rights," *The Nation* (August 9–16, 1993), 174–77.
39. One cannot universalize the state's loss of legitimacy. Adamantia Pollis suggests that the legitimacy of the state may vary considerably even within Europe: "Advocates of universality contend that individual rights either are or are becoming valid throughout the world. Although the notion of individual human rights emerged at a particular historical epoch in Western Europe, it is argued that in the post World War II era, this Western concept of rights is being disseminated along with modernization. Therefore, communalism, characteristic of traditional societies, is gradually being replaced by notions of individual human rights" ("The State, the Law, and Human Rights in Modern Greece," *Human Rights Quarterly* 9 [1987], 587–614, esp. 587). Asking "whether the 'Western' conception of individual human rights is applicable to a peripheral European country" (587) where duties have been located in the state rather than rights in the individual, she answers in the negative: "This study of Greece highlights the simplistic nature of arguments over universalism versus cultural relativism regarding notions of human rights. The presumption of a shared philosophic foundation of human rights is empirically invalid even within the West" (613). On the legitimacy of the state in Greece, see also, however, Stathis Gourgouris, "Nationalism and Oneirocriticism: Of Modern Hellenes in Europe," *Diaspora* 2, 1 (Spring 1992), 43–72.
40. Gayatri Chakravorty Spivak, "Who Claims Sexuality in the New World Order?" (paper based on her speeches at the United Nations ICPD Conference, Cairo, in September 1994, delivered at the Conference on Culture/Sex/Economics, LaTrobe University, Melbourne, Australia, December 1994).

NOTES TO CHAPTER 4

1. References to John Berger's works are given in the text. The editions cited and their abbreviations are the following: *About Looking* (*AL*) (London: Writers & Readers, 1980); *A Painter of Our Time* (*APT*) (London: Writers & Readers, 1958); *A Seventh Man* (*ASM*) (Harmondsworth: Penguin, 1975); *Lilac and Flag: An Old Wives' Tale of a City* (New York: Pantheon, 1990); *Once in Europa* (New York: Pantheon, 1983, 1987); *Permanent Red* (*PR*) (London: Writers & Readers, 1960); *Pig Earth* (*PE*) (London: Writers & Readers, 1979); *Return to My Native Land*, with Anya Bostock (Harmondsworth: Penguin, 1969); *The Success and Failure of Picasso* (*SFP*) (Harmondsworth: Penguin, 1965); *Another Way of Telling* (*AWT*), with Jean Mohr (New York: Pantheon, 1982); *Ways of Seeing* (*WS*) (Harmondsworth: Penguin, 1972).

2. Carrie Rickey, "John Berger Is a Big Deal," *Village Voice* 25, 35 (August 27–September 2, 1980), 31.
3. Fred Pfeil, review of *Pig Earth* and *About Looking, Minnesota Review*, n.s., no. 15 (Fall 1980), 124.
4. Ibid., 125.
5. See, for example, Edward Said, "Reflections on Recent American 'Left' Criticism," *boundary 2* 8 (Fall 1979), 11–30.
6. James Clifford, *The Predicament of Culture: Twentieth-Century Ethnography, Literature, and Art* (Cambridge, MA, and London: Harvard University Press, 1988), 21–54.
7. Raphael Samuels, ed., *People's History and Socialist Theory* (London: Routledge & Kegan Paul, 1981), xviii–ix, xxx.
8. Perry Anderson, *Arguments within English Marxism* (London: Verso, 1980), 57–58.
9. Ibid., 26–28.
10. Terry Eagleton, *Criticism and Ideology* (London: New Left Books, 1976), 22. Like Anderson, Eagleton refers to but does not make central use of the distinction between *Erlebnis* (the subjective experience of an incident as belonging to a precise moment) and *Erfahrung* (the more general experience) developed by Walter Benjamin in "On Some Motifs in Baudelaire," in *Illuminations*, trans. Harry Zohn, ed. Hannah Arendt (New York: Schocken, 1969). Eagleton's own treatment of experience is criticized, and the concept is defended, in Ian Craib's "*Criticism and Ideology*: Theory and Experience," *Contemporary Literature* 22 (1981), 489–509.
11. Eagleton, *Criticism and Ideology*, 15, 28.
12. Raymond Williams, *Politics and Letters: Interviews with New Left Review* (London: Verso, 1979), 170. In a similar vein, Edward Said comments on the neglect of imperialism in Williams's *The Country and the City*. See Edward W. Said, *Culture and Imperialism* (New York: Knopf, 1993), 65, 82–84.
13. Richard Johnson, "Histories of Culture/Theories of Ideology: Notes on an Impasse," in Michele Barrett, Philip Corrigan, Annette Kuhn, and Janet Wolff, eds., *Ideology and Cultural Production* (London: Croom Helm, 1979), 51–55.
14. Terry Eagleton, *Walter Benjamin, or Towards a Revolutionary Criticism* (London: Verso, 1981), 177.
15. Anderson, *Arguments within English Marxism*, 36.
16. Williams, *Politics and Letters*, 165, 170–71.
17. Terry Eagleton, "A Sort of Fiction," *New Statesman* 15 (1979), 876.
18. See my "John Berger's Disappearing Peasants," *Minnesota Review*, n.s., no. 28 (Spring 1987), 63–67, for discussion of the second volume of the "Into Their Labors" trilogy, *Once in Europa*. (The third volume is *Lilac and Flag*.) In the title story, a manganese factory has taken over the village, killing one character and mutilating another along the way. Yet for Berger, the new is

not merely the destructive. Little by little, the reader catches on to the un-usual circumstances of narration: the story is made up of the musings of a peasant woman, who is hang gliding at three thousand meters with her son. Her voice soars, filled with the spirit that made her jump off a mountain. After initial resistance, she has accepted the lesson learned from her dead lover—that one can *choose* where to live—and has chosen to live above a shop in town. Now she lives at a higher altitude, where life may seem thin but where there is also the exhilaration of unimagined possibilities. It is a tribute to Berger that even when his metanarrative recognizes only victimiza-tion, he cannot present his peasants merely as victims. He seems unable not to bestow innovative energies even on those he claims want only to return to how things were.

Another example of this reluctant virtue resides in the story's title. The words IN EUROPA are an acronym made up of the letters assigned to each of the factory's eight sheds, where the (mainly foreign) workers live. Origi-nally, the narrator says, the sheds were simply lettered *A* to *H*; then one of the workers painted them over. What is so nice about the word is that you don't know how to pronounce it; you don't even know what language it's in. German, Italian, Spanish? Or is it just a "mistake" or mistranslation? No matter; all you know, and all you need to know, is that it's neither French, the language of the characters, nor English, the language of the reader. There is no visible connection to the nationality of any character in the story. As if to stress this pure uprootedness, the shed where the protagonist and her (Ukrainian-Swedish) lover live is letter *A*, the distinguishing sign of difference from "our" languages and thus the sign of a new, "made-up" lan-guage. Industrialism surrounds them, but the product of their union is irreducible to industrialism and seems as lively or vital as the peasant cul-ture it supplants. The phrase "in Europa" leaves us with an image of Europe already penetrated by difference, where peasant traditions coexist with unprecedented mixtures and marvels—an image that injects some buoyancy into the bathos of the "disappearing peasantry" narrative.

19. See, for example, Marc Shell, *The Economy of Literature* (Baltimore: Johns Hopkins University Press, 1978), 39–42; and Hayden White, *Metahistory* (Baltimore: Johns Hopkins University Press, 1972), 100.

20. Susan Sontag, *On Photography* (New York: Delta, 1977); hereafter cited as *OP*.

21. Roland Barthes, *Mythologies*, trans. Annette Lavers (New York: Hill & Wang, 1972), 100.

22. Michel Foucault, *Power/Knowledge: Selected Interviews and Other Writings, 1972–1977*, ed. Colin Gordon (New York: Pantheon, 1980), 78–92.

23. Paul Bové, "The End of Humanism," *Humanities in Society* 3 (Winter 1980), 34–35.

NOTES TO CHAPTER 5

1. E. J. Hobsbawm, *Nations and Nationalism since 1780: Programme, Myth, Reality* (Cambridge: Cambridge University Press, 1990), 1.

2. "Was it, we may ask, historically fortuitous that the classic era of free trade liberalism coincided with that 'nation-making' which [Walter] Bagehot saw as so central to his century? In other words, did the nation-state have a specific function as such in the process of capitalist development?" (ibid., 25). Today, the nation-state has lost this function, Hobsbawm says. Thus, "in spite of its evident prominence, nationalism is historically less important" (181).

3. Julien Benda, *The Treason of the Intellectuals*, trans. Richard Aldington (1928; reprint, New York: Norton, 1969); Max Weber, *From Max Weber: Essays in Sociology*, ed. and trans. H. H. Gerth and C. Wright Mills (New York: Oxford University Press, 1946), 176.

4. Gayatri Spivak, in *Outside in the Teaching Machine* (New York: Routledge, 1993), writes of the need "to put together the story of the development of a cosmopolitanism that is global, gendered, and dynamic" (278). Choosing the words with her customary care, Spivak makes this a story of where *we* come from, how it happens that students of colonial and postcolonial culture are so anxious to identify ourselves with an alternative to nationalism. To the surprise of some, *cosmopolitanism* figures here as a word that can be used to identify a "correct" position. In the next paragraph Spivak says, "the last paragraph was grant proposal talk." Yet the point is surely that the self-abstraction of grant-proposal talk can never be wholly abstracted from the self.

5. James Clifford, "Traveling Cultures," in Lawrence Grossberg, Cary Nelson, and Paula Treichler, eds., *Cultural Studies* (New York: Routledge, 1992).

6. Paul Gilroy, *The Black Atlantic: Modernity and Double Consciousness* (Cambridge, MA: Harvard University Press, 1993).

7. Amitav Ghosh, *In an Antique Land* (New York: Knopf, 1992).

8. Benita Parry, "The Contradictions of Cultural Studies," *Transition*, no. 53 (1991), 37–45.

9. Gayatri Chakravorty Spivak, "Poststructuralism, Marginality, Postcoloniality, and Value," in Peter Collier and Helga Geyer-Ryan, eds., *Literary Theory Today* (Ithaca: Cornell University Press, 1990), 222, 224.

10. Jamaica Kincaid, *Lucy* (New York: Farrar, Straus & Giroux, 1990); Bharati Mukherjee, "Jasmine," in *The Middleman and Other Stories* (New York: Fawcett Crest, 1988); Bharati Mukherjee, *Jasmine* (New York: Fawcett Crest, 1989).

11. Gayatri Chakravorty Spivak, "Three Women's Texts and a Critique of Imperialism," *Critical Inquiry* 12 (Autumn 1985), 243–61.

12. See Bruce Robbins, *Secular Vocations: Intellectuals, Professionalism, Culture* (London: Verso, 1993), chap. 6.

13. It remains an interesting question how much the crossing of national borders does or does not change the nature of rural/urban migration. For domestic migrations, see, for example, S. A. Radcliffe, "Ethnicity, Patriarchy, and Incorporation into the Nation: Female Migrants as Domestic Workers in Peru," *Environment and Planning D: Society and Space* 8 (1990), 379–93.

14. V. S. Naipaul notoriously takes his personal journey from Trinidad to the United Kingdom and up the social ladder as an allegory of the progress of civilization. For this *Bildungsroman* in miniature, see, for example, "Our Universal Civilization," *New York Review of Books*, January 31, 1991, 22–25. For a useful warning against the temptations of such narratives, see Kevin Gaines, "Black Americans' Racial Uplift Ideology as 'Civilizing Mission': Pauline E. Hopkins on Race and Imperialism," in Amy Kaplan and Donald E. Pease, eds., *Cultures of United States Imperialism* (Durham: Duke University Press, 1993), 433–55.

15. Spivak, "Poststructuralism, Marginality," 228.

16. See Bruce Robbins, *The Servant's Hand: English Fiction from Below* (New York: Columbia University Press, 1986; paperback, Durham: Duke University Press, 1993).

17. Compare Kincaid's *Lucy* with the servant's placement in the midst of her employers' marital troubles in Melanie Sumner, "The Edge of the Sky," *New Yorker* (February 1, 1993), 73–84.

18. Rough or violent sex, also a motif in *Lucy*, seems in both texts to play dangerously with the ambiguity of whether such violence inescapably calls down on itself an allegory of political domination.

19. The amount of allegorical "give" in a narrative such as *Jane Eyre* is already a difficult question in nineteenth-century Britain: Jane is, of course, both a figure for the middle class and a figure for women, and this duplicity is not definitively resolvable into the figure of Jane as middle-class woman. If middle-class feminism can take it over, so, for example, can middle-class radicalism in general, which is the dominant form in the university.

20. Here, the surprisingly pertinent parallel would be Jane Eyre's other marriage option, St. John Rivers, and the direct role he offers her in imperialism's missionary project.

21. This has always been a problem for the interpretation of class allegory, as suggested by the continuing debate over Samuel Richardson's *Clarissa* (1747–48).

22. In James Salter's story "Foreign Shores," the intrusion of an au pair into the home is made ironically representative of fears of the international sex trade. See James Salter, *Dusk and Other Stories* (San Francisco: North Point Press, 1988). Thanks to Fred Pfeil for the reference.

23. This may be related to the history of monogamy as an Orientalist trope, basic to Western civilization's self-definition or differentiation—as, indeed,

it is in *Jane Eyre* itself. It is, of course, a strange trope, given how far from monogamous Western society is or ever was.

24. As with her appreciation for the Gauguin figure, here again we have identification of the breaking up of a nuclear family with the birth of the artist-migrant.

25 Hilton Als, "Don't Worry Be Happy," *The Nation*, February 18, 1991, 207–8.

26. For a not entirely unsympathetic class description of the recent Indian diaspora in North America, see Aijaz Ahmad, *In Theory* (London: Verso, 1992).

27. Cynthia Enloe, in the final chapter of *Bananas, Beaches, and Bases* (Berkeley: University of California Press, 1989), is extremely insightful on the relation between the history of feminism and the history of domestic work, as well as on the correspondence between racial difference and the hierarchy of child-care workers. According to her scheme, white professional nannies who do no housework are on top; on the bottom are women of color who "are available for household chores as well" and who "are not thought of as professionals." Racially heterogeneous but more often white, au pairs, who see their work "as a short-term job, a way to travel and learn another language before moving on to more serious commitments" (180), are in the middle and thus partake symbolically in both upper and lower social worlds.

28. It has been argued that feminism itself could come into existence in the West only because middle-class women in the First World, unlike middle-class women in the Third World, did not have access to affordable domestic servants. Thus the relation between Third World au pair and First World feminist professional becomes even more complexly allegorical, and it is even less clear that the move to the metropolis is simply a move up. See Martha Gimenez, "The Dialectics of Waged and Unwaged Work," in Jane L. Collins and Martha Gimenez, eds., *Work without Wages: Domestic Labor and Self-Employment within Capitalism* (Albany: State University of New York Press, 1990), 25–46.

29. On transnational child-care workers who pay others to care for children of their own left behind in the Caribbean, see, for example, Shellee Colen, " 'With Respect and Feelings': Voices of West Indian Child Care and Domestic Workers in New York City," in Women's Studies Program of Rutgers University, *Women, Culture and Society: A Reader* (Dubuque, IA: Kendall/Hunt, 1985).

30. The quotient of allegorical play or "give" in this narrative, which lends itself to the diverging imaginative agendas of readerships or constituencies that are not composed of Third World au pairs, is not the same as literariness itself, but like literariness, it has a history. One can speculate that this quotient may have shifted along with post-Fordism's regime of flexible accumulation or flexible specialization, which is often taken to distinguish a characteristically postmodernist from a modernist sense of identity. According to this

reasoning, modernism's Fordist refashioning of the producer/consumer self gave way to less control over a more multiple selfhood, more free to be different and yet also less able to touch or influence the veiled, dispersed forces that continue to constrain it. In this sense, the au pair narrative may be said to offer itself to the hopes and desires of more types of readers, while it also offers each of them less of a vicarious victory—while it persistently equivocates, that is, between the suggestion of an upward movement and the suggestion of a merely lateral movement. How much can be won—what, indeed, is "winning" about—from the moment when there is no center to occupy?

31. Linda Colley, "Whose Nation? Class and National Consciousness in Britain 1750–1830," *Past and Present*, no. 113 (1986), 97–117.

32. Hobsbawm, *Nations and Nationalism*: "This was evidently incompatible with definitions of nations as based on ethnicity, language, or common history" (33). These theorists saw nationalism as "a phase in human evolution or progress from the small group to the larger . . . and, in the last instance, to the unified world of the future in which, to quote the superficial and therefore typical G. Lowes Dickinson, 'the barriers of nationality which belong to the infancy of the race will melt and dissolve in the sunshine of science and art' " (38). See Etienne Balibar, "Is There a 'Neo-Racism'?" in Etienne Balibar and Immanuel Wallerstein, *Race, Nation, Class: Ambiguous Identities* (London, Verso, 1991), 19, for "evolutionary anthropology" as the prototype of "academic racism."

33. The ladder is an unfortunate figure here; to be more precise, one should say that the question of the non-West's own desiderata is thereby foreclosed.

34. Edward W. Said, *Culture and Imperialism* (New York: Knopf, 1993), 244.

35. Franco Moretti, *The Way of the World: The Bildungsroman in European Culture* (London: Verso, 1987).

36. The reference is to Emile Habiby, *The Secret Life of Saeed, the Ill-Fated Pessoptimist*, trans. Salma Khadia Jayyusi and Trevor Le Gaassick (1974; reprint, Los Angeles: Readers International, 1985). See my review of *Culture and Imperialism* in *Nineteenth-Century Contexts*, no. 18 (1994), 93–96.

NOTES TO CHAPTER 6

1. In the interests of economy, I henceforth combine the two into *(post)colonial*. On the development and limits of the term *postcolonial*, see Ella Shohat, "Notes on the 'Post-Colonial,' " *Social Text*, no. 31/32 (1992), 99–113; and in the same issue, Anne McClintock, "The Angel of Progress: Pitfalls of the Term 'Post-Colonialism," 84–98.

2. Kwame Anthony Appiah, *In My Father's House: Africa in the Philosophy of Culture* (New York: Oxford University Press, 1992), 149.

3. Arif Dirlik, "The Postcolonial Aura: Third World Criticism in the Age of Global Capitalism," *Critical Inquiry* 20, 2 (Winter 1994), 356, 329. See also

Dirlik's *After the Revolution: Waking to Global Capitalism* (Hanover and London: Wesleyan University Press, 1994), for the argument that "postcolonialism coincides with the ideology of Global Capitalism" (97).

4. Régis Debray, *Teachers, Writers, Celebrities: The Intellectuals of Modern France*, trans. David Macey, introduction by Francis Mulhern (London: Verso, 1981), 58–59.

5. It would also be interesting to consider at least two of Said's idiosyncratic uses of *secular*, which have to do especially with scholarship: (1) the association of the secular with a distinctively *slow* historical rhythm, the temporality of scholarship, and (2) its association with a sort of Weberian existential heroism of scholarship, one that does without the usual versions of transcendent reassurance.

6. See, more recently, Edward W. Said, *The Politics of Dispossession: The Struggle for Palestinian Self-Determination, 1969–1994* (New York: Pantheon, 1994).

7. Michael Sprinker, ed., *Edward W. Said: A Critical Reader* (London: Blackwell, 1992), 232–33.

8. Tim Brennan, "Places of Mind, Occupied Lands: Edward Said and Philology," in Sprinker, ed., *Edward W. Said*, 92.

9. R. Radhakrishnan, *Diasporic Mediations: Between Home and Location* (Minneapolis: University of Minnesota Press, 1996), 160. See also William Connolly, "Pluralism and Multiculturalism" (lecture delivered at the Bohen Foundation, New York City, February 1994): "But what if secularism remains, on points crucial to multiculturalism, too close to the partner it loves to struggle against? And what if these affinities make their own contribution to the periodic return of violent Christian and secular fundamentalisms in western states? . . . Both the celebration and the lament of the (precarious) victory of the secular underplay the degree to which the Christian sacred remains buried in it" (25).

10. Peter van der Veer, "The Foreign Hand: Orientalist Discourse in Sociology and Communalism," in Carol A. Breckenridge and Peter van der Veer, eds., *Orientalism and the Postcolonial Predicament: Perspectives on South Asia* (Philadelphia: University of Pennsylvania Press, 1993), 39.

11. Ranajit Guha, "The Prose of Counter-Insurgency," in Ranajit Guha and Gayatri Chakravorty Spivak, eds., *Selected Subaltern Studies*, foreword by Edward W. Said (New York and Oxford: Oxford University Press, 1988), 81.

12. Dipesh Chakrabarty, "The Death of History? Historical Consciousness and the Culture of Late Capitalism," *Public Culture* 4, 2 (Spring 1992), 52–53. Again, "nationalist history, in spite of its anti-imperialist stance and substance, shared a deeply embedded meta-narrative with imperialist accounts of British India. This was the meta-narrative of the modern state" (52).

13. Another example comes from Faisal Fatehali Devji: "Ideologically, I think, Hindu nationalism has emerged as the only mode of resistance to the 'secular' state—indeed as the only credible, organized form of alternative politics

in a country where the ruling elite has appropriated secular nationalism so completely as to allow no room for dispute in its terms. Even the Left collapses into secular-nationalist attitudes when faced with a 'communalism' it is incapable of understanding or dealing with apart from a largely irrelevant rhetoric of class conflict. Secular nationalism itself, in other words, has become a kind of state 'fundamentalism,' a sort of self-legitimizing mode of coercion that ends up generating its own nemesis in the 'communalism' it demonizes" ("Hindu/Muslim/Indian," *Public Culture* 5, 1 [Fall 1992], 5). Somewhat excessively, Devji blames secularists for the creation of communalism. Like Rorty's claim that the parochialism of the academic left is responsible for the failure of a broader left in the United States, this is a form of covert celebration of left-wing intellectuals, for it holds them responsible—that is, credits their power and influence—for matters far beyond them, including the craziness of their enemies and critics.

14. See, however, Partha Chatterjee's essay in Sprinker, ed., *Edward W. Said*, "Their Own Words? An Essay for Edward Said," which defends within nationalism the "many possibilities of authentic, creative, and plural development of social identities which were violently disrupted by the political history of the post-colonial state seeking to replicate the modular forms of the modern nation-state" (216).

15. Note the uses of *authority* in *Beginnings*, vis-à-vis molestation—a coinage that is emphatically not antiauthoritarian. See Edward W. Said, *Beginnings: Intention and Method* (New York: Basic Books, 1975). But note also the pathos of Said's isolated, genuinely heroic critique of the Middle East "peace process" in his *Peace and Its Discontents: Essays on Palestine in the Middle East Peace Process* (New York: Vintage, 1996).

16. Edward W. Said, "Gods That Always Fail," *Raritan* 13, 4 (Spring 1994), 13; also in Edward W. Said, *Representations of the Intellectual* (New York: Pantheon, 1994), 120.

17. Said, *Representations*, 121, 120. One's own beliefs and findings, in Said's view, quickly and inevitably harden into authorities.

18. "Benda's examples, however, make it quite clear that he does not endorse the notion of totally disengaged, other-worldly, ivory-towered thinkers. . . . Real intellectuals are never more themselves than when, moved by metaphysical passion and disinterested principles of justice and truth, they denounce corruption, defend the weak, defy imperfect or oppressive authority" (ibid., 5–6).

19. Edward W. Said, *The World, the Text, and the Critic* (Cambridge, MA: Harvard University Press, 1983).

20. Anna Boschetti, *The Intellectual Enterprise: Sartre and "Les Temps modernes,"* trans. Richard McCleary (Evanston: Northwestern University Press, 1988).

21. See chapter 5.

22. Edward W. Said, *Culture and Imperialism* (New York: Knopf, 1993), 244.

23. Pierre Bourdieu, *Homo Academicus*, trans. Peter Collier (Stanford: Stanford University Press, 1988). Note the irony that the secular scholar can hold to his institution only with a religious irrationality.

24. Dirlik, "Postcolonial Aura," 354–55. Note the repetition of the old charge against cosmopolitans, leveled equally by Nazism and Stalinism, of complicity with world capitalism.

25. McClintock, "Angel of Progress," 84–98.

26. Alan Sinfield, *Literature, Politics, and Culture in Postwar Britain* (Berkeley: University of California Press, 1989), 234.

27. Arjun Appadurai, "Disjuncture and Difference in the Global Cultural Economy," in Bruce Robbins, ed., *The Phantom Public Sphere* (Minneapolis: University of Minnesota Press, 1993), 269–95.

28. Abdul JanMohamed, "Worldliness-without-World, Homelessness-as-Home," in Sprinker, ed., *Edward W. Said*, 96–120.

29. It is interesting to note the historical usefulness of "secular" as a qualifier of multiculturalism. William Connolly writes, "Eventually, of course, secularism emerges as a loose set of doctrines designed to prevent struggles between contending Christian sects from tearing the fabric of public life apart" ("Pluralism and Multiculturalism," 25).

NOTES TO CHAPTER 7

1. I am grateful to the organizers of the Seventh Quadrennial Comparative Literature Conference in Taipei in August 1995, where these ideas were first developed, and to Lauren Berlant, Jacqueline Bhabha, Carol Breckenridge, Pheng Cheah, and Dilip Gaonkar for their detailed critiques. I am also grateful to Richard Rorty for making available several of his unpublished manuscripts and for generously taking the time to argue.

2. Richard Rorty, "The Unpatriotic Academy," *New York Times*, Sunday, February 13, 1994, E15.

3. The left would add: not just the defense but the extension of the social welfare state.

4. Nancy Fraser, *Unruly Practices: Power, Discourse and Gender in Contemporary Social Theory* (Minneapolis: University of Minnesota Press, 1989).

5. Richard Rorty, "Intellectuals in Politics," *Dissent* 38 (Fall 1991), 483–90. The response by Andrew Ross, "On Intellectuals in Politics," and "Richard Rorty Replies" are in *Dissent* 39 (Spring 1992), 263–67. The quoted lines are from "Richard Rorty Replies," 265.

6. Richard Rorty, "On Ethnocentrism: A Reply to Clifford Geertz," in *Objectivity, Relativism, and Truth: Philosophical Papers*, vol. 1 (Cambridge: Cambridge University Press, 1991), 203–10, esp. 210.

7. Rorty describes a form of ethnocentrism that is "inevitable and unobjectionable" (212) as one that would "look forward, in a vague way, to a time when the Cashinahua, the Chinese, and (if such there be) the planets which form

the Galactic Empire will all be part of the same cosmopolitan social democratic community" (Richard Rorty, "Cosmopolitanism without Emancipation: A Reply to Jean-François Lyotard," in *Objectivity, Relativism, and Truth*, vol. 1, 211–22, esp. 212).

8. Rorty, "On Ethnocentrism," 209. For related arguments on the limited value of a cultural politics, see Jürgen Habermas on immigration in "Struggles for Recognition in the Democratic Constitutional State," in Charles Taylor et al., *Multiculturalism: Examining the Politics of Recognition*, Amy Gutman, ed. (Princeton: Princeton University Press, 1994), 107–48.

9. A recent, ill-tempered denunciation of the so-called postmodern left in the name of human rights is Marshall Berman, "Modernism and Human Rights near the Millenium," *Dissent* (Summer 1995), 333–41. Berman sets this postmodern left against Habermas, whom he describes as "the most serious theorist of human rights today" (340).

10. Richard Rorty, "Philosophy and the Future," in *Rorty and Pragmatism*, ed. Herman Saatkamp (Nashville: Vanderbilt University Press, 1995).

11. Terry Eagleton, "Defending the Free World," in Ralph Miliband, Leo Panitch, and John Saville, eds., *Socialist Register 1990* (London: Merlin Press, 1990), 85–93, esp. 85.

12. Richard Rorty, "Private Irony and Liberal Hope," in *Contingency, Irony, and Solidarity* (Cambridge and New York: Cambridge University Press, 1989). We may pause to note that if Europe, Asia, and Africa all have communities, only Europe appears to possess families and individuals.

13. Michael Billig ascribes Rorty's "admitted ethnocentrism (which simultaneously is a subtly denied ethnocentrism)" to "the nationalism of the *Pax Americana*. This nationalism, unlike some older forms, does not speak with narrow ferocity for the nation. Instead, it draws its moral force to lead the nations from its own proclaimed reasonableness. The global ambitions are to be presented as the voice of tolerance ('our' tolerance), even doubt ('our' doubt, 'our' modesty). All the while, 'we' are to keep a sense of 'ourselves.' And a sense of 'others': the mad and the bad, who cling to dangerous absolutes, opposing 'our' pragmatic, non-ideological politics. It should be noted how easily new enemies—the religious fundamentalists, particularly Islamic fundamentalists—can replace old Soviet demons in this ideological matrix" ("Nationalism and Richard Rorty: The Text as a Flag for the *Pax Americana*," *New Left Review*, no. 202 [November/December 1993], 82–83).

14. Richard Rorty, "Human Rights, Rationality, and Sentimentality," in Stephen Shute and Susan Hurley, eds., *On Human Rights: The Oxford Amnesty Lectures 1993* (New York: Basic Books, 1993), 111–34.

15. My own argument here remains Rortyan in the sense that, rather than seeking a universal philosophical foundation for human rights, I take as my point of departure the existence of a provisional transnational consensus

about human rights, legitimated by the increasing participation of NGOs, especially non-Western ones, and the existence of continuing dialogue about the limits and unequal applications of human rights instruments.

16. Rorty, "On Ethnocentrism," 203.

17. Richard Rorty, "Who Are We? Moral Universalism and Economic Triage" (forthcoming in a volume of UNESCO essays).

18. Norman Geras, *Solidarity in the Conversation of Mankind: The Ungroundable Liberalism of Richard Rorty* (London: Verso, 1995), 99.

19. The speech is excerpted in *Harper's* (June 1996), 15–18.

20. Rorty, "Who Are We?"

21. See James Livingston, *Pragmatism and the Political Economy of Cultural Revolution, 1850–1940* (Chapel Hill: University of North Carolina Press, 1994), chap. 10. For an argument that, like Livingston's, sees hope for global redistribution less in a cultural politics of asceticism than in the extension of Western freedom, creativity, and pleasure, see Andrew Ross, *The Chicago Gangster Theory of Life: Nature's Debt to Society* (London and New York: Verso, 1994), introduction.

22. I developed this argument further in chapter 1.

23. This is the sort of human rights culture that shows its power when, for instance, Amnesty International investigates the New York Police Department, or when Randall Robinson and the African American organization TransAfrica Forum, which spearheaded the boycott of South Africa under apartheid, call for sanctions against the government of Nigeria. See Steven A. Holmes, "U.S. Blacks Battle Nigeria over Rights Issue," *New York Times*, June 15, 1995, A6.

24. "During the global contest between the nuclear giants, the UN passed its most exacting test. It survived, and so did the human race" ("The United Nations at Fifty," *New York Times*, June 26, 1995, editorial page).

25. Barbara Crossette, "U.N. Finds Skepticism Is Eroding the Hope That Is Its Foundation," *New York Times*, June 25, 1995, A1.

26. The editorial of *The Nation's* fortieth-birthday special issue ("Reflections on a Glass House: The U.N. at Forty," *The Nation* [September 21, 1985]) presented the United Nations as a "Global Talk Show." Describing the Nairobi conference that capped off the UN Decade for Women, *The Nation* said, "The conference brought together people who do not normally talk to one another" (228).

27. Richard Falk, "The United Nations after Forty Years," *The Nation* (September 21, 1985), 234–38.

28. Fateh Azzam, "Non-Governmental Organizations and the UN World Conference on Human Rights," *Review of the International Commission of Jurists*, no. 50 (1993), 89–100. "Southern human rights NGOs have come of age and will be a force to be reckoned with in the human rights debate in the future" (99).

29. Upandra Baxi, " 'The Spirit of Our Age, the Realities of Our Time': The Vienna Declaration on Human Rights," in *Mambrino's Helmet: Human Rights for a Changing World* (New Delhi: Har Anand, 1994).

30. (ISHR), *Human Rights Monitor*, no. 21 (May 1993), 21. Note that, as Azzam says, NGOs themselves proclaimed the Vienna Declaration a "Flawed Document" ("Non-Governmental Organizations," 98) for its failure to commit governments to concrete measures.

31. The NGOs could function as well as they did because, like culture, they and their rights discourse were seen as *not* being fully or explicitly political. They were not states but units of international civil society—something between the powerlessness of culture and the power of the state. Indeed, Azzam sees the very success of the NGOs in Vienna as dangerous, for it crossed "the very thin line between human rights advocacy, populist advocacy, and political advocacy" ("Non-Governmental Organizations," 99).

32. Catherine MacKinnon, "Crimes of War, Crimes of Peace" in Shute and Hurley, eds., *On Human Rights*, 83–110; also Julie Peters and Andrea Wolper, eds., *Women's Rights Human Rights: International Feminist Perspectives* (New York and London: Routledge, 1995).

33. It is possible that Rorty intended to distinguish, interestingly, between atrocity stories, whose effect he is rightly skeptical about, and the "sad and sentimental stories" he credits with developing human rights culture. But no such distinction appears in his text.

34. Laura Flanders, "Hard Cases and Human Rights: C. MacKinnon in the City of Freud," *The Nation* (August 9–16, 1993), 174–77.

35. On human rights as a form of action necessary, if not sufficient, to economic redistribution, see, for example, *Development Bulletin*, no. 34 (August 1995), a special issue devoted to human rights and development. In this issue, Philip Alston, in "The Rights Framework and Development Assistance," argues that since the link was made in the early 1990s, the human rights vocabulary has added a new and empowering immediacy to earlier talk of "basic needs" and "human well-being": "They are no longer a vague and undefined entitlement to a favour of some kind to be bestowed upon them by a benevolent government, if and when they can afford it" (10).

36. Baxi writes, "While most 'obstacles' and 'challenges' emanate from unjust, and evil, forms of governance, the civil society, too, may provide a fertile soil for the growth of 'obstacles' and 'challenges' to human rights attainment. In so far as this is the case, the Declaration envisages a substantial interventionist role by the state and superstatal institutions" (" 'Spirit of Our Age,' " 4).

37. C. J. Wee Wan-ling, "Re: Michael Fay," *Commentary* (journal of the National University of Singapore Society [NUSS]), 12, 1 (1994). For apparently unrelated reasons, this issue was suppressed by the NUSS management society.

38. Leon Perera, "The Michael Fay Controversy: What Was at Stake?" *Commentary* 12, 1 (1994). Perera points out as well how Singaporean opinion tended

not to object to foreign intervention as such: "Mainstream opinion here . . . is generally supportive of U.S.-led UN military intervention in the killing fields of Rwanda and Bosnia" (122). Respect for sovereignty is not an absolute principle.

39. A Cuban resolution of 1985 to the United Nations, opposed by the Western powers but finally passed in 1991, asserted the principle of nonselectivity, impartiality, and objectivity in dealing with human rights. It is unclear that this resolution has had any effect on human rights work.

40. Perera here refers to Asad Latif, *Straits Times* (23 April 1994).

41. According to the polls I saw, the U.S. public did not agree with its political leaders and editorialists who condemned the caning as an act of barbarism. A majority agreed that the American criminal justice system does not work and thought it might improve if the United States followed Singapore's example and caned vandals. In the months after the Fay case, several bills were presented in state legislatures around the country that, inspired by Singaporean policy, called for whipping as punishment for graffiti. Is this internationalism or merely Americano-centrism of a different type, one that prefers to seize on similarities to what it knows, rather than assuming difference? In other words, is it just the recognition of sameness that Rorty's sad and sentimental stories are supposed to encourage? This incongruity between mass opinion (which tended to approve the caning) and the so-called educated elites (which condemned it) is, again, worth following up.

42. See Amanda Anderson, "Cryptonormativism and Double Gestures: The Politics of Post-Structuralism," *Cultural Critique* 21 (Spring 1992), 63–95.

43. Pheng Cheah, "Given Culture: Rethinking Cosmopolitical Freedom in Transnationalism," *boundary 2* 24, 2 (Summer 1997), 157-97. Cheah also usefully defines the dilemma with which I began: "A metropolitan cultural politics which espouses a hands-off approach to a museumized cultural other leaves the neocolonial staging of that other—fundamentalism, ethnicism, patriarchal nationalism—untouched. Yet, if we intervene in those other spaces as self-proclaimed didacts of freedom, we forget that we too are part of the crisis because the problems of unequal development and the post-industrial feudalisation of the periphery are fundamental structures of *our* everyday" (158).

44. Richard Rorty, "Two Cheers for the Cultural Left," in Darryl J. Gless and Barbara Herrnstein Smith, eds., *The Politics of Liberal Education* (Durham and London: Duke University Press, 1992), 233–40, esp. 235.

45. Ibid., 234.

NOTES TO CHAPTER 8

1. This passage is discussed in Kwame Anthony Appiah, "Cosmopolitan Patriots," *Critical Inquiry* 23, 3 (Spring 1997), 617–39, esp. 638.

2. Martha C. Nussbaum et al., *For Love of Country: Debating the Limits of Patriotism*, ed. Josh Cohen (Boston: Beacon Press, 1996). Nussbaum develops

her theme at greater length in her *Cultivating Humanity: A Classical Defense of Reform in Liberal Education* (Cambridge, MA: Harvard University Press, 1997). For a useful commentary, see Michael Bérubé, "Citizens of the World, Unite! Martha Nussbaum's Campaign to Cultivate Humanity," *Lingua Franca* (September 1997), 54–61.

3. The case for a more modest version of cosmopolitanism can be found in Pheng Cheah and Bruce Robbins, eds., *Cosmopolitics: Thinking and Feeling beyond the Nation* (Minneapolis: University of Minnesota Press, 1998).

4. See Larry Rohter, "Hondurans in 'Sweatshops' See Opportunity," *New York Times*, July 18, 1996, A1, 14; and Andrew Ross, ed., *No Sweat: Fashion, Free Trade, and the Rights of Garment Workers* (London and New York: Verso, 1997).

5. Linda S. Bosniak, "Opposing Prop. 187: Undocumented Immigrants and the National Imagination," *Connecticut Law Review* 28, 3 (Spring 1996), 555–619.

6. James Der Derian, *Antidiplomacy: Spies, Terror, Speed, and War* (Cambridge, MA, and Oxford: Blackwell, 1992), 95.

7. In so doing, Nussbaum also exposes some cryptonormativity among the culturalists, who disguise the inevitably normative drive behind their critique by locating it among cultural and geographical particulars. The following critics appear in *For Love of Country*, unless otherwise cited.

8. Michael J. Sandel, *Democracy's Discontent: America in Search of a Public Philosophy* (Cambridge, MA, and London: Harvard University Press, 1996), 343.

9. See my "Telescopic Philanthropy: Professionalism and Responsibility in *Bleak House*," in Homi Bhabha, ed., *Nation and Narration* (London: Methuen, 1990), 213–30.

10. Yasemin Soysal, *The Limits of Citizenship: Migrants and Postnational Membership in Europe* (Chicago and London: University of Chicago Press, 1994). European states "have expanded their comprehensive welfare apparatuses to guestworkers and their families. However," Soysal cautions, "there is nothing inherent about the logic of the welfare state that would dictate the incorporation of foreigners into its system of privileges" (138).

11. Quoted in Tom Keenan, "Publicity and Indifference (Sarajevo on Television)" (forthcoming as discussion paper, Joan Shorenstein Center on Press, Politics, and Public Policy, Harvard University, 1998). If, Keenan questions, there has been a "displacement of deliberation by emotion," then why didn't it work the same way in Bosnia? Why is it that "Somalia was hyperactivity, Bosnia inactivity"? Keenan concludes that what failed in Bosnia was the belief that images and emotions are compelling enough—that is, there was a loss of faith in their self-evidence.

12. Paul Virilio, *L'Écran du desert: Chroniques de Guerre* (Paris: Galilée, 1991), 71–72, quoted in Keenan, "Publicity and Indifference." Note the uncer-

tainty as to whether this displacement of politics by emotion is newly true about *all* politics—a matter of media and time, as Virilio says, and not differentiated by space or geographical scale—or, as Kennan seems to suggest, true about foreign policy but not about domestic policy. Once again, there is some confusion about whether the line between the national and international does or does not mark a significant difference.

13. Mary Kaldor, "Cosmopolitanism versus Nationalism: The New Divide?" in Richard Caplan and John Feffer, eds., *Europe's New Nationalism: States and Minorities in Conflict* (New York and Oxford: Oxford University Press, 1996), 42–58.

14. See, for example, "The National Entertainment State," *The Nation*, June 3, 1996, 20–28.

15. John Judis, *Grand Illusion: Critics and Champions of the American Century* (New York: Farrar, Straus & Giroux, 1992). In a review of Judis's book, Jim Chapin notes that the "realists" Judis admires, including Kennan, "were antidemocrats" ("Before and After the Cold War," *In These Times* [December 28, 1992], 33–34, esp. 34).

16. Anders Stephanson, *Kennan and the Art of Foreign Policy* (Cambridge, MA: Harvard University Press, 1989), 148. "Vietnam, in a nutshell, was not worth the trouble" (172). In response to a congressman's question in May 1947, Kennan stated, "If I thought for a moment that the precedent of Greece and Turkey obliged us to try to do the same thing in China, I would throw up my hands and say we had better have a whole new approach to the affairs of the world" (quoted in Stephanson, *Kennan*, 101–2.

17. See the section called "Globalizing the Rawlsian Conception of Justice" in Thomas W. Pogge, *Realizing Rawls* (Ithaca and London: Cornell University Press, 1989), 211–80.

18. For a more optimistic view of neo-medievalism, consider Mary Kaldor's call for "a new transnational layer of governance that would coexist with other layers—national, local, and regional. This new diversity of political institutions might resemble the premodern period in Europe, which was characterized by multiple, overlapping sources of political power, including city-states, principalities, kingdoms, and the Holy Roman Empire" ("Cosmopolitanism versus Nationalism: The New Divide?" 42–58, esp. 54–55).

19. Chapin, for instance, notes that, "Judis criticizes the evangelical dimension of American politics without explaining how it can be transcended. Although he recognizes the weakness of Nixon and Kissinger in failing to develop popular support for 'realism,' how realistic can an ideology be if it can't draw support from its own people?" ("Before and After the Cold War," 33).

20. Tom Nairn, *Faces of Nationalism: Janus Revisited* (London and New York: Verso, 1997), 5.

21. Of course, even the model of rooting does not require that we take the existence of teams—that is, self-interested nation-states—for granted. We actu-

ally root in more complex ways, at overlapping and conflicting levels: for individual players, leagues, local situations.

22. As we see elsewhere, the solution to mass starvation is not central administration.

23. Perhaps this is because the image of the warlord is really less a description than a projection, capitalism's own savage undermining of the state projected onto its supposedly primitive others.

24. See Der Derian, *Antidiplomacy*, 95.

25. E. J. Hobsbawm, *Bandits* (1969; reprint, Harmondsworth: Penguin, 1972), 106.

26. Quoted in Anita Desai, "Introduction," in Rabindranath Tagore, *The Home and the World*, trans. Surendranath Tagore (1919; reprint, Harmondsworth: Penguin, 1985), 7.

27. On Bengali sexual politics in this period, see Tanika Sarkar, "Nationalist Iconography: Image of Women in Nineteenth-Century Bengali Literature," *Economic and Political Weekly* (November 21, 1987), 2011–15. For this reference and an extremely pertinent argument, I am indebted to Michael Sprinker, "Homeboys: Nationalism, Colonialism, and Gender in Rabindranath Tagore's *The Home and the World*," in Richard Dienst and Henry Schwarz, eds., *Reading the Shape of the World* (Boulder: Westview Press, 1997).

28. Partha Chatterjee, *The Nation and Its Fragments* (Princeton: Princeton University Press, 1993), 147. This argument is elaborated and contested in Inderpal Grewal, *Home and Harem: Nation, Gender, Empire, and the Cultures of Travel* (Durham and London: Duke University Press, 1996).

29. Guha quotes Tagore: "To enforce unity on a person by twisting his neck can hardly be called an act of union; nor, by the same token, can the use of threat or journalistic slander to stop any public airing of disagreement be regarded as working for national unification" ("Discipline and Mobilize: Hegemony and Elite Control in Nationalist Campaigns," in *Dominance without Hegemony: History and Power in Colonial India* [Cambridge, MA, and London: Harvard University Press, 1997], 100–151, esp. 121).

30. Neil Lazarus, "Transnationalism and the Alleged Death of the Nation-State," in Keith Ansell Pearson, Benita Parry, and Judith Squires, eds., *Cultural Readings of Imperialism: Edward Said and the Gravity of History* (London: Lawrence & Wishart, 1997), 28–48. Lazarus's argument in favor of particular nations is strangely and suspiciously silent on the question of *which* particular nationalisms ought to be supported, right now, and which are being opposed or insufficiently supported by the supposed adversaries of nationalism on the left. Have Eric Hobsbawm and Homi Bhabha, whom Lazarus singles out for critique, shown a tendency to belittle the claims of the Palestinians, for example? Many people do not want the Palestinians to get an independent homeland, but I would very much like to see some evi-

dence that anyone withdraws support from them on cosmopolitan grounds. The usual Zionist-nationalist reasons are more in evidence, for example, in full-page ads in the newspapers when Israeli prime minister Benjamin Netanyahu comes to the United States. Formulaic references to the Front de Libération Nationale in Fanon's day (39) are safe, after all; one would like to know what Lazarus thinks of its successors in Algeria today and their claim to international support.

31. Timothy Brennan, *At Home in the World: Cosmopolitanism Now* (Cambridge, MA: Harvard University Press, 1997), 25.

32. Pinsky writes, "That Brooklyn of the Dodgers is a cultural reality shared by many, and I am proud to be among them. Call it patriotism" (in Nussbaum, *For Love of Country*, 90). I, too, went to Ebbetts Field as a child, the Dodgers were my team, and their picture is still on my wall. But I don't call this patriotism. Speaking of home teams, however: the February 1998 Ohio State demonstration against renewed bombing of Iraq worked, I am told, only because it was held in a basketball arena with marvelous acoustics. Demonstrators in the upper tiers, who were not allowed near the microphones, could nonetheless make themselves heard extremely well, disrupt the proceedings, and thus pressure the organizers into letting one of their number ask a question at the microphone—the question quoted in my Introduction. This is presumably a case of architects building up the home-court advantage.

33. Benedict Anderson, "Memory and Forgetting," in *Imagined Communities: Reflections on the Origin and Spread of Nationalism*, rev. ed. (London and New York: Verso, 1991), 187–206, esp. 202–3. Anderson's tolerance for the argument from shared sports fandom seems limited. When Michael Ignatieff, who is Canadian, confesses in *Blood and Belonging* that he wishes he shared with a fellow hockey fan who is Quebecois a similar love for a common nation, rather than merely residence in the same state, Anderson dismisses this as "a high-flying cosmopolitan's *nostalgie de la boue*" (Benedict Anderson, "Ice Empire and Ice Hockey: Two Fin de Siècle Dreams," *New Left Review*, no. 214 [November/December 1995], 146–50, esp. 150).

34. Michael Ondaatje, *The English Patient* (New York: Vintage/Random House, 1992).

35. David Stout, "Pentagon May Know Identity of One in Tomb of Unknowns," *New York Times*, January 20, 1998, A11.

NOTES TO THE AFTERWORD

1. Michael Ondaatje, *The English Patient* (New York: Vintage/Random House, 1992).

2. Martha C. Nussbaum, "Reply," in Martha C. Nussbaum et al., *For Love of Country: Debating the Limits of Patriotism*, ed. Josh Cohen (Boston: Beacon Press, 1996), 141–42.

3. Sigmund Freud, *Civilization and Its Discontents*, standard ed., trans. and ed. James Strachey (New York: Norton, 1961), 11. Freud concludes that the true source of religious sentiments is "the infant's helplessness and the longing for the father aroused by it" (20). As Marcia Ian has pointed out to me, Freud seems to have trouble deciding between the primordiality of the father, as here, or the mother's breast, as five pages earlier.

4. Eric Lott, "The New Cosmopolitanism," *Transition* 72, 6, 4 (Winter 1996), 108–35.

5. I owe this description of politics to Ernesto Laclau and Chantal Mouffe, *Hegemony and Socialist Strategy: Towards a Radical Democratic Politics*, trans. Winston Moore and Paul Cammack (London: Verso, 1985).

6. Gopal Balakrishnan, "The National Imagination," *New Left Review*, no. 211 (May/June 1995), 56–69. This essay is reprinted in Gopal Balakrishnan, ed., *Mapping the Nation* (London and New York: Verso, 1996), 198–213.

7. Tom Nairn, *Faces of Nationalism: Janus Revisited* (London and New York: Verso, 1997), 4: "Through nationalism the dead are awakened, this is the point—seriously awakened for the first time." See also Yael Tamir, "Pro Patria Mori!: Death and the State," in Robert McKim and Jeff McMahan, eds., *The Morality of Nationalism* (New York and Oxford: Oxford University Press, 1997), 227–41.

8. Zygmunt Baumann, *Mortality, Immortality and Other Life Strategies* (Stanford: Stanford University Press, 1992).

9. Samuel P. Huntington, *The Clash of Civilizations and the Remaking of the World Order* (New York: Simon & Schuster, 1996).

10. Immanuel Wallerstein, "The National and the Universal: Can There Be Such a Thing as World Culture?" in *Geopolitics and Geoculture: Essays on the Changing World System* (Cambridge: Cambridge University Press and the Maison des Sciences de l'Homme, 1991), 184–99.

11. David Miller, *On Nationality* (Oxford: Clarendon Press, 1995), 11.

INDEX

anticapitalism, 154. *See also* capitalism; global capitalism

anti-civil society: as synonym for nationalism, 49. *See also* civil society

anticolonial nationalism, 49

antielitism, 124, 156, 162. *See also* elitism

anti-imperialism, 62

antiprogressivism, 63. *See also* progress or progressivism

antiuniversalism, 62, 65, 77. *See also* universalism

Appadurai, Arjun, 49–50, 54, 124

Appiah, Kwame Anthony, 115–16

Arac, Jonathan, 6

Arato, Andrew, 47, 50

Arnold, Matthew, 95, 99

Athanasiou, Tom, 75

au pair narratives, 101–13

Australia, 52

authority: experience as, 82; institutional authority, 122; intellectual authority, 120, 124; of internationalism, 124; in relation to secularism, 119–20, 124; in relation to Third World intellectual migration and upward mobility, 121–22; in relation to truth and power, 119–20

Azzam, Fateh, 140

Balakrishnan, Gopal, 171

Balibar, Étienne, 36, 66–67, 70–71, 142

Barber, Benjamin, 34, 150, 153

Barthes, Roland, 93

Bates, Milton J., 27

Bauman, Zygmunt, 171–72

Baxi, Upandra, 140, 142

Beijing International Conference on Women's Rights, 35, 48, 76. *See also* human rights; United Nations

Benda, Julien, 99, 119, 120

Benjamin, Walter, 2, 80, 84, 92

Berger, John, 23, 79–95

Black diaspora, 55, 100. *See also* diaspora; *Diaspora*

Black intellectuals, 55. *See also* intellectuals; Third World intellectuals

Black public sphere, 54–55. *See also* public sphere

bombs, 1, 9, 166–67, 171

boredom: and cosmopolitanism, 147–54; in relation to indifference and nationalism, 153–55. *See also* emotion; experience; feeling; love

Boschetti, Anna, 120, 121

Bosnia, 4, 11–17, 158

boundary 2: and resistance to internationalism, 41; treatment of Black intellectuals in, 55; and U.S. internationalism, 40

Bourdieu, Pierre, 121–22

Boutros-Ghali, Boutros, 73

Bové, Paul, 95

Brecht, Bertolt, 80

Brennan, Timothy, 1, 101, 117, 163

Brontë, Charlotte: upward mobility in *Jane Eyre*, 101–2

Burke, Edmund, 152

Butler, Judith, 3–4

Calhoun, Craig, 54

California: Proposition 187, 148

capital, cultural. *See* cultural capital

capitalism: and civil society, 50; and commodity fetishism, 65; and cosmopolitanism, 71–72; critiques of, 154; in relation to the nation-state, 50, 66–67; and national sense of responsibility, 154; "real universality" of, 142; and universalism, 66. *See also* anticapitalism; U.S. capitalism

career, 101, 121. *See also* upward mobility

Caribbean, 158

Césaire, Aimé, 86–87

Chakrabarty, Dipesh, 118

Chatterjee, Partha, 47–49, 161

Cheah, Pheng, 144

China, 73, 143, 158, 160

Chow, Rey, 73

Citizenship: and California disputes about Proposition 187, 148; and civil society, 49; and constitutional patriotism, 153; and cosmopolitanism, 7, 152; and nationality, 36; "world citizenship," 148. *See also* nationalism; nation-state

civil society: and capitalism, 50; and citizenship, 49; and ethics, 47; and global capitalism, 51; and public sphere, 54, 76; in relation to nation-states and citizenship, 48; in relation to NGOs (nongovernmental organizations), 76; theory of, 49; in relation to U.S. internationalism and the journal *Public Culture*, 40. *See also* anti-civil society

class, 108–09, 154, 162. *See also* upward mobility

Clifford, James, 82, 100

CNN (Cable News Network): 2, 4; CNN effect, 156. See also television and mass media

Cohen, Jean, 47, 50

cold war: anticommunism and, 158; and formation of cultural left, 53; and internationalism, 42; and nationalism, 52
Colley, Linda, 110
colonialism, 61–77
commodities, 19
commodity fetishism, 65
Connery, Christopher, 41–42
constituency: of Black intellectuals, 55; and cosmopolitanism, 30–32; feeling as coded reference for, 70; and internationalism, 31
cosmopolitanism: and absence of feeling, 70; as
anticulture, 19; and boredom, 147–54; and
capitalism, 71–72; and citizenship, 7; and
class, 162; and constituency, 30–32; critics
and criticism of, 3, 152; cultural cosmopolitanism versus human rights internationalism, 130; and democracy, 162; as denial of
nationality, 151; and ethics, 154; and elitism, 27–29; and emotion, 150; and global
capitalism, 67; and intellectuals, 98; and
laissez-faire economics, 32; and language,
70; and metropolitan self-flattery, 11–12;
and nationalism, 6, 149; and nation-state,
33; "new cosmopolitanism," 7, 171;
nonelite cosmopolitanism, 100; in Michael
Ondaatje's *The English Patient*, 164–68; and
patriotism, 163; popular cosmopolitanism,
45, 100; postcolonial cosmopolitanism,
100–01; Edward Said's critique of, 118; and
social welfare state, 6–7; and Stalinism, 150;
translation or transmutation of, 5; "UN-
ESCO cosmopolitanism," 131, 134; and
universalism, 63, 75. *See also* cultural internationalism
cultural capital, 120–22, 124. *See also* Pierre
Bourdieu; intellectuals; upward mobility
cultural internationalism, 17, 50. *See also* cosmopolitanism
culturalism: and the cultural left, 53; and popular culture, 45; and postmodernism, 45;
right-wing culturalism, 172–73; Richard
Rorty's critique of, 137–38
cultural left: alliance between cultural left and
liberals, 128, 134–35, 138–39; British left
culturalism, 124; and culturalism, 53; formation as result of cold war, 53; and human
rights, 72; and human rights internationalism, 145; and internationalism and leftist
politics, 8, 53; Fredric Jameson on, 35–36;
and nationalism, 52; and nation-state, 34;
opposition between old and new left, 129;

Richard Rorty on unpatriotism of cultural
left, 127–30; and social welfare state, 32, 52,
128
cultural transnationalism, 50. *See also* transnationalism
culture: and aesthetics, 18, 21–22, 129; and
capitalism, 50, 98; deference to, 2; in relation to democratic politics and economic redistribution, 137–38; and experience, 138;
in opposition to human rights, 72; "human
rights culture," 133–34; and internationalism, 31, 53; and nation-state, 172; and nationalism, 19–21, 49; and politics, 129;
public culture and civil society, 47; as signifier of membership and identity, 138;
Martha Nussbaum on, 150; peasant culture,
79–95; and self-interest, 31; as signifier of
identity, 138; in relation to universal/partic-
ular conflict, 144–45; Immanuel Wallerstein
on, 173
culture wars: 23–25; double charge of "Third
Worldism" and elitism, 99; and elitism, 27;
and globalization, 35

Debray, Régis, 116
De Maistre, Joseph, 147–48, 167
democracy, 135–37; American, 139, 153; and
cosmopolitanism, 162; in relation to culture
and economic redistribution, 137–38;
global democracy, 1338–39; within global
village, 156; and/as love, 171; participatory
democracy, 153; and socialism, 164
Depew, David J., 74–75
Der Derian, James, 149, 159
Dhareshwar, Vivek, 62
diaspora: in relation to Black public sphere and
Black diaspora, 54–55; and citizenship, 41;
multiculturalism, 40; and nation-state, 49;
and transnationalism, 100; and upward mobility, 108; in relation to U.S. internationalism and the journal *Diaspora*, 40. *See also*
Black diaspora; *Diaspora*
Diaspora: in relation to internationalization and
American pluralism, 41; and U.S. internationalism, 40
difference, politics of. *See* politics of difference
Diggins, John Patrick, 25
Dirlik, Arif, 41, 116, 122–23
disinterestedness: in relation to aesthetics and
internationalism, 30; John Berger and,
81–82; and worldliness, 171. *See also* self-
interest

Disraeli, Benjamin, 110–11
dominance, 68. *See also* hegemony; power
Dreyfuss Affair, 98. *See also* Black intellectuals;
    intellectuals; Third World intellectuals
Durkheim, Émile, 11

Eagleton, Terry, 83–84, 86, 131
Ecological internationalism, 31, 57. *See also* internationalism
elitism: and cosmopolitanism, 27–29; and culture wars, 99; versus democracy, 111; in relation to Eastern European nationalism, 45; elitist nationalism, 158; in relation to intellectuals, 120; and new nationalist fundamentalism, 68; popular culture's turn against, 45; in relation to *Realpolitik*, 159. *See also* progress or progressivism; secularism
emigration, 91–92. *See also* migration
emotion: and cosmopolitanism, 150; and eroticized nationalism, 164; and lobbying for policies and human rights, 152, 157; and national pride, 127, 150; and politics, 156–57; in relation to television and mass media, 156–58; transnational emotionality, 157. *See also* experience; feeling; love; patriotism
Enzenberger, Hans Magnus, 56
Erlich, Paul, 57
ethics: and civil society, 47; and cosmopolitanism, 154; and internationalism, 23; and nationalism, 35, 173; Martha Nussbaum on, 150, 154; and postmodernism, 47
Europe, Eastern: Eastern European nationalism in relation to intellectual elitism, 45; new nationalism in, 157
experience, 79–95; colonial and postcolonial experience, 121; and culture, 138; versus emigration and money, 91–92; Sigmund Freud on love and, 170; global experience, 86; international experience, 84; and migration, 88–90; national experience, 82, 85; posthumanist experience, 90; and photography, 92–93; of violence in relation to human/women's rights, 141. *See also* emotion; feeling; love; patriotism
extranationalism, 99, 152, 157. *See also* nationalism; nation-state

Falk, Richard, 16–17, 139
Fanon, Frantz, 67–68
Faraday, Michael, 86
Fay, Michael (caning of). *See* human rights; Singapore; violence

feeling, 69–70; "alienation" of intellectuals from, 71; anger and solidarity, 112; anti-imperial feeling in Michael Ondaatje's *The English Patient*, 166; as coded reference to constituency, 70; cosmopolitan's absence of, 70; and eroticized nationalism, 164; and humanism, 93; and identity politics, 137; internationalist emotion and human rights, 72, 141; learning to "feel global," 86, 170, 174; and nation-state, 72; and Oedipus complex, 170; in relation to photography and experience, 93; Richard Rorty on, 136–37; structures of, 83; in relation to television and mass media, 156–58; and universalism, 75. *See also* emotion; experience; love; patriotism
feminist internationalism, 35, 76. *See also* Beijing Conference for Women's Rights; human rights; United Nations
Flanders, Laura, 76, 141–42
Forster, E.M., 161
Foucault, Michel, 6, 95, 120
Fraser, Nancy, 128–29
Freud, Sigmund, 170

Garnham, Nicholas, 66
gay rights, 137. *See also* rights
genocide, 12–13
Geras, Norman, 136
Ghosh, Amitav, 68, 100
Gibson-Graham, J. K., 43
Gilroy, Paul, 100
Gingrich, Newt, 32
Ginsburg, Faye, 45
Glazer, Nathan, 150
global capitalism: and class, 109; and cosmopolitanism, 67, 154; in relation to nation-state and internationalism, 7, 51; and postcolonial studies, 116, 123; and unhappiness, 154; and universalism, 66; and/as U.S. capitalism, 43–44; in relation to U.S. internationalism and the journal *boundary 2*, 40, 41–42. *See also* capitalism; U.S. capitalism
"global feeling," 95, 174. *See also* emotion; feeling; love; patriotism
globalization: and culture wars, 35; and humanism, 81; of multinational capitalism, 98
Goldmann, Kjell, 16
Greece, 191n. 39
Guha, Ranajit, 118, 162–63
Gulf War, 3–4, 64

Gutmann, Amy, 152

Habermas, Jürgen, 54, 55, 153
Hackney, Sheldon, 149–50
Hall, Stuart, 124
Hansen, Miriam, 55–56
Hartsock, Nancy, 62
Haskell, Thomas, 19–20
hegemony: American, 3–4, 42; British, 42; French, 42; and internationalism, 42; and nation-state, 5–6. *See also* dominance; power
Himmelfarb, Gertrude, 62, 150–51
hip-hop, 56
Hitchens, Christopher, 75–76
Hosbawm, E. J., 97–98, 111, 160
Hollinger, David, 35
Honduras, 148
humanism: in relation to experience, 83; and feeling, 93; in relation to globalization, 81; versus Marxism, 82; Martha Nussbaum and, 148. *See* posthumanism; universalism or universality
human rights: activism, 5, 31; Beijing International Conference on Women's Rights, 35, 48, 76; caning of Michael Fay (Singapore), 143–44; and citizenship, 155; and cultural left, 72; and economic development, 141; and feminism, 141; gay rights, 137; "human rights culture," 133–34; and internationalist emotion, 72; and international public sphere, 136, 139–42; and nation-state, 142; and NGOs (nongovernmental organizations), 76; as normative concerns, 145; in relation to power and universalism, 73–74; and progress, 133; and racial discrimination, 74; Richard Rorty and, 130–31, 133, 137; Serbian "ethnic cleansing," 133; and United Nations, 46, 48, 72, 139–45; and universalism, 73; Vienna World Conference on Human Rights, 73, 139–41; women's rights, 141
human rights internationalism, 31; versus cultural cosmopolitanism, 130; as project for cultural left and liberals, 128; as inheritor of liberal premises, 145
Huntington, Samuel, 172–173

identity: culture as signifier of, 138
identity, national. *See* national identity
identity politics, 137–38
Ignatieff, Michael, 153

IMF (International Monetary Fund), 142, 154, 174. *See also* World Bank
immigration, 124–25. *See also* emigration; migration
India, 118, 122, 160–64. *See also* nationalism; postcolonial studies; secularism; Subaltern Studies Group
intellectuals: authority of, 120, 124; and/as cosmopolitans, 98, 99; and elitism, 99; and feeling, 71; First- and Second-World, 53; within metropolitan space, 112; and nationalism, 99; and nation-state, 51; and social welfare state, 36, 52. *See also* Black intellectuals, Third World intellectuals
international civil society, 50, 140, 153. *See also* civil society; international public sphere
internationalism: "American internationalism," 7, 39–59; authority of, 124; cold war internationalism, 42; and constituency, 31; in relation to cosmopolitanism, 5; versus cosmopolitanism, 17; and culture, 31, 53; cultural internationalism, 17, 50; definition of, 16; and disinterestedness, 30; ecological internationalism, 31; and ethics, 23; human rights internationalism, 31; and the humanities, 33; and the journal *boundary 2*, 41; and leftist politics, 8; and love in Michael Ondaatje's *The English Patient*, 166–68; and nationalism, 6, 21; and nation-state, 33; resistance to, 12–14; Edward Said's critique of, 118; and secularism, 118, 124; socialist internationalism, 7–8; and social welfare state, 6–7; and universalism, 63. *See also* feminist internationalism; U.S. internationalism
internationalist culture, 31. *See also* culture
internationalist ethics, 23. *See also* ethics
internationalist feeling, 174. *See also* emotion; feeling; love; patriotism
internationalist feminism, 35, 76, 171. *See also* Beijing Conference for Women's rights; human rights; United Nations
internationalist public sphere, 127–45; and human rights, 136, 142; versus international private sphere, 133; and NGOs (nongovernmental organizations), 140, 142; in relation to world resources, 136
Iraq, 64, 100

James, William, 58, 134, 135
Jameson, Fredric, 35–36, 43
JanMohamed, Abdul, 124
Johnson, Richard, 84

Judis, John, 52

Kaldor, Mary, 157
Kantian universalism, 7, 63, 148
Keane, John, 48
Kennedy, John F., 125
Kennan, George F., 156–57
Kincaid, Jamaica, 97, 101, 121; upward mobility in *Lucy* 102–3, 106–8
Kluge, Alexander, 55–56
Kristeva, Julia, 21

Laclau, Enesto, 65
laissez-faire economics: and cosmopolitanism, 32
language, 70–71
Latin America, 3, 158
Lazarus, Neil, 67–68, 162–63
Leavis, F. R., 83
Lee, Benjamin, 52
left and leftist politics. *See* cultural left
liberalism. *See* Richard Rorty
liberal nationalism, 30. *See also* nationalism
Lind, Michael, 30, 35
Lionnet, Françoise, 73
Livingston, James, 58, 138
López, María Milagros, 45–46
Lott, Eric, 7, 56, 171
love: cosmopolitan life and lack of, 70; critics of cosmopolitanism and, 152; and/as democracy, 171; Sigmund Freud on experience and, 170; in relation to internationalism and secular desire in Michael Ondaatje's *The English Patient*, 164–71; in relation to nationalism and patriotism in Rabindranath Tagore's *The Home and the World*, 160–61; and patriotism, 167; in a transnational public sphere, 153; and universalism or universality, 156. *See also* emotion; experience; feeling; patriotism
Lummis, C. Douglas, 73–74
Lyotard, Jean-François, 47

Mann, Michael, 34, 35
Marx, Karl, 61, 65, 90–91
Marxism, 7, 43, 55, 81, 82, 122–23, 131
McClintock, Anne, 44, 123
McConnell, Michael, 151–52
media, mass. *See* television and mass media
memory, 94
metropolis and metropolitan space, 112–13. *See also* elitism; intellectuals; postcolonial studies; Third World intellectuals; upward mobility

Michaels, Walter Benn, 171
migration, 88–90, 94–95; California dispute about Proposition 187, 148; Third World intellectual (im)migration, 121, 124. *See also* emigration
Miller, David, 18–19, 29, 35, 173
Miyoshi, Masao, 51
money, 90–91, 137. *See also* capitalism; global capitalism; U.S. capitalism
Moretti, Franco, 113
Morris, Meaghan, 52
Mouffe, Chantal, 65
Mukherjee, Bharati, 40, 101, 121; upward mobility in "Jasmine" (and in *Jasmine*), 103–06
multiculturalism: American, 44, 50, 64, 125; critique of, 151; and diaspora, 40; and global capitalism, 34; international form of, 125; Richard Rorty and, 138
multinational capitalism, 98. *See also* capitalism; global capitalism; U.S. capitalism

Nairn, Tom, 171
national identity, 127
nationalism: American nationalism, 1, 50, 64, 127, 149, 153; as anti-civil society, 49; anticolonial nationalism, 49; civic nationalism, 153; and cold ward, 52; and cosmopolitanism, 6, 149; and cultural inheritance, 19; and culture, 19–21; in Eastern Europe, 45; elitist nationalism, 158; eroticized nationalism, 164; ethnic nationalism, 153; and experience, 82, 85; fundamental articulations of new nationalism, 68; Indian national liberation movement, 162–63; and intellectual work, 99, 127; and internationalism, 6, 21; liberal nationalism, 30; and nation-state, 6, 97–98; new nationalism and xenophobia, 35; North American nationalism, 164; Palestinian national movement, 117; and print capitalism, 21; and racism, 71; versus religion, 117; secular nationalism in India, 118; and self-interest, 31; and upward mobility, 111; and welfare state, 173. *See also* extranationalism; patriotism
nationality: and citizenship, 36; and cosmopolitanism, 151; and universalism or universality, 147–48
nation-state: and capitalism, 66–67; and cultural left, 34; and feeling, 72; and financial transnationalism, 34; and global capitalism, 34; and hegemony, 5–6; and human rights, 142; identification with, 158; and international civil society, 46–47; and internation-

INDEX

Rieff, David, 15
Rorty, Richard, 25–26, 36, 53, 69, 124,
    127–45, 150, 173
Ross, Andrew, 57–58, 129
Rousseau, Jean-Jacques, 97
Rwanda, 158

Said, Edward, 4, 39, 101, 112–13, 115–25. *See
    also* elitism; Palestine; postcolonial studies;
    progress or progressiveness; secularism;
    Third World intellectuals
Sakai, Naoki, 66
Sandel, Michael, 152
Sartre, Jean-Paul, 120
Scarry, Elaine, 152
Schor, Naomi, 73
secularism, 115–25; in relation to authority,
    119–20, 124; critique of, 118; definition of,
    117, 119; postmodern secularism, 118; sec-
    ular nationalism in India, 118. *See also* elit-
    ism; intellectuals; postcolonial studies;
    progress or progressivism; Edward Said;
    Third World intellectuals
self-interest: group self-interest versus "new cos-
    mopolitanism," 171; in relation to intellec-
    tual institutions, 128; in relation to nation-
    alism and culture, 31; postponement of,
    155; and the United States, 158. *See also* dis-
    interestedness
Shain, Yossi, 42, 63
Shapiro, Michael, 47
Shohat, Ella, 44
Sierra Leone, 154
Sinfield, Alan, 124
Singapore: caning of Michael Fay, 143–44. *See
    also* human rights; violence
sixties generation, 25–26. *See also* cultural left
Snow, Edgar, 160
Social Text: and U.S. internationalism, 40,
    44–46
social welfare state. *See* welfare state
solidarity, 112, 117, 134, 138, 171. *See also* al-
    liance; emotion; experience; feeling; love
Somalia, 156, 158, 159–60
Sontag, Susan, 11-23, 92–95
South Africa, 163, 164
Soysal, Yasemin, 155
Spillers, Hortense, 55
Spivak, Gayatri Charavorty, 48, 77, 101–03,
    109, 112, 124
Sprinker, Michael, 117
Steichen, Edward, 93

Stephanson, Anders, 158
Subaltern Studies Group, 118. *See also* postcolo-
    nial studies; Edward Said; secularism; Third
    World intellectuals
surveillance. *See* perspective; photography
Sweden, 154
sympathy, 133, 141, 148. *See also* emotion; ex-
    perience; feeling; love

Tagore, Rabindranath: patriotism in *The Home
    and the World*, 160–61
Tamir, Yael, 19
Taylor, Charles, 47, 50–51, 56, 72–73, 145,
    151
television and mass media, 3, 156–59. *See also*
    CNN (Cable News Network)
Thiong'o, Ngugi wa, 101
Thompson, E. P., 82–83, 85, 124
Third World, 5, 29, 136, 150. *See also* NGOs
    (nongovernmental organizations)
Third World intellectuals, 100–101, 112–13,
    115–25. *See also* Black intellectuals; intellec-
    tuals; postcolonial studies
TNCs (Transnational Corporations), 51, 154
transnational capital, 42–43, 51
transnational emotionality, 157. *See also* emo-
    tion; experience; feeling; love; patriotism
transnational patriotism, 49. *See also* patriotism
transnational public sphere, 153. *See also* inter-
    national public sphere; public sphere
transnationalism: cultural transnationalism, 50;
    and diaspora, 100; financial transnational-
    ism and the nation-state, 34

UNESCO (United Nations Education,
    Scientific, and Cultural Organization),
    130–31, 134. *See also* human rights; United
    Nations
Unger, Peter, 33
unhappiness, 153. *See also* anger; emotion; expe-
    rience; feeling; love; patriotism
UNICEF (United Nations International
    Children's Emergency Fund), 33. *See also*
    human rights; United Nations
United Nations, 14, 46, 48, 72, 73, 136,
    139–45. *See also* democracy; human rights;
    racism
universalism or universality: anti-imperialist
    universalism, 65; in relation to (global) capi-
    talism, 66; in relation to colonialism, 68; in
    relation to cosmopolitanism and interna-
    tionalism, 63, 75; and feeling, 75, 141;

and/of human rights, 73, 131, 133, 142–44; Kantian universalism, 7, 63, 148; and love, 156; and nationality, 147–49; Martha Nussbaum and, 148–56; in relation to power, 73–74, 77, 142; progress and repudiation of, 62, 133; "real universality" of capitalism, 142; Richard Rorty on, 131, 133, 135; Susan Sontag and, 15–16. *See also* antiuniversalism

upward mobility, 97–113; and British left culturalism, 124; in Charlotte Brontë's *Jane Eyre*, 101–02; cultural capital as form of authority and, 121–22; and diaspora, 108; in Jamaica Kincaid's *Lucy*, 102–03; in Bharati Mukherjee's "Jasmine," 103–06; and nationalism, 111; and progress, 123–24; in relation to sex and marriage, 106–08; versus lateral mobility, 105, 107. *See also* class; intellectuals; metropolis and metropolitan space; Third World intellectuals

U.S. capitalism, 56. *See also* American; capitalism; global capitalism; multinational capitalism

U.S. internationalism: in relation to the journals *Diaspora, boundary 2, Social Text*, and *Public Culture*, 40, 54

van der Veer, Peter, 118

Verdery, Katherine, 45

Vienna World Conference on Human Rights, 73, 76, 139–41. *See also* human rights; NGOs (nongovernmental organizations); United Nations

Vietnam War: anticommunism and, 158; antiwar movement, 27–28; and formation of

new left, 53; victims of, 148, 167

violence: caning of Michael Fay (Singapore); Ethnic violence and constitutional patriotism, 153; in relation to human/women's rights, 141–42, 143–44; and nation-state, 159–60. *See also* human rights

Virilio, Paul, 156–57

Wallerstein, Immanuel, 173

Walzer, Michael, 150, 152

warlord, 158–60. *See also* neo-medievalism

Waterman, Peter, 8

Weber, Max, 99

Wee, C. J. Wan-ling, 143

welfare state: and citizenship, 36, 155; and cultural left, 32, 127; and globalization, 7; and intellectuals, 36, 52; and internationalism, 6; left-liberal alliance as defense of, 135; and nationalism, 173; restoration of, 33–34

West, Cornel, 55, 56

Wicke, Jennifer, 117

Williams, Raymond, 83, 85, 109, 124

Wilson, Rob, 41

women's rights, 140. *See also* Beijing International Conference on Women's Rights; human rights; NGOs (nongovernmental organizations); United Nations

World Bank, 48, 51, 76–77, 142, 174

worldliness, 2, 4, 171

Yúdice, George, 44, 64

Zizek, Slavoj, 65

ABOUT THE AUTHOR

BRUCE ROBBINS was born in 1949 in Brooklyn, New York, and educated at Valley Stream Central High School and at Harvard. He taught in Switzerland at the universities of Geneva and Lausanne from 1976 to 1984 and since 1984 has taught at Rutgers, New Brunswick, where he is professor of English and Comparative Literature. He has also held visiting positions at Harvard, Cornell, and New York University.

He is the author of *The Servant's Hand: English Fiction from Below* (Columbia, 1986), which was reissued in paper in 1993 by Duke, and *Secular Vocations: Intellectuals, Professionalism, Culture* (Verso, 1993). He has edited *Intellectuals: Aesthetics, Politics, Academics* (Minnesota, 1990) and *The Phantom Public Sphere* (Minnesota, 1993) and coedited *Cosmopolitics: Thinking and Feeling beyond the Nation* (Minnesota, 1998). He is also a coeditor of the journal *Social Text*.